350

BIG TASTE RECIPES FOR THE 1½ QUART MINI SLOW COOKER

BOOKSURGE, LLC
GLOBAL BOOK PUBLISHERS
An Amazon.com Company

Cook Books
by
ALBERT HERBERT
with
KEVIN ELLIOTT

350 BIG TASTE RECIPES
FOR THE 1½ QUART
MINI SLOW COOKER

THE COLLEGE GOURMET

THE SENIOR GOURMET

350

BIG TASTE RECIPES FOR THE 1½ QUART MINI SLOW COOKER

AMERICAN AND ETHNIC
FAVORITES ADAPTED FOR THE
MINI SLOW COOKER
WITH AN EMPHASIS
ON HEALTHY COOKING

BY
ALBERT HERBERT

WITH
KEVIN ELLIOTT
EXECUTIVE CHEF CONSULTANT

Copyright 2004
by
Albert Herbert

All rights reserved. No part of this book may be reproduced or transmitted in any form, or by any means, electronic or mechanical, including photocopying, recording, or by any information storage and retrieval system without permission in writing from the copyright owners

Notice: The information printed in this book is true and complete to the best of our knowledge. All recommendations are made without any guarantee on the part of the author or publisher. The author and publisher disclaim any and all liability in connection with the use of this information. If you have any allergies or other known health problems which might be affected by information in this book, the author and the publisher are not responsible for any health care costs which may result in careless use of this information.

Library of Congress catalogue number: 2004105655

ISBN Number: 1-59457-370-0

350 BIG TASTE RECIPES FOR THE 1½ QUART MINI SLOW COOKER
1. Author: Herbert, Albert 2. Consultant: Elliott, Kevin
3. Cookbook 4. 1½ quart mini slow cooker 5. Healthy eating

This book was printed in the United States of America.

To order additional copies of this book contact:
BOOKSURGE, LLC
7290B Investment Drive
N. Charleston, SC 29418
Tel: 866-308-6235
e-mail: www.booksurge.com
or at
amazon.com

Booksurge is an amazon.com company

For Roger, Sandy and Ed, and all
the others who gave me support
and believed in my effort

INTRODUCTION

Why the mini slow cooker? I have been asked that question many times. When you really seriously consider the 1½ quart slow cooker and its many advantages then the answer becomes clear.

First consider its size. The recipes in this cook book were designed for and tested in a Rival "Crockpot" (patented name) Model No.3215WN. This small slow cooker is 7½" in diameter and 7" high to the top of the glass lid. It has a removable stoneware liner which has a "Rinse Clean Lifetime Stick Resistant Coating." There is a sturdy glass lid through which you can watch the food cooking. More about that later.

The small size of the slow cooker makes it ideal for cooking in minimal spaces like an RV, motor home, camper, boat or small apartment kitchen. It is perfect for the college dorm where it might even lure students away from the ubiquitous pizza and into eating more healthful food.

The very size of the cooker is a way of controlling portions and thus diet and over eating. The 1½ quart slow cooker holds 6 cups of food. That is 1½ cups per person which is more than adequate for most people, especially if there are side dishes, a salad, bread or rolls, and a dessert to finish up. In many cases you will have left over food which may come as a surprise.

The mini slow cooker has other advantages as well. Because of its small size the mini slow cooker heats up much faster than its larger cousins. You will note that most large slow cooker recipes suggest cooking times of up to eight to ten hours. There is not one recipe in this cookbook which takes more than four hours, and most take a lot less time than that.

If you are on a special diet (I am a Type II Diabetic) then the mini slow cooker is perfect for you. If you need to make special meals for yourself, or for some other person in your family, then the mini slow cooker takes the place of an extra pan (or pans) on the stove. It can even replace your oven!

If the cooking time suggested does run over don't worry about it. You can rarely overcook anything in the slow cooker. It will never burn or scorch food. The slow cooker brings out the inherent tastes of the food making meats juicy and delicious, vegetables crisp but well done, and rice and other starches perfectly cooked and just the right consistency.

After using the mini slow cooker while developing these recipes I have come to believe that it is probably the most versatile and useful small appliance in your kitchen, capable of making wonderful soups, delicious stews and casseroles, and even baking the occasional cake or dessert. Have fun with the mini slow cooker and you will undoubtedly find a use for it which I have not yet discovered. Happy slow cooking!

Albert Herbert / Kevin Elliott
Williamsburg, Virginia

BASICS

GETTING TO KNOW AND LOVE YOUR COOKER
Like any other appliance there are certain things you should know about your mini slow cooker. Some have to do with safety and some have to do with kitchen helpers and food preparation. I have, therefore, divided these into three sections.

SAFETY
Much of this is just common sense but sometimes we have to be reminded and to be alert.

The cooker does get hot so handle it with care. Always use oven mitts when handling the slow cooker insert. There are two projecting handles and they make handling the cooker easier.

Watch the cord. Do NOT let the cord hang over the edge of the kitchen counter. Do NOT let the cord come in contact with water. Do NOT let children play in the area while the cooker is hot.

Do NOT put the hot liner into cold water. It may crack. Do NOT put cold foods into a hot liner. Do NOT put a hot liner on a cold surface.

As a precaution I put my slow cooker in an 8" pie pan to collect any food or juices which might overflow (it does happen).

Do NOT use the mini slow cooker outdoors, or for any other use than it was intended for. Do NOT put the cooker liner into a hot oven. Do NOT put the liner into the freezer.

Clean the liner with soap and water. DO NOT use harsh detergents or scrape it with metal utensils. Use wooden spoons or plastic as necessary. Never immerse the outside of the cooker in water. Clean it with a sponge and wipe dry. The liner may be put into the dishwasher, preferably in the top rack.

If you have a slow cooker with no temperature control knob on it, it will cook on HIGH automatically. If you have a cooker with a control knob, then cook only on the HIGH setting. Do not use the lower settings unless you are keeping food warm before serving.

Never move the slow cooker while it is plugged in. When the cooking is completed immediately unplug the cooker and make sure the cord is secure. If you serve directly from the cooker, and want to use the liner at the table, you must provide a suitable hot pad to put the cooker on. Remember, ALWAYS USE OVEN MITTS!

If you follow these simple safety procedures you will have no problems using you mini slow cooker.

KITCHEN ESSENTIALS
You will need some special kitchen helpers to cook successfully with the mini slow cooker. They are simple and not expensive but necessary.

An accurate quick-read thermometer is an absolute necessity and not just for cooking with the mini slow cooker. I use a Taylor Model No. 9640, which is supposedly accurate from -54/+402 degrees F. It has a watch type battery and an off/on switch to save battery power. It has a case and a clip so you can carry it with you easily.

You will need a small accurate timer. I use a digital one which measures 2½" wide x 3" high. It has button 1-0 and an off/on switch to save battery power. Many such small timers are available through kitchen supply stores or by catalogue.

You will need some heat-resistant plastic utensils. I would suggest a spatula, a slotted spoon, and a small stirring spoon. This will help prevent damage to the liner.

You will need some measuring cups. I would suggest three: a 1 cup measure, a 2 cup measure, and a 4 cup measure. Either glass or heat-resistant plastic will do.

You will need a good pair of oven mitts (which you probably already have!)

FOOD PREPARATION
Cooking with the mini slow cooker takes some basic understanding of how the cooker works. The heat is slow, but constant. Water will accumulate rather than evaporate in the slow cooker.

Vegetables often take longer to cook than meats. Vegetables should be cut into consistent bite size pieces so they will take the same amount of time to cook. There is no heat on the bottom of the cooker – only on the sides. Therefore the cooker should be at least half full to cook efficiently.

Patience is a key word when cooking with the slow cooker. You will be tempted to lift the lid to see what is happening – DON'T! Every time you lift the lid it adds about 10 minutes to the cooking time. BE PATIENT! IT'S COOKING!

You will not need to add as much liquid to the mini slow cooker as you do in regular cooking. Many vegetables give off copious amounts of water when cooking. Not everything needs to be covered by water or liquids. The heat "surrounds" the food.

Rice, grains and some pasta will cook in the cooker, along with other foods. However, in some recipes, I have recommended cooking pasta on the stove (al dente) by the regular method, and then adding it later into the cooker. Rice will be more glutinous than by the usual stove top method.

I have used many prepared and boxed foods in these recipes. Not only do they save time, they are easy to store and usually good!

Trim meats of as much fat as possible, although it cannot be denied that fat can sometimes add immeasurably to the taste of a dish.

I am often asked if the recipes will be finished in the time indicated. There are sometimes variations in voltage which can affect the temperature at which the cooker is cooking. A cooker in good order will reach nearly 200 degrees – but will never boil. Always check meat and chicken with your quick-read thermometer – if more time is required then just cover and cook additionally using your own good sense.

Do not be afraid to alter a recipe if you have something on hand which is a suitable replacement. Use your imagination – of this great ideas are born!

Experience is the best teacher. Learn to love and to trust your mini slow cooker. It will reward you many times over!

HOW TO USE THIS BOOK

Although the first edition of this recipe collection did not have an index at the back of the book, this edition does. I was ambivalent about this as many indexes are very frustrating and useful only if you are doing research. I can name more than one internationally known and popular cookbook where the index is nothing more than a jumble of words, cross-indexed in a manner designed to frustrate even the most advanced cook.

There are two ways to use this cookbook. I hope this index is clear and with the necessary use of capital letters indicating alphabetical sections will make your using it as easy as possible. You will note that the recipes listed in alphabetical order at the beginning of each section of this book are in **bold** type. Everything else is listed in regular type and is cross-indexed.

The other way is to use the various section listings, as all recipes are in alphabetical order. Therefore, under each of the sections as listed below, you can find just about anything you want.

APPETIZERS AND EGGS	1
SOUPS	35
FISH AND SHELLFISH	67
BEEF	123
HAM AND PORK	157
LAMB AND VEAL	187
SPECIALTY MEATS	209
POULTRY	229
VEGETABLES	281
GRAINS, PASTA, RICE AND BEANS	313
DESSERTS	347

Once you get the hang of it either way should make your cooking experience easy and enjoyable. At any rate you will probably find some favorites which you will make over and over again – I mark those in my cookbooks with tiny Post-It stick on tabs as a reminder for easy access.

SOME ADDITIONAL NOTES REGARDING CAPACITY

Although your mini slow cooker is advertised as being 1½ quarts (one quart = four cups – 1½ quarts = 6 cups), it will actually only comfortably hold five to five and one half cups of liquid and foods. More than this will bring the food right up to the top of the liner, which will undoubtedly result in an overflow!

Each one of the recipes in this book has been calculated carefully in regards to this limitation. If for some reason you have too much food to fill your cooker then simply adjust the amounts as necessary.

All manufacturers recommend that the cooker works best when it is at least half full – so bear that in mind. Also bear in mind that there are no heating elements on the bottom of the cooker – all heating elements are on the sides of the cooker only.

Each cup of food or liquid equals eight ounces – so the maximum capacity of the cooker is about 40 to 42 ounces. As I have stated earlier I keep my cooker in a large aluminum pie pan – to catch overflows which sometimes do happen. Simply wipe up the overflow around the lid with a paper towel. Keep the outside of the cooker clean by wiping it with a damp cloth.

PORTIONS

The portions accompanying the recipes are based on 1 to 1½ cups per person, except those which serve "a crowd" with cocktails or party food. If you need larger portions then you can expect to serve fewer people per recipe. Prepare accordingly.

'Nough said.

APPETIZERS

BBQ Meatballs
Blue cheese and Caviar Fritatta
Buffalo Wings
Caponata
Cheddar, Bacon and Horseradish Dip
Cocktail Onions
Dates Wrapped with Prosciutto
Eggplant Caviar
Hot "Krab" Dip
Hotsy-Totsy Peanuts
Kicked-Up Velveeta Spread
"Little Smokies" in Spicy Tomato Sauce
Meat Balls in Cranberry Sauce
Meatballs Strogonoff
Mushrooms a la Grecque
Spiced Mixed Nuts
Spicy Carrot Sticks
Sweet and Sour Meatballs
Swiss Cheese Fondue
Welsh Rarebit

EGGS

Cheese Bread Pudding
Eggs Florentine with Mushrooms
Eggs in Cheese Sauce
Fritatta Creole
Huevos Rancheros
Italian Fritatta
Quiche Lorraine without the Crust
Tex-Mex Salsa Fritatta
Western Fritatta
Zucchini Fritatta

350 BIG TASTE RECIPES FOR THE 1½ QUART MINI SLOW COOKER

APPETIZERS

You never know when some one is going to surprise you and arrive for tea, coffee or cocktails. This always calls for something to accompany the drinks.

The cautious host or hostess always has something in the pantry which can be used in such an emergency. Cookies or something sweet for the tea and coffee are the usual offering. Something on the more sophisticated side is suitable for the cocktails. Cheese of some nature is usually the first choice. The Cheddar, Bacon and Horseradish dip would be a good choice. Of course, any of the meat ball recipes are certain winners.

I keep a jar of the Mushrooms a la Grecque in the refrigerator at all times – they seem to keep forever, but then they will probably all disappear as soon as you serve them.

Because of the shape and size of the mini slow cooker things like skewered meats or cheeses are not possible. However, the mini slow cooker will stand you in good stead for things like "Little Smokies in Spicy Tomato Sauce" which are easy to prepare and can be served directly from the cooker. "Hotsy Totsy Peanuts" are easy to make and can be kept in a tightly sealed jar for a long period of time.

Dips are always cocktail time favorites. Try "Eggplant Caviar" for a special treat. It also keeps well and is elegant served on crackers or the mini cocktail breads.

No matter what you serve your guests, it is your generosity and friendship which will make it a special occasion.

350 BIG TASTE RECIPES FOR THE 1½ QUART MINI SLOW COOKER

BBQ MEATBALLS

You can whip these up in a jiffy. Buy the cocktail size cooked meatballs. Use your favorite BBQ sauce. Serve the meatballs in a low dish with toothpicks and plenty of paper napkins.

1 pkg. (12 oz) Rosina Brand, or equal.* (24 meatballs)
1 bottle (8 oz) BBQ sauce, your favorite flavor
1 tsp. finely chopped garlic
Worcestershire sauce (optional)

Spray the cooker with cooking spray. Add the meatballs and then the sauce. Toss well. Cover and cook undisturbed for at least 2 hours or until the meatballs are hot enough to serve.

Serves four or more as an appetizer

* You can also buy Armour meatballs in a 1 lb package (32 meatballs) available in various flavors.

Note: You can serve these as a party snack or with the addition of horizontally sliced hoagies a lusty sandwich. Slice the meatballs in half for easier handling. Pour the sauce over the sandwich.

BLUE CHEESE AND CAVIAR FRITTATA

This Frittata is made for the cocktail hour, and cut into small slices will easily serve eight or more as an hors d'oeuvre. Don't use expensive caviar when the bottled red lumpfish caviar will do just fine. Serve with delicate crackers, or tiny slices of rye cocktail bread.

6 large eggs beaten
½ lb blue cheese (Maytag, Danish or whatever)
1 jar (3 oz) red lumpfish caviar
Pepper (Salt is not needed as the caviar is salty enough)

In a small bowl, break up the blue cheese with a fork. Add the beaten egg and the caviar. Mix well. Spray the cooker with cooking spray and add the egg mixture. Cover and cook undisturbed for 2 hours or until the eggs are set. Run a knife around the outside edge of the eggs to release it from the liner. Invert the liner over a serving dish and the eggs should release. Cut into small wedges.

Serves six or eight as an appetizer

BUFFALO WINGS

No, Buffalo don't fly, and they don't have wings, but these tasty morsels invented in Buffalo. New York will literally fly out of your kitchen. Buffalo Wings are made to be heavily spiced so lay it on. Eaten with cold beer or other stronger libations, they are a perennial party favorite. Serve with traditional celery stalks and blue cheese dressing.

1½ lbs chicken wings
1 (14.5 oz) can tomato sauce
3 tbsp. cider vinegar
3 tbsp Tabasco sauce.
1 tbsp crushed red pepper flakes

Wash the wings well. Cut the two larger portions in half, and remove the tips and discard. Mix the tomato sauce with the other ingredients. Add the chicken wings, and pour into the slow cooker. Cover and cook undisturbed for 3 hours. Check for doneness with your quick read thermometer. The wings should read 165-175 degrees and the juices should run clear. Serve with the celery stalks cut into 3" pieces, and the blue cheese dressing on the side. Get ready to make another batch. Have plenty of napkins ready!

Serves four or more as an appetizer

CAPONATA

This wonderful garlicy spread is terrific on crackers or small toasts. Some say it is Sicilian in origin, but I think it is more probably Turkish. It is best cooled and served in a low dish so that it can be scooped up easily.

4 cups eggplant, not peeled, cut into bite size pieces
1 medium onion, chopped fine
3 tbsp garlic, chopped fine
3 tbsp capers, chopped
½ cup pitted Greek olives, chopped (Calamata are best)
½ cup tomato puree
Salt and pepper to taste

Spray the cooker with cooking spray. In a medium bowl mix all the ingredients and toss well. Pour the mixture into the cooker. Cover and cook undisturbed for 3 hours. Let the mixture cool. Pour into a bowl where it can be mashed. If you have a food processor handy use that but do not over process. Refrigerate. Bring to room temperature before serving to enhance the flavors.

Serves four or more as an appetizer

CHEDDAR, BACON AND HORSERADISH DIP

This is a really tasty dip to be served with good crisp crackers, little breads, or crunchy "scoopers" – your guests will never get enough. I suggest you spoon it from the cooker onto a low serving dish for more convenient "dipping" or "scooping."

2 pkg. (8 oz ea.) cream cheese, cut into small pieces
1 pkg. (8 oz) cheddar cheese, cut into small pieces
½ cup half and half
½ cup scallions, chopped fine (including the green part)
¼ cup prepared grated horseradish
3 tbsp Dijon type mustard
5 slices bacon, cooked crisp (or use 2 tbsp. Bacos)
2 tbsp Worcestershire sauce
Salt and freshly ground pepper to taste

Spray the cooker with cooking spray. Add the two cheeses and the half and half. Cover and cook undisturbed for 1 hour. Add the remaining ingredients and stir well into the cheese mixture. Cover and cook for 1 or 2 hours more. Stir well and serve as suggested above.

Serves four or more as an appetizer

COCKTAIL ONIONS

These tasty little morsels will jazz up any cocktail hour. For an extra treat wrap the onions with a piece of garlic flavored luncheon meat, such as salami and secure with a toothpick.

1 lb pkg. frozen small onions (I find Birdseye are the best)
½ tsp coriander seeds
½ tsp majoram
½ tsp thyme
1 tsp chopped garlic
2 bay leaves crushed
2 cups white wine vinegar
¼ cup olive oil
1 tbsp lemon juice
Salt and pepper

Defrost the frozen onions to room temperature. Tie all the spices in a cheesecloth bag. Place the onions in the cooker, pour the vinegar, oil and lemon juice over and push the bag into the onions. Cover and cook undisturbed for 2 hours. Cool and remove the cheesecloth bag. Put the onions into a glass jar and refrigerate. Serve with toothpicks.

Serves four or more as an appetizer with cocktails

DATES WRAPPED WITH PROSCIUTTO

This recipe has been a favorite for many years, however I have always made it with bacon and cooked it under a broiler. Making it in the mini slow cooker necessitates the use of pre-cooked meat, hence the prosciutto. The results are just as delicious. Serve these hot. You will note that the dates nearest the cooker wall will release more of their natural sugar, than those in the center of the cooker. You cannot overcook these, so start them before your cocktail party and let 'em go until you are ready to serve.

1 pkg. (8 oz) pitted California dates
½ lb (approx) prosciutto, sliced thin from the deli counter
Tooth picks

Cut the prosciutto into 1" x 3" pieces, or big enough to wrap around each date. Secure with a toothpick. Arrange the dates in the cooker. There will be about 40 pieces and the cooker will be full. Cover and cook undisturbed for as long as you like. Serve on a decorative platter and enjoy the compliments.

Serves four or more as an appetizer

EGGPLANT CAVIAR

Supposedly from the Middle East and made for those who could not afford the real thing this delicious hors d'oeuvre spread is a favorite of just about everyone who has had it. Serve it cold or at room temperature. Supply lots of delicate crackers or cocktail breads to spread it on. Low in calories too!

4 cups eggplant, un-peeled and cut into small pieces
1 medium bell pepper, diced
4 tsp chopped garlic (or more if you want)
1 can (8 oz) tomato sauce
Salt and pepper to taste

In a medium bowl combine all the ingredients. Mix well. Spray the liner of the cooker with cooking spray and add the mixture. Cover and cook undisturbed for 3 hours. Remove the mixture with a slotted spoon and place it in a strainer to drain. Pour from the strainer into the bowl of a food processor. Process until the mix is just slightly lumpy – do not over process. Test for seasoning and add salt and pepper as necessary. Put the mixture into a serving bowl and refrigerate overnight. It improves with age.

Serves six or more as an appetizer

HOT "KRAB" DIP

This is a real crowd pleaser for a cocktail party. You can serve it directly from the slow cooker, but it would be better to transfer it to a low dish for easy dipping. Serve it with sturdy crackers or crisp restaurant style tortillas.

1½ lb "krab" available at your supermarket fish counter
½ cup celery, diced fine
½ cup scallions, chopped fine
1 small red bell pepper, diced fine
1 cup sour cream
1 tbsp Tabasco sauce
Salt and pepper to taste

Chop the "krab" into fine dice. In a medium bowl combine the "krab" with the sour cream, bell pepper, scallions, Tabasco and celery. Mix well. Add the mix to the slow cooker. Cover and cook undisturbed for 2 hours. Serve the dip warm or at room temperature.

Serves four or more as an appetizer

HOTSY-TOTSY PEANUTS

Mr. Peanuts will run for the woods after he's tasted these spiced up peanuts. Make lots of these as they will go like wildfire at your next cocktail party.

1 lb salted dry roasted peanuts (about 4 cups)
3 tbsp melted butter or oleo
1 tbsp chili powder
1 tbsp ground red pepper

Spray the cooker with cooking spray. Pour the peanuts into the cooker liner. Pour the melted butter and spices over and mix well. Cover and cook for 2 hours. Let cool and pour into a jar or air tight tin to preserve until serving.

Serves four or more as *an appetizer*

Note: You can use others of your favorite spices, such as curry, etc. Use your discretion!

KICKED UP VELVEETA SPREAD

Unlike the Velveeta cheese sandwiches of your childhood this spread has a real kick. Best served warm but its good cold too. Serve with a variety of crackers, party breads or Tostitos. It will make any cocktail party sing.

1 lb block "Velveeta" brand cheese
1 cup mayonnaise
3 tbsp hot red pepper flakes
2 tbsp Worcestershire sauce
½ cup pimento, chopped fine
½ cup salsa – hot or medium, your choice
Pepper to taste

Spray the cooker liner with cooking spray. Chop the cheese into 1" cubes and pour into the cooker. Cover and cook undisturbed for 2 hours, or until the cheese has melted. Add all the other ingredients. Mix well and cook for 1 hour more. Transfer to a low serving bowl for easy dipping or spreading. Will keep well in the refrigerator – that is, if you have any leftovers!

Serves four or more as an appetizer

"LITTLE SMOKIES" IN SPICY TOMATO SAUCE

This dish can't be beat for a crowd as the slow cooker liner can be brought right to the buffet table and the "Little Smokies" can be served directly from the pot. Have plenty of napkins on hand. This can get a little messy! Use cocktail toothpicks to serve.

1 pkg (1 lb.) "Little Smokies" cocktail sausages (45-50 count)
1 (15oz.) can tomato sauce (your choice)
½ cup barbecue sauce (your choice of flavor)
1 medium onion diced fine
1 tsp. hot pepper flakes (optional)
2 tbsp Tabasco sauce
¼ cup grated Mexican style cheese for garnish

Mix tomato sauce with the barbecue sauce. Add the diced onion, the hot pepper flakes, (if using) and the Tabasco sauce. Pour into the slow cooker. Add the "Little Smokies" and stir well. Cover and cook undisturbed for 2 hours. When ready to serve sprinkle the Mexican style grated cheese on top.

Serves four or more as an appetizer

MEATBALLS IN CRANBERRY SAUCE

This seems like a strange combination, but once you get over the idea, these meatballs are really quite wonderful. Buy the small frozen pre-cooked cocktail size meatballs. There are several brands and flavors available. Serve from a low dish with toothpicks and have plenty of napkins available.

1 pkg. (16 oz) frozen cocktail meatballs – about 32 meatballs
1 can (8 oz) whole cranberry sauce – not the jellied kind
1 cup water
2 tbsp chopped garlic
2 tbsp prepared horseradish
2 tbsp Dijon style mustard
2 tbsp lemon juice
 Salt and pepper to taste

Defrost the meatballs to room temperature. Spray the cooker with cooking spray. Prepare the sauce in a separate bowl, add the meatballs and stir well. Pour into the cooker. Cover and cook undisturbed for 2 hours or more. You cannot overcook these, so just let them go until you are ready to serve.

Serves four or more as an appetizer

MEATBALLS STROGONOFF

Something different from the usual tomato based sauce. Buy the small cocktail size meatballs and serve in a low dish for easy picking up with toothpicks.

1 lb or more frozen cocktail size meatballs
1 pkg (16 oz) sour cream
½ lb mushrooms, sliced
¼ cup onion, diced
Fresh or dried dill to taste

Spray the cooker with cooking spray. Place the meatballs in the cooker, cover and cook undisturbed for 1 hour. In the meantime combine the mushrooms and garlic with the sour cream. Add dill to taste. Pour the sour cream mixture into the cooker and stir the meatballs well to coat. Cover and cook for 1 hour more. Serve warm.

Serves four or more as an appetizer

MUSHROOMS A LA GRECQUE

This is an adaptation of a recipe I got many years ago from Air France. In those days a first class flight from Paris to New York always featured an elaborate lunch or dinner served on real china, and accompanied by several wines or champagne and then brandy. The Stewards or Stewardesses would come down the aisle with elaborately arranged carts featuring many hors d'oeuvre selections, each doled out onto small plates in ceremonial fashion. Those days are long gone, but the memories of those delicious mushrooms lingers on.

1 lb button mushrooms – the smallest you can find.
Boiling water to cover the mushrooms
1 cup red wine vinegar
½ cup olive oil
2 tbsp pickling spices
2 bay leaves
1 tbsp whole black pepper corns
1 tbsp whole coriander seeds

Clean the mushrooms, and cut off the stems at the base of the top. In a heat resistant bowl cover the mushrooms with the boiling water, and let them soak for about 5 minutes. Save the stems for another use. In a non-reactive bowl mix all the other ingredients and stir well. Pour into the cooker and add the mushrooms. They will float to the top – weight them down into the liquid with a small bowl which fits into the cooker. Cover and cook undisturbed for 1 hour. Stir the mushrooms bringing some of those from the bottom up to the top. Cover again, and cook for 1 hour more. Unplug the cooker and let the mushrooms come to room temperature. Serve from a low bowl with toothpicks. The mushrooms may be refrigerated in a glass jar.

Serves four or more as an appetizer.

SPICED MIXED NUTS

A bowl of these spiced mixed nuts are always a hit during the cocktail hour. Use any kind of nuts you want.

5 cups mixed nuts-any kind you want.
2 tbsp butter or oleo
1 tsp ground red pepper
1 tbsp Tabasco sauce (more if you want)
3 tbsp Worcestershire sauce
Salt

Melt the butter in the bottom of the cooker. Add the nuts and all the spices and salt and stir thoroughly to coat. Cover and cook the nuts for 2 hours. Uncover and let the nuts cool in the cooker. When cool put into an airtight tin or jar, or serve in decorative bowls.

Serves a crowd as a cocktail nibble

SPICY CARROT STICKS

Who still remembers the "dilly beans" of a few years ago? Well, these are similar. They can be kept in the refrigerator for a quick snack, or be served at your next cocktail party. They are delicious dipped into any of the flavored sour cream based dips. Good for the waistline too!

1 bag (16 oz) fresh carrots
2 cups hot tap water
1 cup cider vinegar
3 tbsp pickling spices
1 bay leave
1 tsp coriander seeds
1 tsp whole black pepper corns

Peel the carrots, and cut into ¼" x 3 ½" batons, so they will stand u p vertically in the cooker. Make enough to almost fill the cooker, leaving just enough space for the liquid. In a non-reactive bowl mix the water, vinegar and spices and pour over the carrots. Cover and cook undisturbed for 2 to 3 hours. The carrots should still be crisp and not limp. Let the carrots cool to room temperature. Store the carrots in the marinade in a glass jar in the refrigerator.

Serves four or more as an appetizer

SWEET AND SOUR MEATBALLS

These tasty morsels will have guests clamoring for more. Buy the tiny frozen pre-cooked cocktail meatballs. Serve directly from the cooker or put into a shallow serving dish to facilitate easy pick up with toothpicks.

1 lb or so frozen pre-cooked cocktail size meatballs*
1 cup ketchup
1 tbsp Worcestershire sauce
½ cup white vinegar
3 tbsp sugar (or sugar substitute)
3 tsp dry mustard
1 tbsp red pepper flakes
Salt and freshly ground black pepper to taste

Spray the cooker with cooking spray. Defrost the meatballs. In a medium bowl mix the ketchup and all the other ingredients. Pour the mix into the cooker. Add the meatballs and stir well to see that they are covered with the sauce. Cover and cook undisturbed for 2 or more hours. Serve hot as described above.

Serves four or more as an appetizer

*Buy Armour meatballs in a 16oz package (32 meatballs) or Rosina Brand in a 12oz package – 24 meatballs. Each comes in various flavors – your choice!

SWISS CHEESE FONDUE

This dish can be served as an appetizer or as a main supper dish. I have put it in the appetizer section, because there is nothing like sitting around a fondue pot with friends to get a party going. The slow cooker with the removable liner is the ideal way to make a fondue as you do not have to worry about scorching. Additionally the cooker liner stays hot for quite awhile as does the fondue in it. Serve with chunks of lusty French bread and long handled forks or skewers for dipping.

1½ lb Swiss cheese cut into small chunks
1 tbsp garlic chopped fine
½ cup dry white wine
1 tbsp dry English mustard
1 tbsp Worcestershire sauce
Pinch nutmeg
3 tbsp Kirsch (optional)

Spray the cooker with cooking spray. Put the cheese into the cooker. Cover and cook undisturbed for 2 hours, or until all the cheese is melted. Add the mustard, Worcestershire sauce, white wine, and nutmeg. Stir well. Cover and cook for 1 hour more.

Serves four or more as a first course or appetizer

WELSH RAREBIT

Nothing beats this simple dish for lunch on a cold day. Serve it over warm cornbread or on toasted rye or whole wheat bread. Warm Southern biscuits would also be terrific.

4 cups cheddar cheese, cut into 1" cubes
1 can (12 fl oz) dark beer or ale (NA beer works well too)
1 tbsp Worcestershire sauce
1 tsp ground paprika
Salt and pepper to taste

Spray the cooker with cooking spray and add the cheese. Cover and cook undisturbed for 2 hours, or until the cheese has melted. Add the beer and the spices and stir well. Cover and cook for 1 hour more. Taste for seasoning and add salt and pepper as necessary. If the rarebit is not hot enough, cover and cook for 1/2 hour more.

Serves four to six as a first course

350 BIG TASTE RECIPES FOR THE 1½ QUART MINI SLOW COOKER

EGGS

Cooking eggs in the mini slow cooker is rather limited. Although eggs are used in some of the other recipes, eggs by themselves generally run to something like a Frittata.

The shape and size of the slow cooker, along with the type of cooking itself determine the limitations of eggs.

However there are some possibilities. Frittatas are especially successful in the mini slow cooker and are limited only by your imagination. The "Tex-Mex Salsa Frittata" is a case in point. You can add your favorite chilis and salsa for extra heat, or use left over cooked ground meat as an addition. Even cut up sausage and other deli meats are fair game.

For the French, eggs are a more important part of general cooking than for most Americans, who consider eggs for breakfast only. The French poach eggs in red wine, they make souffles out of them, and they use them for thickening sauces. They make egg desserts of ethereal quality such as Ile Flottant, or the famous Omelet Norwegian, more commonly known as Baked Alaska.

Someday I will figure out how to make a souffle in the mini slow cooker, but then you'll find it under desserts!

CHEESE BREAD PUDDING

This is a wonderful luncheon dish served with a green salad and fresh baked rolls. It's also a good way to use up some day old bread.

3 large eggs well beaten
5 slices day old bread, crusts removed and cut into 1" cubes, about 4 cups
1½ cups milk
1 cup grated cheese (Cheddar, Mexican, Swiss – your choice)
Pinch nutmeg
Salt and pepper to taste

Spray the cooker with cooking spray. In a medium bowl stir the eggs and the milk. Add the bread cubes and let soak for ½ hour. Add the cheese, nutmeg and salt and pepper and mix well. Pour the mixture into the cooker. Cover and cook undisturbed for 2 hours or until the eggs are set. Serve directly from the cooker.

Serves two to four as a first course or savory

EGGS FLORENTINE WITH MUSHROOMS

This delicious dish is easy to prepare and is perfect for the vegetarian. Mix only half the can of the mushroom soup with the spinach, and save the rest for another use. Serve with a fresh green salad and toasted country bread.

1 pkg, (10 oz) frozen chopped spinach
1 can (10.5oz) cream of mushroom soup
4 large eggs, well beaten
½ lb. fresh mushrooms, sliced thin
2 scallions, chopped fine
Grated nutmeg to taste
Salt and pepper to taste
Shredded cheese (your choice)

Completely defrost the chopped spinach. In a small bowl mix ½ the mushroom soup with the spinach. Grate some fresh nutmeg into the mixture, and add some salt and pepper. Beat the eggs and add the scallions and sliced mushrooms. Salt and pepper the egg mixture. Spray the cooker with cooking spray and place the spinach on the bottom. Pour the egg and mushroom mixture on top, and sprinkle the top with some of the grated cheese. Cover, and cook for 2 hours. Check to see if the eggs are set. If not, cover and cook for ½ hour more. Serve directly from the cooker. Be sure to get some of the spinach with each serving

Serves two to four as a first course or savory

EGGS IN CHEESE SAUCE

This inexpensive and easy to make dish is perfect for a summer luncheon or as a first course for a light dinner. Serve the eggs over toast points, biscuit halves or rice, and accompany them with a fresh green salad.

8 large eggs, hardboiled and cut in half
1 can (10.25 oz) cheddar cheese soup
½ cup water
1 tbsp Worcestershire sauce
1 tbsp Dijon style mustard
1 can (8 oz) tiny sweet peas, drained
¼ lb fresh mushrooms, sliced thin
¼ cup canned pimiento cut into fine dice (optional)
Salt and pepper to taste
Shredded cheddar cheese, optional

Spray the cooker with cooking spray. Dilute the soup with the water, and add the Worcestershire sauce and mustard. Stir well. Add all the other ingredients except the peas and the eggs. Cover and cook undisturbed for 1½ hours. Add the eggs and the peas and stir well. Cover and cook for 1 hour more. Serve as suggested above. Sprinkle with some of the shredded cheddar if desired.

Serves two to four as a first course or light luncheon dish

FRITTATA CREOLE

This wonderful spicy egg dish is enough for a full dinner along with a fresh green salad, some good Italian bread, and a dry white wine. Grate Parmesan cheese on the frittata for additional flavor.

8 large eggs well beaten
½ cup onion diced
½ cup green bell pepper diced
½ cup Roma tomatoes diced
½ cup fresh mushrooms sliced
1 tbsp chili pepper
½ cup salsa (optional)
Fresh Parmesan cheese for garnish

Spray the cooker with cooking spray. Combine the eggs with the diced vegetables and the chili pepper. Pour the mixture into the cooker. Cover and cook undisturbed for 3 hours or until the eggs are set. Spoon the frittata directly from the cooker, and grate the cheese on top. For a fancier presentation, remove the frittata whole onto a serving plate and cut into wedges.

Serves two to four as a first course or light luncheon dish

HUEVOS RANCHEROS

Not exactly in the traditional manner but a savory dish nonetheless as an appetizer or first course for a light luncheon. Serve with a salad of fresh greens with avocado and thinly sliced red onion on top.

4 - 8" diameter corn or wheat tortillas
6 eggs, well beaten
1 small green pepper, diced
1 small onion, chopped (reserve some for garnish)
½ cup salsa
½ cup grated Mexican style cheese
Sour cream for garnish
Salt and pepper to taste

Spray the cooker with cooking spray. Mix the eggs with the vegetables and pour the mixture into the cooker. Cover and cook undisturbed for 1 hour. Check to see if the eggs are set. Spread the salsa on top of the eggs and top with some of the grated cheese. Cover and cook for 1 hour more or until the eggs are fully set and the cheese has melted. If you want the eggs slightly less set, then stop the cooking and proceed to serve them. Place a tortilla on each of four serving plates. Spoon some of the egg mixture onto each tortilla, and roll up loosely. Top with some of the sour cream, additional salsa, chopped onion, and shredded cheese.

Serves two to four as a first course or savory

Note: You can serve these tortillas with chili beans and Mexican style rice, for a complete Mexican meal.

ITALIAN FRITTATA

The Italian Frittata is often confused with the French omelet – they could not be more different! The French omelet is cooked over high heat, filled, and then folded over and inverted on the plate. The Italian Frittata is cooked slowly, is flat and perfectly round, like a cake. The mini slow cooker is the ideal way to make a perfect Frittata. A Frittata can be filled with whatever you wish, from plain cheese to more exotic fillings – the choice is yours. Here we have a plain cheese Frittata – the basis for any number of variations – let your imagination be your guide!

8 large eggs, well beaten
1 cup freshly grated Parmesan or Swiss cheese
3 tbsp. Butter
¼ cup milk or heavy cream
Salt and pepper to taste.

Beat the eggs well, add the milk or cream and the grated cheese. Using a paper towel, rub the butter over the bottom and 1/3 up the sides of the cooker insert. Leave the remaining butter on the bottom. Pour the egg mixture into the cooker insert Cover, plug in the cooker, and cook undisturbed for 2 1/2 to 3 hours. Check to see if the eggs are set. When finished, carefully remove the insert from the cooker (use oven mitts!) and invert onto a serving dish. Easier yet, using a large long handled spoon, serve the eggs directly onto plates. Garnish as desired.

Serves two to four as a first course or savory

QUICHE LORRAINE

Seems unlikely that you can make this in a mini slow cooker but it works just fine. You will get a small 5" diameter pie enough for a nibble at a cocktail party.

1 square ready made pie dough thawed, cut into an 8" circle
4 large eggs beaten
¾ cup heavy cream
4 slices bacon cooked and chopped into small dice
2 tbsp onion diced fine
2 tbsp Dijon type mustard
¾ cup grated Swiss Cheese
Salt and pepper to taste

Spray the cooker liner with cooking spray. Lay the thawed pie dough centered on the bottom of the cooker with sides about 1" high all around. Work the dough into the corners of the cooker. Prick the bottom with a fork. Cover and cook undisturbed for ½ hour. While the dough is blind cooking mix all the other ingredients in a medium size bowl. Pour the mix into the dough. Cover and cook for 2 hours more. Test to see if the eggs are set. Lay the cooker on its side and with a long handled fork coax the pie out of the cooker onto a serving plate. Put the pie into a 350 degree oven for 10 minutes or so to crisp the crust. Cut in wedges to serve.

Serves four as a cocktail nibble or two as a first course

Note: The eggs are delicious served out of the cooker onto plates without the crust. If you have a mini muffin pan (12 mini muffins) you can make the crusts in that, and spoon the Quiche mixture into them – makes 12 Mini Quiches.

TEX-MEX SALSA FRITTATA

This is a "sock-em in the eye" way to wake them up for breakfast or to serve a tasty lunch or light supper. Serve with grated cheese on top and spicy sausage on the side. Tortillas are a given!

6 large eggs, well beaten
½ cup salsa (mild, medium or hot – your choice!)
Grated cheese for garnish
Pinch ground cumin
Warm tortillas
Sour cream for garnish
Chopped cilantro for garnish

Beat the eggs well and add the salsa. Spray the cooker with cooking spray. Add the eggs. Cover and cook undisturbed for 2 hours. Check to see if the eggs have set – they should be firm but not hard. Remove the eggs by inverting the cooker over a serving plate. Serve cut in wedges or spoon the eggs from the cooker and garnish with the cheese, sour cream and cilantro.

Serves two to four as an appetizer or first course or savory

WESTERN FRITTATA

This Frittata is a meal in itself, and a wonderful way to make use of leftovers or clean out the fridge! You don't necessarily have to stick to the recipe and you can add or subtract whatever you wish. If you want to give it a "south of the border" taste just add some salsa.

6 large eggs. well beaten
½ cup onion, chopped
½ cup green pepper, chopped
2 Roma tomatoes, chopped
½ cup cooked ham, chopped
¼ cup salsa (optional)
1 tsp thyme
Salt and pepper to taste

In a medium bowl mix the beaten eggs with all the other ingredients. Spray the cooker with cooking spray and add the egg mixture. Cover and cook undisturbed for 2 hours or until the eggs are set. Serve directly from the cooker or run a knife around the edge of the frittata to loosen it. Invert the liner over the serving plate and the frittata should release. Cut into wedges to serve.

Serves two to four as a light luncheon dish or savory

ZUCCHINI FRITATTA

When your garden is so full of zucchini that you don't know what to do with them this is a good way to get rid of some of them. You will also have tomatoes ripening on the vine, so use those as well. Don't be afraid of all the garlic. Wonderful served as a luncheon entrée.

2 cups fresh zucchini diced
1 cup fresh tomatoes peeled, seeded, and diced
5 eggs, beaten
4 tbsp chopped garlic
1 tbsp dried basil
Salt and pepper

Spray the cooker liner with cooking spray. In a medium size bowl combine all the ingredients. Pour into the cooker, cover and cook undisturbed for 2 hours or until the eggs are set. Cut around the outside of the cake with a thin knife to release the egg frittata. Invert the liner over a serving plate and release the frittata to serve. Cut into wedges.

Serves two to four as a light luncheon dish or savory

Note: You can spoon the eggs out of the cooker onto plates without the fuss of trying to get the "cake" out of the cooker – just as delicious.

SOUPS

Black Bean Soup
Borscht
Cabbage and Beef Soup
Cheese Soup with Vegetables
Chicken Soup with Tortellini
Corn Chowder
Creamed Carrot Soup
Creamy Corn Soup
Easy Chicken Soup
French Onion Soup
Fresh Tomato Soup
Italian Bean and Sausage Soup
"Krab" and Corn Soup
Lentil and Sausage Soup
Manhattan Clam Chowder
Minestrone Soup
Mushroom Soup
Navy Bean and Tomato Soup
Pasta and Bean Soup
Pea Soup
Potato and Leek Soup
Potato, Onion and Bacon Soup
Tomato and Rice Soup
Tortellini en Brodo
Tortellini and Sausage Soup
Tuscan Bread and Tomato Soup
U.S. Senate Bean Soup
Vegetable Soup
Vegetarian Vegetable Soup
Wonton Soup

SOUPS

Soups, stews and casseroles are where the mini slow cooker shines. The slow cooking brings out the natural flavors of the ingredients and imparts freshness and goodness not found in other forms of cooking. All of the nutrients are retained in the cooker as there is no loss due to boiling or steaming. There is, however, a lot of natural condensation.

Many of the soups in this collection have pre-cooked components, along with fresh ingredients. They will cook simultaneously without any problems.

If there is a time limit on the soup recipe you can conveniently forget about it. Rarely could any of these soups be overcooked. Additional cooking time will only serve to meld and intensify the flavors.

Many of these soups are really a "meal in a bowl." Served with a salad and some good bread they will make a satisfying meal on their own.

I am not going to bring your attention to any specific soup recipe as there are so many of them with merit. Soups are also a good way to use leftovers which may be crowding your refrigerator. Don't be afraid to add another ingredient to any of the recipes if it seems suitable. Leftover cooked vegetables and in some cases cooked rice or pasta can be added easily. Let your imagination be your guide!

You've heard the expression "Its soup day" – and indeed, soups are heart warming, nutritious and satisfying. The mini slow cooker is an ideal and easy way to prepare your favorite.

BLACK BEAN SOUP

This is a favorite in the South where country ham and black beans are a way of life! Serve with beaten biscuits and lots of fresh butter.

2 cans (15.5 oz each) black beans – do not drain
1 cup country ham, cut into bite size pieces
1 small onion, diced
1 small green pepper, diced
2 bay leaves
½ tsp dried thyme
Salt and pepper to taste

In a medium bowl combine all the ingredients. Mix well. Spray the cooker liner with cooking spray and add all the ingredients. Cover and cook undisturbed for 3 hours. Taste for seasoning and adjust as needed. Continue to cook until ready to serve.

Serves two to four

Note: If the soup is a little too thick, you can add some water, or better still some beef or chicken broth. You can also use your stick blender to mash the soup up a bit – some people prefer it that way!

BORSCHT

This famous soup is popular throughout Eastern Europe. There are many variations but this is about the simplest to make. Serve with dark rye or pumpernickel bread.

1 can (15.5 oz) sliced beets, drained and diced fine
1 can (10.5 oz) chicken stock
1 can (8.5 oz) crushed tomatoes
1 carrot, peeled and cut into small dice
1 tbsp lemon juice
Salt and pepper to taste
Fresh dill chopped fine for garnish
Sour cream for garnish

Mix all the ingredients in the cooker. Cover and cook undisturbed for 3 hours. Taste for seasonings and adjust as necessary. Puree the soup with a hand held blender, or use a food processor. Do not over puree. There should still be some small bits of beets. Serve in bowls with a dollop of sour cream on top and sprinkled with the dill. This soup is also good chilled.

Serves two to four

CABBAGE AND BEEF SOUP

This wonderful cold weather soup uses just a few modest ingredients: cabbage to start with, and some leftover beef as an additional flavoring. Serve with dark crusty bread and a green salad for a full meal. Adjust your babushka!

3 cups cabbage, cored and shredded
1 can (10.5 oz) beef broth
½ medium onion, diced, approx. ¼ cup
1 celery stalk, diced, approx. ¼ cup
½ cup cooked beef, cut into ¼" pieces
1 medium carrot, diced fine, approx. ½ cup
1 tsp thyme
1 bay leaf
Salt and pepper to taste

Add all the ingredients to the cooker and stir well. Push down the cabbage to get it all into the cooker – it will seem like too much, but it will cook down. Cover and cook undisturbed for 3 or more hours. Test for seasoning and adjust as needed. You can't overcook this – so just let it go until you're ready to serve.

Serves two to four

Note: Some people prefer this soup a little mashed up - you can do this with a stick blender, or pour the soup out of the cooker into a bowl, and mash it up with a large fork or a potato masher.

CHEESE SOUP WITH VEGETABLES

An array of finely diced vegetables makes this a most festive and heartwarming winter soup. Serve with some crisp croutons on top.

1 can (10.5 oz) condensed cheese soup
1 cup water
½ cup finely diced celery
½ cup finely diced green bell pepper
½ cup finely diced red bell pepper
½ cup finely diced onion
½ cup diced fresh mushrooms
1 tbsp Worcestershire sauce
Salt and pepper to taste

Spray the cooker with cooking spray. In a medium bowl dilute the cheese soup with the water. Combine with all the other ingredients and mix well. Pour the mixture into the cooker. Cover and cook undisturbed for 3 hours or longer. The vegetables will still be al dente. Serve in bowls with a dollop of sour cream on top along with the croutons.

Serves two to four

Note: If the soup is too thick, add a little water to thin it out as desired.

CHICKEN SOUP WITH TORTELLINI

This is a light chicken soup with the Tortellini acting somewhat like wontons in Wonton Soup. You can pre-cook the Tortellini if you wish, but they will cook in the broth in the time allotted if they have been thawed. A sprig of fresh watercress on top of each serving adds a dash of color.

2 cans (10.5 oz each) chicken broth
1 carrot, cut into fine dice
½ medium onion, diced
2 cups frozen small Tortellini, thawed (add more if you want)
Salt and pepper to taste
Freshly grated Parmesan cheese for garnish
Fresh watercress as garnish

Add all the ingredients to the cooker except the Tortellini. Cover and cook undisturbed for 2 hours. Add the thawed Tortellini and stir well. Cover and cook for 1 hour or more, or until the Tortellini are done and are no longer "pasty." Serve in warmed bowls with a sprig of watercress on top and a sprinkle of the Parmesan cheese.

Serves two to four

CORN CHOWDER

This is a very satisfying soup for a winter luncheon. It is easy to make and is full of flavor. Serve with a green salad garnished with tomatoes and thinly sliced red onion. Slices of toasted French Baguette make a great accompaniment.

1 can (10.5 oz) mushroom soup
½ cup water
1 can (15 oz) whole kernel corn, drained
4 slices bacon, fried crisp and chopped roughly
4 scallions chopped in ½" slices
1 small green bell pepper diced fine, approx. ½ cup
1 small red bell pepper diced fine, approx. ½ cup
1 cup half and half or whole milk
Salt and pepper to taste
Minced parsley for garnish

Dilute the soup with the water. In a medium bowl mix all the ingredients except the milk. Add the mixture to the cooker. Cover and cook undisturbed for 2 hours. Taste and adjust the seasonings as necessary and add the milk. Cook for 1 hour more or until the soup is warm enough to serve. Serve in warm bowls with the minced parsley on top.

Serves two to four

CREAMED CARROT SOUP

In France this soup is known as Crème Crecy. This version is not, however, exactly like the original but it comes close. If your garden is full of carrots this is a good way to use some of them before the rabbits get them! Serve with delicate toast points, or small rolls.

1 can (10.5 oz) condensed cream of mushroom soup
1 cup water
1 cup fresh carrots, cut into very thin slices or diced very fine*
1 tsp grated nutmeg
Pinch of cayenne pepper
1 tsp dried thyme
1 cup sour cream or half and half
Salt and white pepper to taste

In a medium bowl dilute the soup with the water and add all the other ingredients, except the soup cream or half and half. Stir well to blend. Pour the mixture into the cooker. Cover and cook undisturbed for 3 hours. The carrots will still be crunchy. Add the sour cream or half and half, stir well. Cover and cook for an additional 1 hour. Cream the soup with a stick blender or pour it into a food processor. Serve warm or at room temperature.

Serves two to four

*You can use 1 can (8.5 oz) carrots instead of fresh – dice very fine.

CREAMY CORN SOUP

This easy to prepare soup has the extra zip of the Tabasco sauce to give it some zest. Serve it hot with a dollop of sour cream for garnish.

1 can (10.5 oz) whole kernel corn, drained
1 can (10.5 oz) creamed corn (do not drain)
1 can (10.5 oz) chicken broth
1 cup half and half (or sour cream if you wish)
2 tsp Tabasco sauce
Salt and pepper to taste

Pour the corn into the cooker. Add the Tabasco sauce. Stir well. Cover and cook undisturbed for 2-3 hours. Taste for seasonings and add salt and pepper (and more Tabasco if you are inclined) to taste. Add the half and half and continue cooking for 1 hour or more or until ready to serve.

Serves two to four

EASY CHICKEN SOUP

You can make this flavorful and nourishing chicken soup in less than three hours or so. Serve with a crusty loaf of bread.

2 cans (10.5 oz each) chicken broth
1 cup cooked chicken cut into bite size pieces – white or dark meat
1 cup frozen mixed vegetables, thawed to room temperature
2 Roma tomatoes, diced
1 tsp dried basil leaves
Salt and pepper to taste
Chopped parsley for garnish

Combine all the ingredients in the cooker. Cover and cook for 3 hours or until the soup is hot enough to serve. Taste for seasonings and add salt and pepper as needed. The vegetables will still be "al dente," so continue to cook as long as you wish. Serve the soup directly from the cooker into warm soup bowls. Sprinkle chopped parsley on top and add croutons if you wish.

Serves two to four

FRENCH ONION SOUP

It is impossible to make a good onion soup in the slow cooker unless you are willing to cook the onions before hand on the stove. That is how this soup is made. Combined with the canned onion soup this is a really hearty version. It is worth the effort. Serve with a slice of toasted baguette on top with grated cheese on top of the bread.

2 cans (10.5 oz each) condensed onion soup
4 cups yellow onions, sliced fine (pre-cooked measure)
2 tbsp oleo and 2 tbsp olive oil (for sauteing the onions)
1 tbsp sherry or cognac
Salt and pepper to taste.

Saute the onions in a frying pan over medium heat until they caramelize and take on a dark brown color. Be careful not to scorch them. Combine the onions with the onion soup in the slow cooker. Cover and cook for 3 hours or until the soup is hot enough to serve. Add the sherry or cognac and adjust the seasonings as necessary.

Serves two to four

FRESH TOMATO SOUP

If your summer garden has a surplus of tomatoes then this is a good way to use some of them. If you have not tasted fresh tomato soup before, then this will be a revelation. Serve with toasted croutons and a dollop of sour cream on top and garnish with fresh basil.

4 cups fresh tomatoes, seeded but not peeled, roughly chopped
1 can (10.5 oz) chicken broth
1 small onion, diced
Salt and pepper to taste
1 tsp olive oil
1 tbsp finely chopped basil as garnish

Coat the bottom of the cooker liner with the olive oil. Add the tomatoes, the chopped onion and the chicken broth. Cover and cook undisturbed for 3 hours. Puree the soup with a stick blender or put it into a food processor and puree very fine. Adjust for seasonings as necessary. Sprinkle the chopped basil on top with the sour cream.

Serves two to four

ITALIAN BEAN AND SAUSAGE SOUP

This hearty soup is a meal in itself. Serve with a simple green salad and good dense Italian bread.

1 lb pre-cooked Italian sausage, cut into thin slices
1 can (14.5 oz) Great Northern or any other white beans
1 can (10.5 oz) chicken broth
1 can (8.5 oz) diced tomatoes in thick puree
1 cup water (optional – or more chicken broth if you have it)
1 small onion, diced
1 tbsp garlic, minced
1 tbsp dried basil leaves
Salt and pepper to taste
Grated Parmesan cheese for garnish

Mix all the ingredients in the cooker. Cover and let cook for 3 hours or until the soup is warm enough to serve. Serve directly from the cooker into warm soup bowls and top with a sprinkle of the grated cheese.

Serves two to four

"KRAB" AND CORN SOUP

Somehow crab and corn have a natural affinity. To save your pocketbook from ruin I have used imitation "krab" available at all super market fish counters. Serve with toast points as a first course.

1 large can (18.8 oz) Chunky New England Clam Chowder
½ cup water
1 lb. imitation "krab," chopped into bite sized pieces
1 can (10.5 oz) whole kernel corn, drained
½ cup celery, diced
½ cup green bell pepper, diced
1 tbsp pimento, diced
1 tbsp Worcestershire sauce
Salt and pepper to taste

Spray the cooker with cooking spray. In a medium bowl dilute the soup with the water. Add all the other ingredients and mix well. Pour the mixture into the cooker. Cover and let cook undisturbed for 3 hours. The vegetables will still be crunchy. Continue to cook the soup for as long as you want, and serve directly from the cooker into warm bowls.

Serves two to four

LENTIL AND SAUSAGE SOUP

Lentils are one of the oldest crops known to man. Even the ancient Egyptians grew and ate them. This is a good heartwarming soup for a cold winter day. Serve it with a crusty bread and lots of butter.

2 cans (10.5 oz each) chicken broth
1½ cups dried lentils
1 small onion, diced fine, approx. ½ cup
½ lb cooked sausage of your choice, cut into ¼" slices
Pinch of thyme
Salt and pepper to taste

Spray the cooker with cooking spray. Add the broth, water, lentils, diced onion and the sausage. Cover and cook undisturbed for 3-4 hours. Taste for doneness. If the lentils are still hard, cook for an additional 1 hour or more. Taste for seasoning and add salt, pepper and thyme. Serve hot.

Serves two to four

Note: If you prefer to use canned lentils add 1 can (15.5oz) drained, to the chicken broth. Proceed as described above. Some people prefer this soup slightly mashed up – you can do this with an electric mixer, or with a wire whip.

MANHATTAN CLAM CHOWDER

Manhattan or New England? Take your pick but for the mini slow cooker Manhattan Clam Chowder with the tomato base works better. The use of canned clams does not alter the taste of this delicious soup.

2 cans (6.5 oz each) clams, drained and roughly chopped *
1 can (15.5 oz) crushed tomatoes in heavy puree
1 medium onion, diced fine
1 can (10.5 oz) sliced potatoes, drained and diced
1 celery stalk, diced fine
Chopped parsley for garnish
½ cup milk or half and half, to "get the red out"
Salt and pepper to taste

Add all the ingredients to the cooker except the clams and the parsley and the milk. Cover and cook undisturbed for 2 hours. Add the clams and cook for 1 hour more. Add the milk and adjust the seasonings. Serve in warm bowls with the chopped parsley sprinkled on top.

Serves two to four

*You can save the clam juice and after the soup has cooked add whatever amount you want to give the soup the necessary clam "taste."

MINESTRONE SOUP

This is a traditional Italian soup – almost like an American vegetable soup but with the addition of the tomatoes and the elbow macaroni. Serve with chunks of rustic bread and lots of butter.

1 can (14.5 oz) chicken broth
1 can (8.5 oz) diced tomatoes
2½ cups frozen mixed vegetables, thawed to room temperature
1 tbsp chopped garlic
½ cup medium onion, diced
1 tbsp dried basil leaves
½ cup (dry measure) elbow macaroni, cooked "al dente"
Salt and pepper

Spray the cooker with cooking spray. Pour all the ingredients (except the macaroni) into the cooker. Stir well. Cover and cook undisturbed for 3 hours or until the soup vegetables are tender but still have some crunch. Add the "al dente" cooked macaroni, stir well, cover and cook undisturbed for 1 more hour. Serve in warm bowls, with some of the basil leaves sprinkled on top. A sprinkle of freshly grated Parmesan cheese is an added treat.

Serves two to four

MUSHROOM SOUP

It is probably not a good idea to make a cream soup from scratch in the slow cooker as there is always the chance that the milk or cream will curdle before the soup is finished. That is why I have used commercial cream soups as a base in many of these recipes. However this dark and dusky fresh mushroom soup with a beef broth base will satisfy.

3 cans (10.5 oz each) beef broth (about 5 cups)
1½ cups sliced mushrooms (approx 12 oz)
½ cup onion, diced
1 tbsp sherry or cognac
1 tsp cornstarch
Salt and pepper to taste

Combine the beef broth, onions, and the mushrooms in the slow cooker. Cover and let cook undisturbed for 2 hours. Take ¼ cup of the broth from the cooker and mix with the cornstarch. Stir the cornstarch mixture into the soup, cover and cook for 1 hour more. Just before serving add the sherry or cognac and adjust the seasonings as necessary.

Serves two to four

Note: You can puree this soup with a stick blender or in a food processor.

NAVY BEAN AND TOMATO SOUP

This simple soup is perfect for the beginning of a cold winter dinner. Buy ready-made croutons for garnish, or make your own by toasting some day old bread and cutting it into 1" pieces.

1 can (8.5 oz) tomatoes in heavy puree
2 cans (15.5 oz each) white navy beans, drained
1 medium onion, diced fine
2 tbsp garlic, chopped
4 slices bacon, fried crisp and chopped fine
1 tbsp dried thyme
Salt and pepper to taste
Croutons for garnish

Pour the tomatoes into the cooker and break them up as best you can with a wooden spoon. Add all the remaining ingredients and stir well. Cover and cook undisturbed for 3 hours or until the soup is warm enough to serve. Top with the croutons.

Serves two to four

PASTA AND BEAN SOUP

This famous Italian soup known as "Pasta e Fagioli" has many variations, but it always contains the two ingredients for which it is named, that is, pasta and some kind of beans. Serve with good country bread and a green salad on the side.

1 can (8.5 oz) diced tomatoes in thick puree
1 can (8.5 oz) cannelini beans (or any other white beans)
1½ cups small shape pasta cooked "al dente" (cooked measure)*
1 can (10.5 oz) chicken broth
2 tbsp garlic, chopped
½ cup onion, diced
Salt and pepper to taste
Chopped parsley for garnish
Freshly grated Parmesan cheese for garnish

Add all the ingredients to the cooker, except the pasta. Stir well. Cover and cook undisturbed for 2 hours. Add the cooked pasta, adjust the seasonings and cover and cook 1 hour more. Serve the soup in warmed bowls and garnish with the parsley and grated cheese.

Serves two to four

*You can use small elbow macaroni or any other small pasta shape

PEA SOUP

You can make this Pea Soup all year long with frozen peas. No need to work in the garden and then do the shelling and cleaning. Serve with croutons on top or with a dollop of sour cream.

1 box (10 oz) frozen peas, thawed (or approx 1¼ cups)
2 cans (10.5 oz each) chicken broth
2 cups roughly chopped lettuce leaves
1 small onion, diced fine
1 tbsp all purpose flour
1 tbsp butter or oleo
Salt and pepper to taste

Start the cooker and add the butter. Wait until it melts and then add the lettuce. Cook the lettuce for 15 minutes or until it is wilted. Stir in the flour and add the chicken broth and the peas. Cover and cook undisturbed for 3 hours. Puree the soup in the cooker with a stick blender or pour the soup into a food processor and puree it there. Serve in warm soup bowls

Serves two to four

POTATO AND LEEK SOUP

It is said that you can smell this hearty soup all over Paris on a Friday night when it is traditional for the concierge to prepare it in her tiny room next to the building entrance. With the addition of milk and cream and served cold it transforms itself into elegant Vichyssoise! Anyway, the old concierges would only have it hot. Serve with crusty baguette slices and lots of good butter.

2 cups potatoes, peeled and diced
1 cup leeks, washed well and diced (white parts only)
2 cans (10.5 oz each) chicken broth
1 cup water (optional – check before adding)
Salt and pepper to taste

Put all the ingredients into the cooker. Mix well. Cover and cook undisturbed for 3-4 hours. The vegetables should be well done. Puree the soup with a stick blender or pour into the bowl of a food processor and puree it there. Do not over blend the soup – there should still be bits of potato and leek Add the additional water if using, adjust the seasonings and serve in warm bowls.

Serves two to four

POTATO, ONION AND BACON SOUP

This robust and easy to make soup will take the chill off a bleak winter day. Serve it for lunch with good crusty bread and a salad of fresh greens and sliced tomatoes.

1 can (15.5 oz) potatoes, cut into dice (do not drain)
1 can (10.5 oz) condensed cream of potato soup
1 cup water (or more if you want after tasting)
1 small onion, diced
5 slices bacon, fried crisp and chopped fine
Chopped chives (optional)
Salt and pepper to taste

Dilute the soup with the water. Prepare the potatoes as described above and add to the soup. Add the onion and bacon and taste for seasoning. Spray the cooker with cooking spray and pour the mixture into it. Cover and cook undisturbed for 3-4 hours for the flavors to meld. Taste again for seasoning and adjust as necessary. Serve in bowls with some chopped chives on top as garnish.

Serves two to four

Note: If you prefer a creamier soup you can process it with a stick blender or in a food processor. I prefer it "chunky."

TOMATO AND RICE SOUP

Make this soup for a cold winter day when the cooking soup will bring heart warming smells from your kitchen. Serve with good hearty bread and a green salad for a complete lunch.

1 cup instant long grain premium rice (dry measure)*
1 cup hot tap water
1 can (14.5 oz) diced tomatoes, in thick puree
1 can (10.5 oz) chicken broth
½ cup celery, diced fine
Pinch of thyme
1 tsp Tabasco sauce
Salt and pepper to taste

Spray the cooker with cooking spray. Plug it in and heat for 15 minutes with the lid on. Uncover and add the rice and the hot tap water. Cover and cook undisturbed for 2-3 hours. Uncover and stir the rice. Slowly add the diced tomatoes, chicken broth and the celery. Stir well. Cover and cook for 1 hour more. Adjust for seasonings and serve hot.

Serves two to four

*You can use one bag Success Rice. Do not be disturbed if there is some water left on the bottom of the cooker after the rice is done.

TORTELLINI EN BRODO

This famous Italian soup is easy to make in the mini slow cooker. You can use either chicken or beef broth, but the soup is lighter with the chicken broth. Serve with slices of toasted Italian bread.

2 cans (10.5 oz each) chicken broth
1 pkg (16 oz approx.) frozen cheese Tortellini, thawed
1 carrot, diced fine
1 small onion, diced fine
1 small zucchini, diced fine
1 tsp thyme
Salt and pepper to taste
Grated Parmesan cheese for garnish

Add all the ingredients to the cooker. Cover and cook undisturbed for 3 hours or until the soup is warm enough to serve and the Tortellini are cooked al dente. Serve from the cooker into warm bowls and sprinkle some of the grated cheese on top.

Serves two to four

Note: If you wish, you can cook the Tortellini according to package directions and add them to the soup ½ hour before serving.

TORTELLINI AND SAUSAGE SOUP

This is really a one-dish meal in a bowl. Perfect for a cold winter day. Serve it with good Italian style bread and a fresh green salad on the side. Don't forget the grated Parmesan cheese.

½ lb. pre-cooked Italian or other sausage of your choice.
1 can (28 oz) crushed tomatoes in thick puree
1 pkg (9 oz approx) frozen meat stuffed Tortellini, thawed
1 small onion, diced, approx. ¼ cup
1 carrot, sliced thin, approx. ¼ cup
1 small zucchini, sliced thin, approx. ¼ cup
1 tbsp dried basil leaves
Salt and pepper to taste

Pour the tomatoes into the cooker. Cut the sausage into thin slices. Add the sausage and vegetables. Stir well. Cover and cook undisturbed for 2 hours. Add the Tortellini. Cover and cook for 1 more hour. Check the Tortellini for doneness. If they are still pasty, cover and cook for ½ hour more. Serve in bowls with grated Parmesan on top.

Serves two to four

Note: If you prefer you can cook the Tortellini according to the package instructions until "al dente" – then add them to the soup about ½ hour before serving.

TUSCAN BREAD AND TOMATO SOUP

In the farmhouses of Tuscany nothing is wasted. Use day-old or stale bread for this soup and fresh tomatoes from the garden in summer and canned tomatoes in winter.

4 cups day old or stale bread, cut into 1" pieces
1 can (28 oz) whole tomatoes in heavy syrup
2 tbsp garlic, chopped (more if you want)
1 small onion, diced
1 can (10.5 oz) chicken broth
1 tbsp dried basil leaves
Salt and pepper to taste
Grated Parmesan cheese for garnish

Break up the tomatoes as best you can with a wooden spoon. Don't worry if they are chunky! This is a rustic soup, after all! Combine all the ingredients in a medium bowl. Pour into the cooker. Cover and cook undisturbed for 2-3 hours. Taste for seasoning and add salt and pepper as necessary. Cover and cook for 1 more hour. Serve in warm soup bowls with the grated Parmesan on top.

Serves two to four

U. S. SENATE BEAN SOUP

This soup has been a favorite in the U.S. Senate restaurant since the beginning of the 20th. Century. No matter which side of the aisle they sit on, the Senators know a good thing when they have it. You can make this from scratch, but you can also save time and effort by using the canned beans. The final result will be much the same as the original. The Senators have this served with specially made crackers – plain old saltines will do just as well.

1 can (15.8 oz) white beans (your choice), drained
1 can (8.5 oz) white beans (your choice), not drained
1 can (10.5 oz) beef broth
4 slices of bacon, cooked crisp and chopped fine
1 celery stalk, chopped fine, approx. ¼ cup
1 small onion, chopped fine, approx ¼ cup
1 carrot, chopped fine, approx. ¼ cup
1 tbsp garlic, chopped fine
Salt and pepper to taste

Spray the cooker with cooking spray. Add all the ingredients (except the bacon) and stir well. Cover and cook undisturbed for 4 hours. The vegetables will still be tender-crisp. Test for seasonings. Ladle the soup into warm bowls and place some of the chopped bacon on top of each bowl.

Serves two to four

VEGETABLE SOUP

This is probably one of the oldest soups invented by man, and it is still a favorite. This is best made with fresh vegetables - canned ones just do not have the flavor. You can vary the number and kind if vegetables you use. Raid your fall garden, and those unused in the vegetable drawer of your refrigerator.

3 cups beef broth (2–10.5 oz cans) save the rest for another use*
½ cup carrots, diced
½ cup onions, diced
½ cup celery, diced
½ cup potatoes, diced
1 tsp garlic, diced fine
1 tbsp tomato paste
Salt and pepper to taste

Spray the cooker with cooking spray. Add the broth, and then all the vegetables – stir well. Cover and cook undisturbed for 3 hours. Check the vegetables for doneness – they should be cooked, but still crunchy. If you want the vegetables softer, then cover and cook for 1 hour more. Adjust for seasonings and serve hot.

Serves two to four

Note: If you can't get fresh vegetables for this soup, then buy frozen mixed vegetables – one 8 oz package should do it.

*If there is still room in the cooker after the soup has cooked, add some of the left-over broth before serving.

VEGETARIAN BEAN SOUP

The use of canned beans does not in any way deter from the taste of this quick and easy soup. Serve it with thick slices of French bread and a green salad on the side.

1 can (28 oz) Navy or other beans of your choice
1 cup tomato juice
1 celery stalk, sliced fine
1 carrot sliced, fine
1 small onion, diced fine
1 tsp red pepper flakes
Salt and ground black pepper to taste

Put all the ingredients into the cooker. Stir well. Cover and cook undisturbed for 3 hours or until the soup is warm enough to serve. The vegetables will still be crunchy. If you want them better done, cover the cooker and let the soup cook for 1 hour more.

Serves two to four

WONTON SOUP

This easily made soup is warming and filling. You can make your own wontons should you prefer, but good ones can be found frozen in large super markets or in oriental specialty shops. The amount of wontons is up to you, but three to four per person is more or less traditional..

2 cans (10.5 oz each) condensed chicken broth
1 cup water
4 -5 scallions, cut into small pieces on the bias
12 – 16 wontons (or more if you wish), thawed
Sesame oil for garnish
Salt and pepper to taste

Pour the chicken broth into the cooker along with the scallions and the water. Cover and cook undisturbed for 2 hours. Add the thawed wontons and stir. Cover and cook for 1 more hour. Test the wontons for doneness. If they are still gummy or pasty, cover and cook for 1 hour more. Serve in warm bowls with a drop or two of sesame oil on top.

Serves two to four

FISH AND SHELLFISH

Bay Scallops Provencal
Cajun Style Shrimp
Cod Fillets with Vegetables
Cod with Tomatoes and Olives
Creamed Tuna
Curried "Krab" Casserole
Curried Shrimp
Easy Cod Stew
Fish Veracruz Style
Flounder Provencal
Flounder Rolls in Light Tomato Sauce
Flounder Rolls with Prosciutto
"Krab Gumbo
"Krab" Stuffed Flounder Fillets
Linguini with Shrimp
Mediterranean Style Scallops
Oyster Stew
Poached Salmon in Court Bouillon
Provencal Fish Stew
Quick "Krab" Newburg
Rice with Shrimp and Peas
Rice with Shrimp and Red Pepper
Salmon Loaf
Salmon Pinwheels
Salmon Steaks and Vegetable Medley
Scallops in Cream Sauce
Scallops Marinara
Scallops Mediterranean Style

continued next page

FISH AND SHELLFISH CONTINUED

Scallops and Shrimp Mornay
Seafood Stew
Shrimp Creole
Shrimp Curry
Shrimp Fra Diavolo
Shrimp Gumbo
Shrimp in Herbed Butter
Shrimp Jambalaya
Shrimp in Light Tomato Sauce
Shrimp Marinara
Shrimp Newburg
Shrimp and Oriental Vegetables
Shrimp and Saffron Rice Casserole
Shrimp with Saffron Rice and Tomatoes
Shrimp with Tomatoes and Pasta
Shrimp Wiggle
Sole Duglere
Sole with Vegetables
Swordfish with Capers and Olives
Tuna Loaf
Tuna and Macaroni Casserole
Tuna Nicoise
Tuna Noodle Casserole
Tuna Steak
Tuna Surprise

FISH AND SHELLFISH

The shape and size of the mini slow cooker dictates in some ways the way in which fish and shellfish can be cooked. Any large fish is not possible, but fish cut into portions to fit the cooker will cook to perfection. Naturally, shrimp are strong contenders for the mini slow cooker because of their size and shape.

However, you have a wonderful selection to choose from. The mini slow cooker heats up faster than it's larger cousins do so do not be afraid to add raw fish or shrimp to the cooker. The cooker reaches a temperature of about 170 degrees in an hour. Most of the fish and shellfish recipes start out with pre-heating a sauce or rice, and then adding the fresh seafood or shellfish for a final 1 hour of cooking.

Fish or shellfish is one area in which over cooking could affect the dish. You will find that shrimp or chunks of fish cook in about 1 hour when added to an already hot cooker.

Scallops are another wonderful seafood when cooked in the mini slow cooker. If you use very large sea scallops it would be better to slice them in half before cooking. Treat them like shrimp and do not over cook as they will become stringy and tough.

If you are cooking fish filets buy one large one and then cut it into pieces to fit the cooker. Do not be afraid to pile them on top of one another as the heat of the cooker surrounds everything with the same temperature.

Remember always when using seafood – buy only the freshest, treat it gently and keep it always under refrigeration until you are ready to use it.

BAY SCALLOPS PROVENCAL

The Southern part of France is an area known for olives, tomatoes and gifts from the sea. This recipe combines all of them to good result. Serve this dish with couscous, white rice or small red potatoes. A salad of fresh greens, sliced tomatoes and red onion with a zesty vinaigrette would be a fine accompaniment.

1½ lbs bay scallops (or sea scallops cut in half)
1 small onion, diced
1 small green pepper, diced
1 can (15.5 oz) diced tomatoes
1 tsp butter or oleo
1 small zucchini, diced fine
½ cup pitted Calamata olives, cut in half
2 tbsp garlic, chopped
Pinch hot red pepper flakes
1 tsp dried thyme
Salt and pepper to taste

Spray the cooker with cooking spray. Add the tomatoes and the oleo, vegetables, garlic, red pepper flakes, Calamata olives and thyme. Stir well. Cover and cook for 2 hours. Add the scallops and cook for 1 hour more. Do not overcook. Serve the vegetable sauce over the scallops.

Serves two to four

CAJUN STYLE SHRIMP

When the shrimp boats come in from the Gulf of Mexico the Cajun cooks start their fires. Serve these spicy shrimp with rice or coucous and cold beer!

1 lb. fresh shrimp, peeled and deveined
1 can (28 oz) tomatoes in heavy puree
3 tbsp garlic, chopped
4 -5 tbsp Cajun spice mix
1 tsp Tabasco sauce

Pour the tomatoes into the cooker and break them up with a wood spoon. Add the spices and stir. Cover and cook undisturbed for 1 hour. Add the shrimp and stir well. Cover and cook for 1 hour more.

Serves two to four

COD FILLETS WITH VEGETABLES

This is a wonderful dish for a cold winters evening. The combination of cod and vegetables is traditional in Maine, where cod has been a staple for centuries. Serve with a good crusty bread and a salad to precede the fish.

Cod fillets, app. 1¼ lb cut into four pieces to fit the cooker
3 small red potatoes, sliced thin
1 small zucchini, sliced thin
1 small onion, sliced thin
2 Roma tomatoes, sliced thin
¾ cup tomato juice (or V8 juice if you prefer)
Salt and pepper to taste

Spray the cooker liner with cooking spray. Layer the vegetables on the bottom of the cooker, starting with the potatoes then the zucchini, onion, and ending with the tomatoes. Pour the tomato juice over the vegetables. Cover and cook undisturbed for 2 hours. Place the fish fillets on top of the vegetables. Salt and pepper well. Cover and let cook undisturbed for 1 hour more. Be careful when removing the fish as it may start to fall apart. Serve the vegetables on top of or beside the fish.

Serves two to four

COD WITH TOMATOES AND OLIVES

Cod is a fish that can stand up to hearty flavors and spices. Serve this with small boiled potatoes and a green salad.

1 can (28 oz) tomatoes in heavy puree
1 lb fresh cod fillets cut into 1" pieces
½ cup pitted Calamata olives, cut in half
1 tbsp garlic, chopped
1 tbsp dried basil leaves
Salt and pepper to taste

Pour the tomatoes into the cooker. Break the tomatoes up as best you can with a wooden spoon. Add the olives and garlic and stir well. Cover and cook undisturbed for 1 hour. Add the cod and stir. Cover and cook for 1 more hour.

Serves two to four

CREAMED TUNA

In the fifties this was a favorite of the "tea room" set and it is fashionable again! Serve it as before in baked patty shells or over freshly toasted white bread. It sounds "dainty" but it is in fact a very satisfying dish for a luncheon or light supper.

2 cans (6.5 oz each) tuna in water, drained and flaked.
1 can (10.5 oz) condensed cream of mushroom soup
½ cup water
1 celery stalk, diced fine, approx. ¼ cup
1 onion, diced fine, approx. ½ cup
½ lb sliced mushrooms, approx. ½ cup
2 tbsp dry sherry
Parsley, chopped fine for garnish
Salt and pepper to taste

Spray the cooker with cooking spray. Dilute the soup with the water. Combine all the ingredients in the cooker. Cover and cook undisturbed for 3 hours. Serve as suggested with a sprinkling of the chopped parsley on top.

Serves two to four

CURRIED "KRAB" CASSEROLE

This is a light dish suitable for a formal luncheon. Serve it directly from the cooker with rice and a green vegetable like freshly cooked asparagus. Fresh biscuits or cornbread would be a suitable accompaniment.

1 lb. "Krab" available at your super market fish counter
1 cup (uncooked measure) elbow macaroni
¼ cup scallions cut on the diagonal in ¼" slices
1 can (10 5 oz) cheese soup, diluted as directed
2 tbsp. Madras curry powder (or more as desired)
½ cup sour cream
Salt and pepper to taste

Spray the cooker with cooking spray. Chop the "krab" into smaller pieces. Dilute the soup with water as directed on the can. Cook the elbow macaroni according to package directions (al dente). Drain well. Combine the macaroni with the soup, "krab," scallions and curry powder. Pour the mixture into the cooker. Cover and cook undisturbed for 1 hour. Add the sour cream. Stir well. Cover and cook for 1 hour more or until the casserole is hot enough to serve.

Serves two to four

CURRIED SHRIMP

This dish is good served as a light luncheon entrée. It may seem a little exotic to some of your more conservative friends, but then once they taste it they will be won over. Serve it with rice and a green salad with crusty rolls.

1 can (14.5 oz) diced tomatoes in thick puree
1 lb fresh shrimp, peeled and deveined
1 can (8.5 oz) sliced potatoes, drained and diced fine
1 tbsp garlic, chopped
1 tbsp curry powder (or more if you desire, to your taste)
1 tsp cayenne pepper
1 tsp lemon juice
Salt and pepper to taste
Chopped parsley for garnish

Pour the tomatoes into the cooker. Add the spices and stir well. Cover and cook undisturbed for 2 hours. Add the shrimp and potatoes and stir well. Check for seasonings and adjust as necessary. Cover and cook for 1 more hour.

Serves two to four

EASY COD STEW

If you are traveling in New England where fresh cod is sometimes available at the dock you will want to make this easy stew. This is a one-dish meal. Serve it with a simple salad and crusty rolls.

1 lb fresh cod filets, cut into 1" pieces
1 can (8.5oz) diced tomatoes in heavy puree
1 can (10.5 oz) chicken broth
2 small red potatoes, diced, approx. ¾ cup
1 medium onion, diced, approx. ¼ cup
2 tbsp chopped parsley, for garnish
Salt and pepper to taste

Spray the cooker with cooking spray. Add all the ingredients except the cod. Mix well. Cover and cook undisturbed for 2 hours. Add the cod and stir. Cover and cook for 1 hour more. Check for seasonings and adjust as necessary. Serve on warm plates with the parsley sprinkled on top.

Serves two to four

FISH VERACRUZ STYLE

This fish recipe comes from the Eastern part of Mexico and specifically from the area around Veracruz which is noted for its seafood. Buy filets which can be trimmed to stack in the slow cooker or about 4" square. Be careful when removing the filets – they will have a tendency to fall apart, so do not overcook. Serve with rice and a green vegetable.

4 fish fillets, approx 4 oz each skinned (cod, weakfish or sea bass)
2 cans (10.5 oz each) stewed or diced tomatoes
1 small onion, diced
1 tbsp finely chopped garlic
1 tbsp capers, drained
¼ cup Manzanilla stuffed olives, halved
½ cup salsa (medium or hot)
½ tsp oregano
Juice of one lime
Salt and pepper to taste

Spray the cooker liner with cooking spray. In a medium bowl combine the tomato sauce with all the other ingredients. Mix well. Stack the fish filets one on top of the other spreading some of the sauce between each filet. Pour the remaining sauce over all. Cover and cook undisturbed for 2 hours. Check fish with a fork – if it flakes easily it is done. If not cook for ½ hour more. Remove the fish carefully to serving plates and pour the sauce over.

Serves two to four

FLOUNDER PROVENCAL

This is a wonderful lusty fish dish. The vegetables under the fish will form a sauce to be served over the fish. Serve with rice and a fresh baguette, with lots of butter!

4 flounder fillets approximately 1 lb. (approx. 3"x 4" each)
3 Roma tomatoes, sliced thin
1 small zucchini, sliced thin
1 small onion, diced fine
¼ cup pitted Calamata olives, cut in half
¼ cup capers, drained and chopped fine
½ cup dry white wine
1 tbsp Herbs de Provence
1 lemon, quartered

Spray the cooker with cooking spray. Place the sliced vegetables on the bottom in no particular order. Roll the flounder fillets up tight and secure with a toothpick if necessary. Place the fish on the vegetables, and pour the wine over all. Sprinkle with the Herbs de Provence. Cover and cook undisturbed for 2 hours. Check the fish with a fork to see if it is done. It should flake easily. Remove carefully to serving plates. Use a stick blender or a fork to mash the vegetables. Pour the vegetable sauce over the fish. Serve with the quartered lemon and the rice.

Serves two to fou8r

FLOUNDER ROLLS IN LIGHT TOMATO SAUCE

This is an elegant and light dish suitable for a spring luncheon. Serve with rice, a salad and a fresh green vegetable.

4 flounder filets 3" wide x 6" long (approx 1 lb total)
1 can (10.5 oz) tomato sauce
1 cup light cream or half and half
1 tsp chopped garlic
1 tsp butter or oleo
Salt and pepper to taste.

Spray the cooker with cooking spray. Mix the tomato sauce, garlic and butter with the cream. Cover and cook for 1 hour. In the meantime prepare the flounder filets by rolling them as tightly as possible and secure with a toothpick if necessary. The rolls should measure approx 3" wide x 1 ½" in diameter. Uncover and insert the flounder rolls into the sauce. Be careful the cooker and sauce will be hot. Cover and cook for 1 hour. Test the fish for doneness with a fork. If it flakes easily it is finished. The rolls will be delicate so take care in removing them. Serve with the sauce.

Serves two to four

FLOUNDER ROLLS WITH PROSCIUTTO

This is an elegant dish which requires some initial preparation, but is worth it. Select filets which are no more than 3" wide and about 6" long so they will stand up in the cooker. The prosciutto and the asparagus will also have to be trimmed to fit. Serve with rice and a Hollandaise sauce.

4 flounder filets, trimmed to fit the cooker as above.
4 slices prosciutto, trimmed to fit.
8 pieces of asparagus cut to 3" long, and par boiled
4 scallions, cut to 3" long
1 small red pepper, cut into 8 batons 3" long.
¼ cup dry white wine
Salt and pepper to taste

Spray the cooker with cooking spray. Lay out the filets on a work table, and trim if necessary. Salt and pepper each filet and lay the prosciutto slice on top. Put two pieces of asparagus on each filet side ways with 2 pieces of the red pepper and 1 scallion. Roll up the filets lengthwise as tightly as possible and secure with a toothpick if necessary. The roll should measure 3" long x 1½" diameter. You may have to force them into the cooker. Pour the white wine over. Cover and let cook undisturbed for 2 hours. The fish should flake easily. Be careful removing the rolls as they will be very delicate.

Serves two to four

"KRAB" GUMBO

Not the real thing but no one will know the difference. Use all the other traditional ingredients and your secret is safe. Serve over white (or dirty) rice with lots of iced tea (yes) or cold beer.

1 lb "Krab" from the fish counter
1 (10 oz pkg) frozen okra, thawed
1 small onion, diced
½ cup celery, diced
½ cup green pepper, diced
1 can (8.5 oz) diced tomatoes, in thick puree
1 tbsp Worcestershire sauce
1 tbsp Tabasco sauce
2 tbsp dry sherry
Chopped parsley for garnish (optional)

In a medium bowl flake the "krab" and mix with the onion, celery and pepper. Cut the okra into ½" pieces and add to the mix. Add the tomatoes and the spices. Pour into the cooker. Cover and cook undisturbed for 3 hours. Serve hot directly from the cooker into warm bowls. Garnish with the parsley.

Serves two to four

"KRAB" STUFFED FLOUNDER FILLETS

Since real crab is so expensive I have used the imitation "krab" which can be found in most fish counters. Since it is rather chunky, it must be chopped finer to stuff into the flounder. Serve with the broccoli, and boiled small red potatoes preceded by a fresh green salad.

4 flounder fillets, approx 1 lb, and 2" x 6" each
¼ lb "krab" mix
2 tbsp mayonnaise
3 cups broccoli florets
¼ cup celery, minced fine
1 tsp butter or oleo
¼ cup water
Salt and pepper to taste

Chop the "krab" fine, and mix with the celery and mayonnaise. Place the fillets on a sheet of waxed paper. Smooth some mayonnaise over each piece. Salt and pepper well. Cover with the "krab" mixture. Roll the fillets up tight and secure with a toothpick if necessary. Place the broccoli florets at the bottom of the cooker pushing down hard to compact them. Place the fillets on top. Cover and cook undisturbed for 2 hours. Check the fillets for doneness – if they flake easily they are done. Remove carefully and keep warm. Check the broccoli. It should be al dente, crisp and not mushy.

Serves two to four

LINGUINI WITH SHRIMP

You will have to make this dish in two parts. First the sauce with the shrimp in the mini slow cooker and secondly the linguini in a pot on the stove. You will not be disappointed with the results.

1 lb Linguini (or as much as you like)
Boiling water for cooking linguini
2 cans (14.5 oz each) crushed tomatoes
1 lb fresh shrimp, peeled and deveined
1 medium onion, diced
1 medium green bell pepper, diced
2 tbsp garlic, chopped
1 tsp dried oregano
1 tsp red pepper flakes
Salt and pepper to taste
Grated Parmesan cheese for garnish

Spray the cooker with cooking spray. Add the tomatoes, onion, pepper and the spices. Cover and cook for 1 hour. In the meantime prepare the pasta according to package directions. Set aside. Add the shrimp to the sauce. Cover and cook for 1 hour more. Serve the sauce over the linguini. Top generously with the grated Parmesan cheese.

Serves two to four

MEDITERRANEAN STYLE SCALLOPS

Scallops are found in just about every part of the world and are abundant in the Mediterranean Sea. If you buy large sea scallops slice them in half. Serve the stew in bowls with boiled potatoes and crusty French bread to sop up the juices.

1 can (15.5oz) crushed tomatoes in thick puree
1 lb bay scallops (if sea scallops cut in half or quarters)
1 green bell pepper, diced, approx. ½ cup
1 medium onion, diced, approx. ½ cup
¼ cup capers, drained
¼ cup pitted green olives, chopped in half
1 tsp red pepper flakes
1 tsp thyme
1 tsp dried basil leaves
Salt and pepper to taste

Spray the cooker with cooking spray. In a medium size bowl mix all the ingredients except the scallops. Pour into the cooker. Cover and cook undisturbed for 2 hours. Add the scallops, cover and cook 1 hour more. Do not over cook as the scallops will get tough and stringy.

Serves two to four

OYSTER STEW

If you are somewhere where fresh live oysters are available then this might just be for you. Use only the freshest oysters that have just been shucked. Reserve some of the oyster liquid to add to the stew. Traditionally served with oyster crackers, but thin buttered toast will do just fine.

2 doz. fresh oysters, shucked and drained (reserve juice)*
1 can (10.5 oz) "Campbells" chunky clam chowder, or equal
½ cup water
½ cup half and half
½ cup oyster liquor
1 tsp paprika
1 tsp garlic salt
2 tbsp Worcestershire sauce
1 tsp Tabasco sauce
Pepper to taste

Spray the cooker with cooking spray. Add the clam chowder to the liner and dilute with ½ cup water. Add the spices and stir well. Cover and cook undisturbed for 2 hours. Add the oysters with the cream and the oyster liquor. Cover and cook for 1 hour more or until the oysters plump up and the edges begin to curl. Serve in warm soup bowls.

Serves two to four

* Fresh oysters are sometimes available in cartons at your local fish counter. Use these, if available, rather than shuck your own. Buy approximately 1 lb (16 oz) stewing oysters, approx. 2 cups.

POACHED SALMON IN COURT BOUILLON

This is the classic way to cook salmon, especially in France where poached salmon is served cold from an hors d'oeuvre table, or warm as a regular fish course. Whichever way you decide to do it this produces a lovely delicate fish. If serving cold, accompany the salmon with mayonnaise and thin slices of cucumber. If you are serving the salmon warm, then a freshly made Hollandaise is the traditional accompaniment. Only the most delicate vegetables should be served with the fish in either case.

1 lb. fresh salmon fillets, cut into pieces to fit the cooker, 4 in all. Be sure all the pin bones are out!
1 can (10.5 oz) vegetable broth
½ cup water
½ cup dry white wine
½ cup celery, diced fine
½ cup onion, diced fine
½ cup carrot, diced fine
1 tbsp whole peppercorns
1 bay leaf
1 tsp dried thyme
Salt and pepper to taste

Spray the cooker with cooking spray. Add all the liquid ingredients and vegetables and stir well. Cover and cook for 1 hour. Carefully place the salmon fillets into the broth. Be sure they are all covered with the liquid. Add more water if necessary. Cover and cook undisturbed for 1 hour more. Check to see if the fish is done – it should flake easily with a fork, however it is best on the rare side. Remove the fish with a slotted spoon and serve as above.

Serves two to four

PROVENCAL FISH STEW

Tomatoes form the base of this spicy fish stew. Serve with a salad of mixed greens with a crusty country baguette.

1 can (14.5 oz) crushed tomatoes in thick puree
1 medium onion, diced, approx. ½ cup
2 tbsp garlic, chopped
1 green bell pepper, diced, approx. ½ cup
1 cup small red potatoes, diced
¼ cup pitted Calamata olives, cut in half
1 tsp red pepper flakes
1 tsp dried basil leaves
1 tsp dried thyme leaves
½ lb fresh small shrimp, peeled and deveined, approx. ½ cup
½ lb bay or sea scallops, approx. ½ cup*
1 lb fresh fish filets (cod, snapper or halibut) cut into ½" pieces
Salt and pepper to taste

Spray the cooker with cooking spray. In a bowl mix the tomatoes with the diced vegetables and the spices. Pour into the cooker. Cover and cook undisturbed for 2 hours. Uncover and add the fish, scallops and shrimp. Cover and cook for 1 hour more. Test the fish for doneness by flaking with a fork. Do not overcook as the shrimp and scallops will become tough and stringy.

Serves two to four

* If using sea scallops, cut them in half or quarters.

QUICK "KRAB" NEWBURG

Since real crabmeat is so expensive I have used the "Krab" available at most fish counters and no one will know the difference. This is wonderful served over corn bread or toasted English muffins. Don't forget a fresh green salad and a green vegetable as an accompaniment.

1¼ lb pkg. "Krabmeat"
1 can (10.5 oz) cheese soup
½ cup water
¼ cup dry sherry
½ cup celery, chopped
1 cup frozen peas, thawed
¼ cup pimento, chopped
Salt and pepper to taste

In a medium bowl flake the "Krabmeat" into bite size pieces. Add the soup diluted with the water and sherry. Combine all the other ingredients and stir well. Spray the cooker with cooking spray. Add the "krab" mixture. Cover and cook undisturbed for 3 hours or until serving temperature.

Serves two to four

RICE WITH SHRIMPS AND PEAS

This may seem complicated at first but it is very easy to make and is a refreshing Spring dish. Serve with a tossed green salad with sliced tomatoes and a good balsamic dressing.

1 lb fresh medium shrimp peeled and deveined, approx. 2 cups
1½ cups instant enriched long grain premium white rice*
1½ cups hot tap water
1 small onion, diced, approx. ½ cup
1 can (10.5 oz) tiny spring peas, drained
1 tsp garlic, chopped
Salt and pepper to taste

Spray the cooker with cooking spray. Add the rice and the hot tap water. Add the chopped onion, cover and cook undisturbed for 2 hours. Fluff the rice with a fork. Do not be afraid if there is still some water on the bottom of the cooker. Add the shrimp and cook for 45 minutes. Add the peas and cook for 15 minutes more.

Serves two to four

*You can use one bag of Success Rice if you wish.

RICE WITH SHRIMPS AND RED PEPPER

This is an easy dish to make in the mini slow cooker. Serve this with a tossed green salad with sliced onion and tomatoes.

1½ cups instant enriched long grain premium rice
1½ cups hot tap water
1 lb fresh shrimp, peeled and deveined if necessary
1 large red bell pepper, diced
½ cup red onion, diced
Salt and pepper to taste

Spray the cooker with cooking spray. Add the rice with the hot tap water. Cover and cook undisturbed 2 hours. In the meantime peel the shrimp and prepare the vegetables. Add the shrimp and vegetables and stir well. Cover and cook 1 hour more. The vegetables will be tender crisp and will have a crunchy consistency. Do not overcook as the shrimp will become stringy.

Serves two to four

SALMON LOAF

This easy salmon loaf is one of the best fish dishes which can be successfully made in the slow cooker. Garnish with slices of cucumber, and tomatoes. Use fresh homemade breadcrumbs if possible. This is wonderful as a luncheon dish, or a satisfying main course dinner dish.

1 can (16 oz.) salmon, drained (see procedure)
1½ cups bread crumbs
2/3 cup milk and salmon liquid (see procedure)
1 egg, slightly beaten
2 stalks celery, chopped fine
½ cup onion, chopped fine
½ tbsp chopped dill
Salt and pepper to taste
1 tbsp lemon juice
Sliced cucumber for garnish
Sliced tomato for garnish

Spray the cooker with cooking spray. Drain the salmon, reserving the liquid. Add milk to the liquid to make 2/3 cup. In a small bowl flake the salmon until all the chunks are broken up. Add the egg, breadcrumbs and the liquid. Mix well. Add all the other ingredients and taste. Put the ingredients into the cooker. Sprinkle some additional dill on top. Cover and cook for 3 hours. When done, unplug the cooker, and let the salmon loaf sit for ½ hour to firm up. Carefully remove the liner, and run a thin knife around the outside of the loaf to loosen. Invert over a serving plate, and un-mould the loaf. Cut into slices or wedges, or serve it directly onto plates with a spoon. Garnish with the sliced cucumbers, tomatoes and lemon wedges. This loaf is good served warm or chilled.

Serves four to six

SALMON PINWHEELS

This is an elegant presentation. Do not be afraid if the pinwheels don't fit flat into the cooker. Just let them pile up on each other around the cooker liner. Everything in the cooker cooks at the same temperature! Serve with rice or couscous, and use the vegetables as a garnish on the salmon.

1 lb filet of salmon, about 4" wide x 4" long, skin removed
1 small zucchini, cut into 3" pieces and julienned
1 Roma tomato, sliced thin
3 scallions, sliced thin
Chopped dill, fresh or dried
Salt and pepper to taste

Cut the salmon filet into 1" strips or ¼ lb each. Check for and remove any small bones. Sprinkle the flesh on both sides with the dill, salt and pepper. Roll the strips up as tight as you can and secure with a toothpick. Place the zucchini on the bottom of the cooker with the tomato and onion slices on top. Cover and cook undisturbed for 2 hours. Place the salmon rolls on top of the vegetables. Cover and cook undisturbed for 1 hour more.

Serves two to four

SALMON STEAKS AND VEGETABLE MEDLEY

This elegant dinner combines many of the flavors of the Orient with those of France and Scandinavia. Cooked in the slow cooker the fish absorbs all of these flavors along with the vegetables. Serve with tossed green salad and good French bread.

2 Salmon steaks approx. 1" thick (about 1¼ lb), cut in half
3 small red potatoes, (washed and unpeeled) sliced thin
2 small carrots, sliced thin
1 small zucchini, sliced thin
3 scallions, sliced thin
2 Roma tomatoes, sliced thin
2 tbsp capers, rinsed
Dill weed, dry (or fresh if possible) chopped fine
1 lemon, sliced thin
1 tbsp butter
¼ cup dry white wine
2 tbsp Teryaki sauce
Salt and pepper to taste

Prepare the vegetables as noted above. Remove the center bone in the salmon steaks and cut them in half. Spray the cooker with cooking spray. Put the butter on the bottom of the cooker, with the vegetables layered on top, starting with the potatoes, and in nor particular order ending with the scallions. Sprinkle with some capers on top, and cover with lemon slices. Add the salmon steaks and add more lemon slices. Mix the Teriyaki sauce with the white wine, and pour over the salmon steaks. Sprinkle some dill on top. Cover and cook undisturbed for 1½ hours. The salmon should flake easily. Remove the steaks carefully and place on plates, with the vegetables spooned around the fish.

Serves two to four

SCALLOPS IN CREAM SAUCE

This is a quick and easy approximation of the famous French Coquille St. Jacques. You can serve this in the traditional scallop shaped dishes, or over toast points, in pastry shells or over rice. This is sometimes served as a "starter" but you can serve it as a main course with a vegetable or other accompaniments.

1 lb bay scallops, washed with cold water
1 can (10.5 oz) condensed mushroom soup
½ cup water
¼ cup dry white wine
½ lb fresh mushrooms, sliced
½ cup celery, diced fine
2 tsp lemon juice
Salt and pepper to taste

In a medium bowl dilute the soup with the white wine and the water.. Spray the cooker liner with cooking spray, and add the soup to the liner. Stir in the mushrooms and the diced celery. Cover and cook undisturbed for 2 hours. Stir in the scallops. Cover and cook for 1 hour more. Test a scallop for doneness – do not over cook as they will become tough and stringy.

Serves two to four

SCALLOPS MARINARA

Scallops are very adaptable to various methods of cooking and this recipe owes its beginnings to the southern part of Italy known for its wonderful seafood and produce. Serve over spaghetti (I prefer Linguini) or rice and with a dry white wine and crusty Italian bread.

1¼ lb bay scallops, washed
1 can (14.5 oz) diced tomatoes
3 tbsp garlic, diced
½ lb fresh mushrooms, sliced
1 medium onion, diced
1 green pepper, diced
1 small zucchini, diced
1 tsp fresh chopped basil or dried basil leaves
2 bay leaves
Salt and pepper to taste

In a medium bowl combine all the ingredients (except the scallops) and stir well. Spray the cooker with cooking spray. Pour the mixture into the cooker. Cover and cook undisturbed for 2 hours. Add the scallops and stir into the tomato-vegetable mixture. Cover and cook for 1 hour more. Check a scallop for doneness – do not over cook as they will get tough and stringy. Do not worry if the vegetables are al dente – they will add crunch to the dish.

Serves two to four

SCALLOPS MEDITERRANEAN STYLE

This dish which combines scallops with tomatoes and Calamata olives could not have originated anywhere but around the Mediterranean Sea. Serve this with rice or couscous and a fresh green salad.

1½ lb bay scallops
1 can (14.5.oz) diced tomatoes
2 tbsp garlic, chopped
½ cup pitted Calamata olives, cut in half
2 tbsp grated lemon rind
½ cup dry white wine
1 tsp dried basil leaves
Salt and pepper to taste

Spray the cooker liner with cooking spray. Pour all the other ingredients (except the scallops) into the cooker. Stir well. Cover and cook for 2 hours. Add the scallops and stir to mix. Cover and cook for an additional 1 hour. Do not over cook as the scallops will become stringy and tough – better underdone than over done!

Serves two to four

SCALLOPS AND SHRIMPS MORNAY

This is a wonderful dish for a light formal luncheon. Serve it over rice with a fresh green salad with sliced avocado and tomatoes. Southern biscuits would be an appropriate accompaniment.

½ lb. bay scallops, rinsed and patted dry
½ lb shrimp, peeled and deveined
1 can (10.5 oz) cheddar cheese soup
½ cup water
½ lb fresh mushrooms, sliced
¼ cup pimiento, diced
¼ cup shredded Parmesan or Swiss cheese
Salt and pepper to taste

In a medium bowl dilute the soup with the water. Spray the cooker with cooking spray. Add the soup and the mushrooms. Cover and cook undisturbed for 2 hours. Add the shrimp and scallops. Cover and cook for 1 hour more. Add the additional cheese and taste for seasoning. Cover and cook for 15 minutes more. Serve as described above.

Serves two to four

SEAFOOD STEW

Although it cannot be compared to the "cioppino" prepared at the famous Fisherman's Wharf in San Francisco this seafood stew is a close runner up. Be sure to let the soup heat up in the slow cooker before adding the other ingredients, which should all be at room temperature.

1 can (18.8 oz) " Campbells" Chunky Clam Chowder
¼ cup water
¼ lb. bay scallops
¼ lb. shrimp, peeled
¼ lb. firm white fish filet, (skinned) and cut into 1" pieces
1 can (15.4 oz) mixed vegetables, drained
Pinch saffron (optional)
1 tbsp. chopped garlic
Salt and pepper to taste

Dilute the soup with the water and pour it into the slow cooker, along with the chopped celery, onion and garlic. Cover and cook undisturbed for 2 hours. Uncover and using an instant read thermometer test the temperature; it should be 175 degrees or more. Add the shrimp, scallops, fish and canned vegetables. Stir to mix well. The slow cooker will be full. Cover and cook for 1 hour more. Add salt, pepper, saffron (if using) and taste. Serve over rice, pasta or toast points.

Serves two to four

SHRIMPS CREOLE

This savory dish owes its origins to the people of Louisiana. There are many variations but this recipe makes a lusty country style dinner. Serve over white rice, with a green vegetable and crusty country bread.

1 lb medium shrimp, peeled and deveined
1 medium green bell pepper, diced
1 celery stalk, diced
1 small onion, diced
1 can (14.5 oz) diced tomatoes, in thick puree
2 tbsp garlic, chopped
1 tbsp Tabasco sauce
1 tbsp Worcestershire sauce
Salt and pepper to taste, or use cayenne pepper if you like
3 scallions, cut into ½" pieces on the bias for garnish

Spray the cooker with cooking spray. In a medium bowl combine all the ingredients except the shrimp. Pour the mixture into the cooker. Cover and cook undisturbed for 2 hours. Add the shrimp and cook for 1 hour more. Serve over the rice with the scallions sprinkled on top.

Serves two to four

SHRIMP CURRY

This easy dish seems the essence of India. You can make the curry as hot as you want, but the apple and the raisins take the "edge" off. Serve over rice with some Indian garnishes such as grated coconut, peanuts and additional raisins. If you have an Indian grocer near you buy some Indian bread to sop up the juices.

1¼ lb fresh medium shrimp, peeled and deveined
1 can (10.5 oz) condensed cream of mushroom soup
½ cup water
½ cup celery, diced
½ cup onion. Diced
1 Granny Smith apple, cored and cut into dice
½ cup dark seedless raisins
2 tbsp Madras curry powder (more if you want)
Pinch crushed red pepper
Salt and pepper to taste

In a medium bowl dilute the soup with the water. Add all the other ingredients except the shrimp. Spray the cooker with cooking spray, and add the soup mixture. Cover and cook undisturbed for 2 hours. Add the shrimp and stir well. Cover and cook for 1 hour more. Do not over cook as the shrimp will become tough and stringy. Taste for seasonings and adjust as necessary. Serve as described above.

Serves two to four

SHRIMPS FRA DIAVOLO

There are so many versions of dishes called "Fra Diavolo" that not even the Italian dictionary could sort them out. This is a spicy version with shrimp to be served with your favorite pasta.

1 lb fresh shrimp, peeled and deveined
1 can (28 oz) tomatoes in thick puree
1 medium onion, diced
2 tbsp garlic, chopped
1 tsp red pepper flakes
1 tbsp Worcestershire sauce
1 tsp Tabasco sauce
Grated Parmesan cheese for garnish

Pour the tomato sauce into the cooker and break up the tomatoes with a wooden spoon. Add all the other ingredients except the shrimp. Cover and cook undisturbed for 2 hours. Add the shrimp and cook for 1 hour more. Serve with your favorite pasta.

Serves two to four

SHRIMP GUMBO

You can make this spicy Cajun inspired gumbo with cooked chicken or sausage, but I like the shrimp version best. Serve it with a fresh green salad and some crusty country style bread to sop up the juices. Tall glasses of iced tea or a cold Chardonnay would be the perfect drink.

1 pkg. (7 oz) "Zatarains" New Orleans Style Gumbo Mix
3½ cups water
¾ lb fresh shrimp, peeled and deveined as necessary
½ lb. pre-cooked Andouille type sausage, chopped fine
1 red bell pepper, cut into 3" x ¼" batons
1 green bell pepper, cut into 3" x ¼" batons
Salt and pepper to taste

Spray the cooker with cooking spray. Add the gumbo mix, the water and the peppers. Stir well. Cover and cook undisturbed for 2 hours. Add the shrimp and sausage and stir into the mix. Be sure all the shrimp and sausage are covered by the mix. Cover and cook for 1 hour more. You can cook the first part of the gumbo as long as you want, but do not over cook the shrimp or they will get limp and stringy.

Serves two to four

SHRIMP IN HERBED BUTTER

I could never suggest that you use the slow cooker as a stir fry medium but this is an easy way to cook shrimp in a zesty sauce. Serve with white rice with steamed snow peas on the side.

1½ lb medium fresh shrimp, peeled and deveined
1 stick (1/4 lb) butter or oleo
2 tbsp garlic, chopped
1 tbsp paprika
1 tbsp chopped dry thyme
½ cup dry white wine
Juice of 1 lemon
½ cup dry bread crumbs
Salt and freshly ground black pepper to taste

Spray the cooker liner with cooking spray. Add all the ingredients except the shrimp and cook for 1 hour. Stir well. Add the shrimp and toss to coat. Cover and cook undisturbed for 1 hour or until the shrimp are pink and tender. Do not overcook

Serves two to four

SHRIMP JAMBALAYA

When developing the recipes for this cookbook there was some question as to whether rice could be successfully cooked in the slow cooker. The answer is a resounding yes if you follow the basic instructions. Use instant long grain premium rice and you will end up with plump rice more akin to the Chinese "sticky rice" than the drier results when cooked according to the package directions.

1 cup dry rice
1 cup hot water from the tap
1 tbsp butter (or oleo)
1 lb medium shrimp, shelled and deveined if necessary
½ cup celery, chopped
½ cup green pepper, diced
½ cup onion, diced
1 tsp thyme
2 cloves garlic, chopped fine
1 can (14.5 oz) tomato sauce
Salt and pepper to taste

Spray the cooker with cooking spray. Pour the rice into the cooker. Add the butter, chopped celery, pepper, onion and garlic. Add the hot water and stir. Cover the cooker and let cook undisturbed for 2 hours. Stir the rice and add the tomato sauce and the shrimp. Mix well. Recover the cooker, and cook for 1 hour more.

Serves two to four

SHRIMP IN LIGHT TOMATO SAUCE

This recipe is adapted from one by the grand master of American cooking, James Beard. Adapting it to the mini slow cooker gives it even more depth of flavor. Serve the shrimp and the tomato sauce over your favorite pasta, but it is especially good over linguini with lots of fresh grated Parmesan cheese.

¾ lb fresh shrimp, peeled and deveined as necessary
1 can (28oz) Redpack un-peeled crushed tomatoes in thick puree
1 medium onion, chopped fine.
1 tbsp minced garlic
1 tbsp basil leaves
Salt and pepper to taste.
Grated Parmesan cheese for garnish
Pasta of your choice, cooked according to package directions

Pour the tomatoes into the cooker. Add the chopped onion and the minced garlic. Cover and cook undisturbed for 2 hours. Add the shrimp. The cooker will be full. Be certain all the shrimp are covered by the sauce. Cover and cook undisturbed for 1 hour more. Serve over your choice of pasta, with plenty of freshly grated Parmesan cheese.

Serves two to four

SHRIMP MARINARA

This tasty Italian dish is served all over America and has as many variations as anyone could think possible. Serve it over pasta with a green salad on the side.

1 lb. fresh shrimp, peeled and deveined
1 can (15.5oz) whole Roma tomatoes in thick puree
1 medium onion, diced fine
2 tbsp garlic, chopped
1 tsp dried basil leaves
1 tbsp dried oregano
1 tsp red pepper flakes
Salt and pepper to taste
Freshly grated Parmesan cheese for garnish.

Pour the tomatoes into the cooker and break them up as best you can with a wooden spoon. Add the other ingredients, except the shrimp. Cover and cook undisturbed for 2 hours. Add the shrimp and stir well. Cover and cook for 1 hour more. Serve over pasta with the grated cheese on top.

Serves two to four

SHRIMP NEWBURG

Okay, so it isn't the traditional creamed shrimp, but it will be just as tasty! Starting with canned soup and with some additions this is truly a delicious dish. Serve over rice or in traditional puff pastry shells Steamed broccoli and sliced tomatoes make a good accompaniment.

1 lb medium fresh shrimp, peeled and deveined
1 can (10.5 oz) condensed cream of mushroom soup
½ cup water
½ lb fresh mushrooms sliced thin
1 tbsp lemon juice
1 tbsp dry sherry
1 tbsp brandy (optional)
1 tbsp cayenne pepper
Pinch of saffron for color
Salt and pepper to taste

Dilute the soup with the water. Add all the other ingredients except the shrimp. Spray the cooker with cooking spray. Add the mixture to the slow cooker and cook covered for 2 hours. Uncover the cooker and stir in the shrimp. Recover and cook 1 hour more or until the shrimp are pink and done.

Serves two to four

SHRIMP AND ORIENTAL VEGETABLES

Shrimp are a natural for the mini slow cooker. This dish should be served over white rice or crisp Chinese noodles with a green salad on the side garnished with pineapple chunks and slivered green pepper.

1 lb. fresh medium shrimp, peeled and deveined
1 pkg. (16 oz) Oriental style frozen vegetables thawed
3 tbsp cornstarch
3 tbsp water
2 tbsp soy sauce
2 tbsp sesame oil

Put the thawed Chinese vegetables into the cooker. Cover and cook undisturbed for 2 hours. Add the shrimp and cook for 1 hour more. Make a slurry of the water, cornstarch, soy and sesame oil. Pour over the vegetables and shrimp and toss well to thicken. Let cook covered for another ¼ hour.

Serves two to four

SHRIMP AND SAFFRON RICE CASSEROLE

This delicate casserole has Near Eastern overtones. Serve with a fresh tomato and red onion salad with a yogurt dressing and pita bread.

1 pkg. (5 oz) "Mahatma" saffron yellow rice
1 2/3 cups hot tap water
1 tsp butter or oleo
1 lb fresh medium shrimp, peeled and deveined
1 medium green bell pepper, diced
1 medium red bell pepper, diced
1 small onion, diced
Parsley chopped for garnish
Salt and pepper to taste

Spray the cooker with cooking spray. Start the cooker and melt the oleo on the bottom. Add the rice and stir to coat. Add the hot tap water and the peppers and onion. Stir to mix well. Cover and cook undisturbed for 2 hours. Fluff the rice with a fork and add the shrimp. Stir to mix. Cover and cook undisturbed for 1 hour more or until the shrimp are pink and tender. Do not over-cook as the shrimp will become tough and stringy.

Serves two to four

SHRIMP WITH SAFFRON RICE AND TOMATOES

If you like shrimp and rice then this is a natural for you. This recipe uses a prepared rice by name and again I reiterate that these are labor and time saving devices.

1 lb fresh medium shrimp, peeled and deveined
1 pkg. (5 oz) "Mahatma" Saffron Long Grain Rice
1 2/3 cup hot tap water
1 medium green bell pepper, diced
1 small onion, diced
1 can (14.5 oz) diced tomatoes
1 tbsp butter or oleo
Salt and pepper to taste
Pasta of your choice

Preheat the cooker for 15 minutes and put the butter on the bottom. Stir in the rice and add the hot tap water. Cover and cook undisturbed for 2 hours. Fluff and stir the rice and add the vegetables, tomatoes and the shrimp. Cover and cook undisturbed for 1 hour more. The vegetables will still be crunchy. Serve directly from the cooker into bowls or plates.

Serves two to four

SHRIMP WITH TOMATOES AND PASTA

This Mediterranean style dish could be from Italy or Greece. The addition of the crumbled feta cheese tips it to the Ionian. Serve with a fresh green salad and good crusty bread.

¾ lb fresh shrimp, peeled and deveined
1 can (15.5 oz) tomatoes in heavy puree
1 medium onion, chopped fine
1 cup cooked pasta (elbows or small penne, cooked al dente)
2 tbsp garlic chopped fine
1 tbsp dried basil leaves
½ cup crumbled feta cheese
Salt and freshly ground pepper to taste

Pour the tomatoes into the cooker and break up the tomatoes with a wooden spoon. Add the onion, garlic, and basil. Cover and cook for 2 hours. Add the pasta and the shrimp and stir well. Cover and cook for 1 more hour. Add the feta cheese and stir before serving.

Serves two to four

SHRIMP WIGGLE

Although "wiggle" is a New England word for anything done in a hurry, this easy dish still has to cook in two separate sections for the shrimp to be done. Originally served over toast points, I recommend that you serve it over white rice.

1 lb fresh shrimp, peeled and deveined
1 can (10.5 oz) mushroom soup
½ cup water
½ cup sweet red pepper, chopped fine
½ cup frozen peas, thawed
½ lb fresh mushrooms, sliced
1 tsp. paprika
Salt and pepper to taste.

Spray the inside of the cooker with cooking spray. Dilute the mushroom soup with the ½ cup water. Add all the other ingredients (except the shrimp) and stir well. Add the soup and vegetable mixture. Cover and cook for 2 hours. Add the shrimp and mix well. Cover and cook undisturbed for 1 hour more or until the shrimp are done.

Serves two to four

SOLE DUGLERE

This famous French recipe for fish can be done in the mini cooker. You can use any white fish filet including cod, halibut or sea bass. The filets have to be cut to fit the cooker; that is about 4" square and about ¾" thick. Serve with small boiled red potatoes and a green vegetable. Be sure you get some of the sauce on each filet.

4 fish filets as described above, approx. 1 lb.
1 can (14.5 oz) diced tomatoes
1 small onion, diced
2 tbsp garlic, chopped fine
Pinch of thyme
½ cup parsley, chopped fine
Salt and pepper to taste

In a small bowl mix the tomatoes with the chopped onion, garlic and parsley. Spray the cooker with cooking spray. Pour a small amount of the sauce on the bottom. Layer the filets one on top of the other with sauce on each in between. End with sauce on top. Cover and cook undisturbed for 2 hours. Check for doneness using a small fork. If the fish flakes easily it is done. If not, recover and cook for another ½ hour. Serve the filets on each plate with the sauce on top. Sprinkle with more parsley.

Serves two to four

SOLE WITH VEGETABLES

This elegant recipe makes for a light and delicious dinner. Serve the fish with the vegetables and lemon at the side. A cold dry white wine would be a fine accompaniment.

4 sole fillets approx. 1b total
3 small red potatoes, un-peeled and sliced thin, approx ½ cup
2 Roma tomatoes, sliced thin, approx ½ cup
1 medium zucchini, diced, approx. ½ cup
2 tbsp capers, drained
1 lemon
1 tbsp. butter or oleo
Freshly ground black pepper to taste

Spray the cooker with cooking spray. Layer the potatoes, zucchini, and tomatoes over the butter on the bottom of the cooker. Cover and cook undisturbed for 2 hours. Roll the fillets as tightly as you can and secure with a toothpick if necessary. Put the fillets on top of the vegetables, lay lemon slices on top, and sprinkle with the capers. Cover and cook undisturbed for 1 hour more. Check the fish with a fork. It should flake easily. Remove the fish carefully, and place some of the vegetables on top of each fillet.

Serves two to four

SWORDFISH WITH CAPERS AND OLIVES

This delicious recipe from the Mediterranean area depends for much of its taste on the olives. I prefer pitted Calamata olives if you can get them. If not, plain black olives will do. Do not overcook the swordfish as it will become tough and stringy. Serve with boiled new red potatoes and a tossed green salad.

1 lb fresh swordfish fillet, skinned, and cut into 1" pieces.
2 Roma tomatoes, sliced thin
2 tbsp garlic, chopped
¼ cup red onion, minced
½ cup Calamata olives, sliced in half
¼ cup capers, drained
1 tsp basil leaves
1 tbsp olive oil
Salt and pepper to taste

Put the olive oil on the bottom of the cooker and place the sliced onion, tomatoes, garlic and capers on top. Cover and cook undisturbed for 2 hours. Pile the cubed swordfish on top of the vegetables. Sprinkle with the basil, and Calamata olives. Salt and pepper generously. Cover and cook undisturbed for 1 hour more. Remove the swordfish to a serving platter. Mash the vegetables with a fork or a stick blender for a sauce. Serve as suggested above.

Serves two to four

TUNA LOAF

This recipe is similar to the Salmon Loaf, but with some variations due to the difference in the size of the cans. Salmon comes in 15oz cans, and tuna comes in 6oz cans – so I have adjusted the amounts of the other ingredients to make up the difference. The tuna is less assertive in taste, but no less delicious.

2 cans (6oz each) tuna (packed in water, and drained as noted)
1¼ cups fresh bread crumbs
¼ cup tuna and milk (see procedure)
1 egg, slightly beaten
2 stalks celery, chopped fine, about ¼ cup
3 scallions, chopped fine
1 tsp chopped garlic
Salt and freshly ground black pepper to taste

Drain the tuna, reserving the liquid. Add milk to the liquid to make ¼ cup. Flake the tuna well and add all the other ingredients. Spray the cooker with cooking spray. Stir the tuna mixture well and add to the cooker. Cover and cook undisturbed for 2 hours. Unplug the cooker and let the loaf sit for ½ hour to firm up. Un-mold the loaf by running a knife around the outside and inverting the cooker liner over a serving plate. Slice as desired or spoon onto plates.

Serves two to four

TUNA AND MACARONI CASSEROLE

The slow cooker is the ideal way to make a casserole, and the liner makes a fine tableside serving container. Tuna and macaroni casseroles were the favorites of many just-beginning cooks, and college dorms smelled of this dish being cooked in students rooms. This is a bit more sophisticated, but still in the "comfort food" category. Most of the contents are already on your pantry shelf.

1 can (6 oz) tuna, drained
1 cup elbow macaroni (dry measure) cooked al dente
1 can (10.5 oz) condensed cream of celery soup
¼ cup water
1 can (10.5 oz) peas, drained
1 can (7 oz) mushrooms stems and pieces, drained
1 tsp. Dijon style mustard
¼ cup pimento, diced
Salt and pepper to taste

Cook the macaroni according to package instructions. Do not cook thoroughly as it will cook again in the slow cooker. In a medium bowl dilute the soup with the water and add all the other ingredients, except the macaroni. Mix well. Spray the cooker with cooking spray. Add the tuna mixture. Cover and cook undisturbed for 2 hours. Add the macaroni and stir well. Cover and cook for 1 hour more. Adjust for seasonings and serve directly from the cooker onto serving plates.

Serves two to four

TUNA NICOISE

This recipe will have you dreaming of the Cote d'Azur and of the wonderfully tasty food of that part of France. You can omit the anchovies if you want, but they do add a special taste to the dish. Serve with rice, couscous or little new red potatoes.

1 lb fresh tuna cut into 1" pieces
3 tbsp olive oil
2 tbsp dried thyme
2 tbsp garlic, chopped
2 cups eggplant cut into 1" pieces
2 Roma tomatoes, chopped
Zucchini, sliced thin, approx ½ cup
Onion, chopped, approx. ½ cup
¼ cup pitted Calamata olives
5 anchovy filets, chopped fine
Salt and pepper to taste

Marinate the tuna in the olive oil, thyme and garlic turning frequently to cover well for about 2 hours in the refrigerator. Spray the cooker with cooking spray and add all the vegetables, anchovies and olives. Cover and cook undisturbed for 2 hours. Pile the tuna on top and add the marinade. Cover and cook for 1 more hour. Remove the tuna to a serving dish. Mash the vegetables with a fork or stick blender and serve over the tuna.

Serves two to four

TUNA NOODLE CASSEROLE

This has been a favorite of aspiring cooks especially after WW2 when vets returned home and started to cook. You can add just about anything to this casserole but keep it simple for best results. Serve with a green salad and good bread or rolls. Sprinkle grated cheese on top of the tuna.

2 cans (6 oz each) tuna in water, drained and flaked
2 cups elbow macaroni (cooked), al dente
1 can (10.5oz) condensed cream of mushroom soup
½ cup water
¼ cup dry vermouth (optional)
1 small green bell pepper, diced, approx. ½ cup
1 small onion, diced, approx. ½ cup
½ lb fresh mushrooms, sliced
Salt and pepper to taste

Cook the elbow macaroni according to package directions. You should have about 3 cups cooked al dente. In a medium bowl dilute the soup with the water. Add the vermouth and stir well. Spray the cooker liner with cooking spray. Add the soup and all the other ingredients, except the macaroni. Mix well. Cover and cook undisturbed for 2 hours. Add the macaroni and cook for 1 more hour. Spoon the tuna directly from the cooker onto plates.

Serves two to four

TUNA STEAK

To do this recipe successfully you will have to have a thick "sashimi grade" fresh tuna steak approximately 3" thick by 4" square to fit into the cooker. Make the marinade ahead of time and let the tune rest in it for an hour or so. Serve with delicate white rice and a steamed vegetable like broccoli. Slice the tuna in ¼" slices across the grain. You should have about 6-8 slices to serve as desired.

1 block of "sashimi grade" yellow fin tuna as described above.
½ cup orange juice
½ cup soy sauce
1 tsp chopped garlic
¼ cup sesame seed oil
Juice of 1 lemon
1 tsp dried basil leaves

In a medium non-reactive bowl make the marinade and let the tuna rest in it for at least one hour, turning every 15 minutes to marinate all sides. Transfer the tuna to the cooker and pour ½ cup of the marinade on the bottom. Cover and cook for 2 hours. The interior of the tuna will be rare. The outside 1" edges will be well done. Slice and serve as suggested above.

Serves two to four

TUNA SURPRISE

This dish was a favorite in the postwar 1950's, when it was inexpensive to prepare and easy to serve. A recipe is aittle less caloric than Tuna Casserole with Noodles. Serve it over rice, toast points or in pastry shells if you wish. A fresh green salad and a crisp vegetable are healthy accompaniments.

2 cans (6 oz each) tuna in water, drained
1 can (10.5 oz) cream of mushroom soup
½ cup dry white wine, or vermouth
½ lb fresh mushrooms, sliced
1 cup frozen peas, thawed
¼ cup pimento, diced
½ cup celery, diced
Pinch of thyme
1 tbsp Dijon type mustard
Salt and pepper to taste.

In a medium bowl flake the tuna and mix with the mushroom soup and the wine or vermouth. Add all the other ingredients and stir well. Spray the cooker with cooking spray. Add the mixture. Cover and cook undisturbed for 3 hours. Serve hot directly from the cooker.

Serves two to four

BEEF

Barter's Stew
Beef and Beans Burritos
Beef Bourguignonne
Beef Braised in Beer
Beef Cabbage Rolls
Beef Creole
Beef Goulash
Beef and Ham Loaf
Beef Hash Tex-Mex Style
Beef "Monday" Pie
Beef and Noodle Casserole
Beef Rolls Stuffed with Spiced Ham
Beef Strogonoff
Beer Stew
Carbonnade of Beef
Chipped Beef
Classic Chili
Corned Beef and Macaroni Casserole
Franks and Beans Tex-Mex
Hamburger and Vegetable Casserole
Meatballs
Meat Loaf
Mediterranean Meatballs
Old Fashioned Beef Stew
Pepper Steak
Picadillo
Roast Beef Hash
Sloppy Joes
Spicy Beef and Beans
Swiss Stew
Wyler's Hearty Beef Stew

MEATS   **BEEF**
                    PORK AND HAM
                    LAMB AND VEAL
                    SPECIALTY MEATS

There are separate sections for each of the above meats, except for specialty meats, which has its own section andintroduction. If you have any qualms about putting raw meat into the mini slow cooker, please lay them aside. I have made the Meat Loaf recipe many times without any problems. The mini slow cooker reaches 170 degrees within an hour, enough to kill any e-coli bacteria.

If you buy your meats from a reputable and clean butcher, or supermarket that you can trust, the mini slow cooker will do the rest. Stews are especially successful in the mini slow cooker, as the slow simmer converts normally tough cuts of meat into fork tender morsels.

You will find that meats sometimes cook faster than vegetables in the mini slow cooker. As I have stated before, do not be afraid to go beyond the cooking times suggested, as further cooking will only serve to meld the flavors and tenderize the meat.

Use your instant read thermometer if you have any fears that a meat is not sufficiently done. This might apply especially to pork, which most Americans often overcook. The dreaded Trichinosis Bacteria is killed at 137 degrees, so use that as your guide. Modern pork processing methods have all but erased this menace. Pork, which is a little pink on the inside, is infinitely more flavorful and tender than a chop which has been cooked until it resembles shoe leather!

Again, I will not draw your attention to any specific recipes in this section, as there are so many good ones from which to choose.

BARTERS STEW

In the area around Boothbay Harbor, Maine, Barter is a well known old family name. Many of the families in that area are also from French Canadian and Portuguese lineage. This is a good dish for a winter night when the snow is piled up against the house and the old stove heats the kitchen to a warm glow. This is wonderful with warm biscuits or dumplings.

1 lb beef chuck, cut into ½" cubes
1 medium onion, sliced, approx. ¼ cup
½ cup flour (in a plastic bag)
1 can (10.5 oz) beef broth
Carrots, cut into ¼" slice, approx. ½ cup
Rutabaga, cut into ¼" dice, approx ½ cup
Potatoes, cut into ½" dice, approx ½ cup
2 bay leaves, crushed
Large pinch thyme
Salt and pepper to taste
1 tbsp cornstarch mixed with ¼ cup cold water (optional)

Coat the beef with the flour and set aside. In a medium bowl combine all the ingredients and mix well. Pour the stew into the cooker, cover and cook undisturbed for 3 - 4 hours. Check the stew and if it is too thin add the cornstarch mixture and cook for ½ hour more. Check for seasoning and add salt and pepper if necessary.

Serves two to four

BEEF AND BEANS BURRITOS

This is a real "south of the border" dish. Serve with rice and a salad of greens and avocado.

1 lb. boneless sirloin steak, cut into ½" dice or ¼" strips
1 can (8.25oz) black beans, drained
1 can (8.25oz) tomatoes in heavy puree
1 medium onion, diced, approx. ½ cup
1 tbsp garlic, diced fine
½ cup salsa (hot or mild, your choice)
1 tbsp chili powder
1 tsp ground cumin
Salt and freshly ground black pepper, to taste

For the burrito wraps:
8 (8") Corn tortillas, wrapped in foil and warmed in the oven
Sour cream for garnish
Chopped cilantro for garnish
Diced onion for garnish
Diced tomato for garnish

Spray the cooker with cooking spray. Add the beans and the tomatoes and stir well. Add the beef, onion, garlic, salsa, and the spices. Cover and cook undisturbed for 2 hours. Check the beef for doneness with a quick read thermometer. It should read 145 degrees or more for medium rare. If not done, cover and cook for ½ hour more. Divide the beef mixture among the 8 tortillas. Roll up and serve two to a plate. Put a dollop of sour cream on each and sprinkle with the chopped cilantro, onion and tomato.

Serves two to four

BEEF BOURGUIGNONNE

There are as many recipes for Beef Bourguignonne as there are chefs in France! This recipe will be for many just like any other traditional beef stew. However, the addition of the Burgundy wine does elevate the flavor to something more refined. Buy first quality beef for best results. Serve over noodles with slices of a French baguette to sop up the gravy.

1 lb beef (your choice), cut into bite size pieces
¼ cup flour generously seasoned with salt and pepper
3 slices bacon, cut into ¼" pieces
2 small potatoes, peeled and cut into ½" cubes, approx ½ cup
2 small carrots, peeled and sliced into ¼" slices
1 small onion, peeled and cut into thin slices, approx ½ cup
¾ cup beef broth
¾ cup red Burgundy wine (or simple red table wine)
1 bay leaf
1 tsp thyme
1 tbsp chopped garlic
Salt and freshly ground black pepper to taste
Noodles (your choice) cooked to package directions.

Trim and cut the beef as directed. Put the flour into a plastic bag, and toss the beef well to coat. Set aside. Prepare the vegetables, and place into the bottom of the cooker. Season the vegetables. Add the garlic, thyme and the bay leaf. Arrange the beef cubes on top of the vegetables, and sprinkle the bacon pieces on top. Pour the wine and broth mixture over. The liquid should just cover the beef. Cover and cook undisturbed for 3-4 hours. Test the beef with a fork for doneness; it should be very tender. Stir the beef and the vegetables and serve over the noodles.

Serves two to four

BEEF BRAISED IN BEER

Probably Belgian in origin this dish is flavorful and rich. Serve it with noodles and a good pumpernickel or rye bread.

1 lb boneless beef rump or chuck cut into 1" pieces
½ cup flour (in a plastic bag)
1 cup onion, sliced
2 cups beer (dark beer or ale is best for deep flavor)
1 can (10.5 oz) beef broth
1 tbsp chopped garlic
1 tbsp red wine vinegar
1 tsp brown sugar
1 tsp dry thyme
2 bay leaves crumbled
2 tbsp corn starch mixed with ½ cup cold water (optional)
Salt and pepper to taste

Spray the cooker liner with cooking spray. Coat the beef with the flour. In a medium size bowl combine all the ingredients and mix well. Pour the ingredients into the cooker. Cover and cook undisturbed for 3 hours, or more if you want. If the sauce is too thin add the cornstarch mixture and cook for 1 hour more to thicken the sauce. You really cannot overcook this dish.

Serves two to four

BEEF CABBAGE ROLLS

Although Hungarian in origin cabbage rolls of one nature or another exist in almost all cuisines. Make the rolls as directed and you will be able to fit six to eight of them into the mini slow cooker, enough for three or four. Serve with a green vegetable or with noodles or rice.

¾ lb ground beef, 10% fat
6-8 cabbage leaves, blanched
¼ cup uncooked brown rice, or rice/pilaf mixture
Small onion, diced, approx ¼ cup
1 can (14oz.) diced tomatoes in heavy sauce
1 egg slightly beaten
Salt and pepper to taste

Select 6- 8 medium cabbage leaves, and cook them in salted boiling water for about 8 minutes, or until they are limp. Drain and cool the leaves. Set aside. In a bowl mix the ground beef, onion, rice and egg. Fill each cabbage leaf with approx. 2 tbsps of the beef mixture. Roll the leaves up tight, about ½" to¾" diameter, and no more than 3" long so they stand up vertically in the slow cooker. Pour the juice over. Cover and cook undisturbed for 3 hours. Use a quick read thermometer to test the beef mixture. It should read about 150 degrees or more for well done. Remove the rolls carefully to serving plates.

Serves two to four

BEEF CREOLE

This is a wonderful recipe to use left-over beef, and give it an entirely new life. Serve this typically Louisiana dish with dirty rice, and ice cold beer.

1 lb. left-over beef, cut into ¾" pieces (about 2 cups)
1 medium onion, diced, approx. ½ cup
1 medium green bell pepper, diced, approx. ½ cup
1 can (8.25 oz) crushed tomatoes, in thick puree
1 can (8.25 oz) whole kernel corn, drained
1 can (8.25 oz) sliced okra, drained (optional)
2 tbsp chili powder
1 tsp gumbo file
Salt and pepper to taste
Sour cream for garnish

Spray the cooker with cooking spray. Add the vegetables and the tomato sauce and stir well. Cover and cook undisturbed for 2 hours. Add the cooked beef and the spices. Stir well. Cover and cook for 1 hour more. Taste for seasonings and adjust as necessary. Serve over rice with a dollop of sour cream on top.

Serves two to four

BEEF GOULASH

There are as many recipes for Hungarian Goulash as there are Hungarian housewives! However, this recipe comes as close as possible to the generally accepted version. Serve over noodles, with the sour cream on the side.

1 lb stewing beef cut into ½" cubes.
1 small onion, chopped, approx. ½ cup
1 medium green pepper, chopped, approx. ½ cup
1 cup beef broth
¼ cup ketchup
2 tbsp caraway seeds
2 tbsp Hungarian sweet paprika.
½ cup sour cream
2 tbsp cornstarch
3 tbsp water
Salt and pepper to taste

Mix the broth, ketchup, paprika and caraway seeds together. Set aside. In a small bowl, mix the beef and the chopped vegetables together. Toss the beef and the vegetables with the flour. (Use a plastic bag.) Put the beef and vegetables into the slow cooker. Pour the beef broth mixture over. The liquid should just cover the beef. Cover and let cook undisturbed for 3 hours, or more if you wish. Mix the cornstarch and water and stir into the sauce. Let cook for ½ hour to thicken. Stir in the sour cream. Prepare the noodles according to package directions, and serve the goulash on top.

Serves two to four

BEEF AND HAM LOAF

This is a little different from your all beef meatloaf, or even the loaf made from three meats – beef, pork and veal. Serve this with mashed potatoes and a green vegetable, along with a fresh green salad on the side. Real comfort food!

1 lb. good quality ground beef – 10% fat, if you can get it.
½ lb. cooked country style ham (Virginia ham or similar)*
½ cup bread crumbs – freshly made are best
½ cup Beefamato or V8 juice
1 small onion diced fine
2 tbsp Worcestershire sauce
Salt and pepper to taste
Barbecue sauce, for garnish

Spray the cooker with cooking spray. In a medium size bowl mix all the ingredients. Add the mixture to the cooker, and pat down to eliminate any air bubbles. Spoon some barbecue sauce on top and smooth with a knife. Cover the cooker and cook undisturbed for 3 hours. Check the temperature with your instant read thermometer – the meat should read 160 degrees at the center of the loaf for the meat to be well done. Stop the cooker and remove the lid. Let the loaf cool for ½ hour in the cooker. Run a thin knife around the outside of the loaf, and then invert the cooker over a serving plate to release the loaf. Cut into wedges, or slice to serve.

Serves two to four

*The ham can be ground or diced fine

BEEF HASH TEX-MEX STYLE

In the American Southwest hash is a way of life that comes from the old chuck wagons that served the cowboys their meals. Leftovers were made into the next day's breakfast, and so hash was born. Authentic hash has no tomato base. This recipe adds a little heat, which the original did not have.

1 lb ground beef (10% fat)
1 small onion, chopped, approx. ½ cup
1 stalk celery, chopped, approx. ½ cup
1 small green pepper, chopped, approx. ½ cup
2 small red potatoes, washed but not peeled, cut into ¼" cubes
1 can (8.25oz) diced tomatoes
¼ cup salsa, medium or hot (your choice)
1 tbsp chili powder
Salt and freshly ground black pepper to taste

In a medium bowl mix the ground beef and the tomatoes together well. Add the vegetables and the other ingredients. Spray the cooker with cooking spray. Add the beef hash mixture and stir well. Cover and cook undisturbed for 3 hours. If you want an authentic crust, pour the hash into a fireproof dish, and put it under the broiler. If more convenient, put it into a frying pan and fry until crisp.

Serves two to four

BEEF "MONDAY PIE"

In England "Monday Pie" is what Sunday's "joint" becomes – in other words leftovers! So, if you have some cooked beef, you can make another entirely different dish from it. Since everything is already cooked, it will not take a long time to create this dish. Just give the mini cooker 2 or 3 hours, and you'll have a delicious dinner.

2 cups cooked roast beef, chopped into fine dice
1 can (8.25 oz) diced tomatoes
1 can (8 oz) mushrooms, drained
1 can (8.25oz) baked beans, your choice of flavor, drained
1 can (8.25 oz) mixed vegetables, drained
1 small onion, chopped fine, approx. ½ cup
2 cloves garlic, chopped fine
1 tsp dry Herbs de Provence (or similar)
Salt and freshly ground black pepper to taste

Spray the cooker with cooking spray. Mix all ingredients together and place into the slow cooker. Cover and cook undisturbed for 2 or 3 or more hours. You really cannot overcook this dish. Spoon directly from the cooker and serve with mashed potatoes and a green salad.

Serves two to four

BEEF AND NOODLE CASSEROLE

This is the true "comfort food" of your childhood. You probably never had it – but then you'll think you did. Use the wide "no yolk" style noodles, or any type of elbow macaroni.

1 lb stewing beef, cut into ½" pieces
½ lb fresh mushrooms, sliced thin
1 can (10.5 oz) beef broth
½ cup water
½ cup red table wine
1 medium onion, diced
1 tsp dried oregano leaves
2 bay leaves
Salt and pepper to taste

Freshly cooked noodles of your choice – approx. 2 to 4 cups
1 container (8oz) sour cream
Chopped parsley, for garnish (optional)

Spray the cooker with cooking spray. In a medium size bowl combine the water and the wine with the spices, to make a marinade. Marinate the beef cubes for 1 or 2 hours covered, or overnight in the refrigerator. Pour the beef and the marinade into the cooker, with the onions. Cover and cook undisturbed for 2 hours. Add the sliced mushrooms, and cook for 1 hour more. In the meantime, prepare the noodles according to package directions. Mix the noodles with one-half of the sour cream, and pour into a shallow oven proof casserole. Drain the beef and mix with the remaining sour cream. Pour the beef over the noodles, Place under a broiler if possible to brown the mixture, or serve as above.

Serves two to four

BEEF ROLLS STUFFED WITH SPICED HAM

Whatever you call them, Roulades, Paupiettes or Ballotines, these beef rolls will give a "gourmet" touch to any meal. Instead of the usual mix of ground veal and pork, sliced spiced ham from your deli will do the trick. Serve these with rice or boiled potatoes, a green vegetable and plenty of crusty French bread.

1¼ lb.lean beef, sliced across the grain, and pounded thin
Spiced ham slices for stuffing, 8 needed
1 can (7oz) beef broth
1 tbsp. chopped garlic
1 tbsp thyme
1 carrot, sliced thin, approx. ¼ cup
1 small onion, sliced thin, approx. ¼ cup
1 tbsp Dijon style mustard
Salt and pepper to taste

Cut the beef across the grain into small slices, about 4" square. You should have 8 pieces. Lay the slices on wax paper. Pound them until they are about 1/8" thick. Salt and pepper liberally. Place a slice of the spiced ham on each. Trim the ham to fit the beef. Roll up each piece and secure with a toothpick or tie with kitchen string. Prepare the vegetables and place them on the bottom of the slow cooker. Sprinkle with salt and pepper. Mix the beef broth with the chopped garlic, thyme and Dijon mustard. Stack the beef rolls in the liner or stand them up vertically. Pour the beef broth over – it should just come up to the top of the beef rolls. Cover and cook undisturbed for 3 hours. You can thicken the sauce with ½ tsp. cornstarch mixed with ¼ cup water, or use Pillsbury Shake and Bake Ultra Fine Flour.

Serves two to four

BEEF STROGONOFF

This elegant dish named for an aristocratic Russian family is always well received. You must use only the finest beef available with all gristle and fat carefully removed. Serve over noodles with sour cream for those who want it.

1 ½ lbs sirloin steak cut into 1/8" x 3" slices
1 can (10.5 oz) condensed cream of mushroom soup
½ cup water
1 medium onion, sliced thin, approx. ¼ cup
½ lb fresh mushrooms, sliced fine
3 tbsp Dijon mustard
¼ cup dry sherry
Salt and pepper to taste
Sour cream, for garnish
Chopped parsley, for garnish

Spray the cooker with cooking spray. Dilute the mushroom soup with the water and pour into the cooker. Add the mushrooms, onions, mustard, sherry and mix well. Cover and cook undisturbed for 2 hours. Add the thinly sliced beef. Cover and cook for 1 hour more. The beef will be medium rare – just as it should be! Garnish with the sour cream and chopped parsley.

Serves two to four

BEER STEW

You can let this cook in the mini slow cooker for just about as long as you want and it will never be overdone. Serve with a green salad to start and a fresh vegetable to accompany the stew.

1½ lb sirloin (or stewing beef) cut into ¼" to ½" pieces
½ cup all purpose flour
1 large baking potato, washed, skin left on and sliced thin
1 onion sliced thin
1 or 2 cans of dark beer
Salt and pepper to taste

Spray the cooker liner with cooking spray. Put the cubed beef into a plastic bag with the flour and shake well to coat. Put the potato and onion slices on the bottom of the cooker. Pile the beef on top. Pour the beer over with just enough to cover. Cover and cook undisturbed for 3 hours. Serve the beef with the potatoes on the side. Thicken the sauce with 1 tbsp cornstarch mixed with ¼ cup water, or use Pillsbury's Ultra Fine Flour.

Serves two to four

CARBONNADE OF BEEF

The Belgians who are known for their dark beer probably invented the carbonnade or beef cooked in beer. There are hundreds of variations but this one will do as a general example. Serve with noodles and good rye or pumpernickel bread.

1 ½ lbs boneless chuck or sirloin steak cut into ½" to ¾" pieces
½ cup all purpose flour
1 medium onion, sliced,, approx. ½ cup
1 can or bottle (10 oz) dark beer
1 can (10.5 oz) beef broth
2 bay leaves
½ tsp caraway seeds
2 tsp cornstarch
2 tsp cold water
Salt and pepper to taste

Spray the cooker with cooking spray. Dredge the beef in the flour to coat well. Mix the beer and the broth in the cooker. Add the beef, onion, bay leaves and caraway seeds. Cover and cook undisturbed for 3 hours. Taste for seasoning and add salt and pepper if necessary. Remove the beef to a serving platter to keep warm. Mix the cornstarch and water. Add to the sauce while stirring until the sauce thickens. While the beef is cooking prepare the noodles according to the package instructions. Serve the beef and sauce over the noodles.

Serves two to four

CHIPPED BEEF

Just about every American serviceman has been served this dish at one time for breakfast when it was known by a less than polite name. Some just tolerated it, but some came to love it. Today chipped beef is sold in most supermarkets either in plastic bags or in bottles. The addition of the mushrooms, pimento and vermouth gives it a little more sophistication. Serve on toast or with rice.

1 pkg chipped beef (approx 1 lb.), roughly chopped
1 can (10.5 oz.) condensed cream of mushroom soup
½ cup water
½ lb fresh mushrooms, sliced thin
Salt and pepper to taste
¼ cup pimento, chopped roughly
2 tbsp dry vermouth (optional)

Spray the cooker liner with cooking spray. In a medium bowl dilute the soup with the water, and stir in the mushrooms and the chipped beef. Cover and cook undisturbed for 3 hours, or until the chipped beef is warm enough to serve. Taste for seasonings and adjust accordingly.

Serves two to four

CLASSIC CHILI

Although made with mostly prepared ingredients, you will find this easy version of a "classic" chili truly delicious. A simple tossed salad and a loaf of crusty bread make for a complete and satisfying meal.

1½ lb good quality ground beef (10% fat if you can get it)
1 can (14oz) chili beans (do not drain)
1 can (7.5oz) diced tomatoes in thick puree
¼ cup water (optional)
1 pkg. Chili Powder Mix – mild, medium or hot
1 medium onion, chopped, approx. ¼ cup
1 tsp Tabasco sauce (or more if you want)
Salt and pepper to taste. (Some like it hot!)

Mix chili powder with ¼ cup water, set aside. Saute beef until it is no longer pink – do not over cook as it will also cook in the mini slow cooker. Add all the ingredients to the cooker and mix well. Replace the lid. Plug in the cooker, and let cook undisturbed for 3 hours. Serve over rice or noodles or on a large hamburger bun for a "Sloppy Joe!"

Serves two to four

CORNED BEEF AND MACARONI CASSEROLE

Since all the ingredients in this recipe are pre-cooked except the macaroni, you can assemble it in the slow cooker and then cook for about two hours to meld the flavors. The slow cooker liner is an ideal way to bring a dish like this to the table for serving. A fresh green salad and some good French bread would be a fine accompaniment.

1 cup elbow macaroni (dry measure)
1 can (14.5 0z) diced tomatoes
1 small onion, chopped fine, approx. ¼ cup
1 can (11 oz) corned beef
1 tsp dry basil
1 tsp dry English mustard
1 tsp Worcestershire sauce
Salt and pepper

Pre-cook the macaroni until it is just al dente – do not cook fully as it will also cook in the slow cooker. In a medium bowl flake the corned beef and then combine with all the other ingredients, except the macaroni. Spray the cooker with cooking spray. Add the mixture. Cover and cook undisturbed for 2 hours. Add the cooked macaroni, stir well, cover and cook for 1 more hour.

Serves two to four

FRANKS AND BEANS TEX-MEX

When you want to turn on a little heat, serve these franks and beans with typical Tex-Mex accompaniments. Chopped onion, chopped tomatoes, sour cream and shredded cheese make great garnishes. Wrap the franks and beans in a tortilla for even more fun. Cold beer is the perfect beverage.

8 frankfurters cut into ¼ slices (use good quality all beef franks)
1 can (15.5 oz) chili beans (do not drain)
1 medium onion, chopped fine, approx. ¼ cup
1 green pepper, chopped into bite size pieces, approx. ¼ cup
½ cup salsa, mild or hot, your choice
1 tbsp Tabasco sauce
Salt and freshly ground black pepper to taste
Sour cream for garnish
Grated cheese for garnish
Chopped tomato for garnish
8 (8") flour or corn tortillas, wrapped in foil, and warmed in the oven

In a medium bowl combine all the ingredients. Spray the cooker with cooking spray. Add the mixture. Cover and cook undisturbed for 3 hours or until it is warm enough to serve. Place two tortillas on each of four plates. Portion the mixture onto the tortillas and roll them up. Garnish with the sour cream, tomatoes and grated cheese.

Serves two to four

HAMBURGER ABD VEGETABLE CASSEROLE

There are many variations of this dish including the traditional English Shepherds Pie. No traditional mashed potato topping here, but just about everything else is true to the original. You may opt to cook the hamburger ahead of assembling the dish in the slow cooker since everything else is pre-cooked.

1 lb ground beef, 10% fat
1 can (10.5 oz.) condensed tomato soup
¼ cup water
1 can (7.5 oz) cut green beans, drained
1 can (7.5 oz) small potatoes, diced
1 medium onion, diced, approx. ¼ cup
1 can (6 oz) sliced mushrooms
1 tbsp thyme
Salt and pepper to taste

In a medium bowl dilute the tomato soup with the ¼ cup water. Add the ground beef, and mix well. Add all the other ingredients and mix. Spray the cooker with cooking spray, and add the beef mixture. Cover and cook undisturbed for 3 hours. Test the casserole with your instant read thermometer - it should read 165 degrees minimum in the center for the beef to be done. Adjust for seasonings and serve.

Serves two to four

MEATBALLS

Commercially made meatballs are available (frozen) in most markets, but sometimes it just seems that only "homemade" ones will do. Make them about 1" or so in diameter, and you should be able to fit eight into the mini slow cooker. Serve with your favorite pasta, and use the juice from the cooker as a sauce. Good crusty bread and freshly grated Parmesan cheese are perfect accompaniments as is a fresh green salad.

1 lb ground beef, 10% fat
½ cup freshly made bread crumbs
1 egg, well beaten
½ cup whole milk, or tomato juice if you prefer
2 cloves garlic chopped fine
1 tbsp basil leaves
1 tsp. Worcestershire sauce
1 tsp. dry English mustard
1 can (14oz) tomatoes, diced or crushed
Salt and pepper to taste
Pasta (your choice) cooked to package direction
Freshly grated Parmesan cheese, for garnish

In a medium size bowl mix all the ingredients – or use a stand mixer with the paddle attachment. Form the mixture into approx. 1" balls – you should be able to get 8 into the mini slow cooker. Pour the tomato sauce over. Cover and cook undisturbed for 3 hours. Use a quick read thermometer to test for doneness. It should read 150 degrees or more. Serve with the pasta and garnish with freshly grated Parmesan cheese.

Serves two to four

MEAT LOAF

You may ask, "Meat Loaf in a mini-cooker?" Yes, and why not. This recipe makes a savory loaf, and the only thing different from your favorite is the shape. It will be round rather than loaf shaped! Serve with mashed potatoes and a green vegetable.

1½ lb good quality ground beef. (10% fat if you can get it)
1 cup bread crumbs, freshly made if possible.
1 large egg, slightly beaten.
1 small onion, chopped fine, approx. ¼ cup
1 tbsp chopped garlic.
1 tsp Worcestershire sauce.
1 tsp dry English mustard
1/3 cup milk.
¼ tsp. each salt and pepper.
Ketchup or Barbecue sauce for garnish.

In a medium size bowl combine all ingredients. Mix with your impeccably clean hands or use whatever tools you prefer. If you have a stand mixer use the paddle attachment. Spray the inside of the cooker with cooking spray. Put a small layer of the ketchup or barbecue sauce on the bottom. Place the meat loaf mixture over and pat down to eliminate open areas. Add more ketchup or barbecue sauce on top. Cover the cooker and cook undisturbed for 3 hours. Check for doneness using an instant read thermometer. The thermometer should read 160-165 in the center for well done. Remove the liner from the cooker and drain off fat and juices. Carefully place the meat loaf onto a serving plate and slice vertically or stand the meat loaf upright and cut into wedges.

Serves to to four

MEDITERRANEAN MEATBALLS

Use frozen small meatballs and save yourself a lot of work. Serve with noodles, a green vegetable and good country bread.

1 lb pre-cooked frozen meatballs, thawed (approx. 8)
1 can (15.5 oz) Redpack crushed tomatoes in thick puree
1 medium onion, diced fine, approx. ¼ cup
2 tbsp capers, drained
2 tbsp garlic, chopped fine
1 can (15.5 oz) chickpeas, drained (or other beans of your choice)
Chopped thyme to taste
Salt and pepper to taste

Spray the cooker with cooking spray. Add all the ingredients and mix well. Cover and cook undisturbed for 3 hours. Check for seasoning and add salt and pepper as necessary. In the meantime prepare the noodles according to package instructions. Serve the meatballs over the noodles with the sauce.

Serves two to four

OLD FASHIONED BEEF STEW

This is a plain "old fashioned" beef stew. Serve with a green vegetable. Don't forget the crusty country bread to sop up the juices.

1¼ lb boneless chuck (or boneless sirloin) cut into ¾" cubes
½ cup flour
1 medium onion, diced, approx. ¼ cup
1 cup carrot, cut into ¼" slices, approx. ¼ cup
1 cup small red potatoes, cut to ½" dice
1 can (10.5 oz) beef broth
1 can (10.5 oz) beef gravy
1 bay leaf
Pinch thyme
Salt and pepper to taste

Spray the cooker liner with cooking spray. In a medium bowl coat the beef and the vegetables with the flour. Pour the beef broth and the gravy into the cooker and add the coated beef and vegetables. Add the thyme and bay leaf. Cover and cook undisturbed for 3 hours, or longer if you want. If the stew is too thick add water to thin it to serving consistency.

Serves two to four

PEPPER STEAK

There is nothing more satisfying than a beef dish with terrific flavor and good texture. Serve this with small red potatoes or rice and a steamed green vegetable.

1½ lbs top round or sirloin steak cut into 1/8" x 3" slices
1 can (14.5 oz) Redpack stewed tomatoes in thick puree
1 small onion, diced, approx. ¼ cup
1 medium green bell pepper, cut into 3" batons
2 tbsp chopped garlic
1 tbsp cornstarch
2 tbsp soy sauce
Salt and pepper to taste

Spray the cooker liner with cooking spray. Cut the beef into very thin slices (partially freeze it if necessary to facilitate this) and set aside. Combine the tomato, onion and green pepper in the cooker. Cover and cook undisturbed for 2 hours. Uncover and add the beef slices. Mix the cornstarch with the soy sauce and add to the mixture. Recover and cook undisturbed for 1 more hour. The beef should be medium rare.

Serves two to four

PICADILLO

This Mexican beef stew is best served as a stuffing for tacos or tortillas. However, it is often served in bowls with lettuce, sliced tomatoes and chopped onions as a garnish just as it would be served in the wraps above. If you are afraid to cook ground beef in the slow cooker without cooking it before in a saute pan, then do so. Use the best grade and freshest ground beef you can find. Serve as you like, but sour cream is a nice accompaniment.

1 lb ground beef (10% f at, if you can get it)
1 lb Chorizo, or any pre-cooked sausage of your choice
1 small onion, diced, approx. ¼ cup
1 can (14.5 oz) diced tomatoes, drained
2 tbsp diced garlic
½ cup seedless dark raisins
½ cup pitted Calamata olives, cut in half
2 tsp capers, drained
Pinch ground cumin
Pinch ground cinnamon
Pinch ground cloves
Salt and freshly ground black pepper to taste

Spray the cooker with cooking spray. In a medium bowl combine all the ingredients and stir well. Pour the mix into the cooker. Cover and cook undisturbed for 3 hours. Serve as above or over white rice.

Serves two to four

ROAST BEEF HASH

This is a quick and easy dish to prepare. You cannot saute the hash in the cooker – if you want that crisp crust you will have to put the hash into a frying pan and fry it until crisp. Serve with poached or fried eggs on top,

2 cups cooked roast beef cut into small dice
2 cups cooked potato, diced or 1 can (15.5 oz) potatoes   drained and diced
1 medium green bell pepper, diced, approx.1/4 cup
1 small onion, diced, approx. ¼ cup
1 tbsp garlic, chopped fine
¼ cup ketchup
Salt and pepper to taste

Place all of the ingredients into the cooker and mix well. The cooker will be full. Cover and cook undisturbed for 2 hours or more if you want. Serve directly from the cooker or fry in patties in a frying pan. Top with the eggs if desired.

Serves two to four

SLOPPY JOES

Aptly named, these can be a mess, but that is the purpose of the whole thing! Buy good quality hamburger buns, not the insipid soft ones which squish easily in the hand. Toast the buns before adding the Sloppy Joe mixture. Serve with potato salad, or creamy cole slaw. Some add ketchup on top of the mixture, but that seems to be "gilding the lily!" Have plenty of paper napkins on hand.

1 lb. ground beef (use the 10% fat quality)
1 can (15 oz) diced tomatoes in heavy sauce
3 garlic cloves, chopped fine
1 medium onion, chopped roughly, approx. ½ cup
1 small green pepper, chopped fine, approx. ½ cup
1 tbsp Worcestershire sauce
1 tbsp Tabasco sauce
Salt and pepper, to taste

If you have some trepidation about adding uncooked hamburger meat to the bowl, then saute it in a pan until it is just loses it's pink color. In a small bowl add all the ingredients, being sure the beef is well mixed into the tomatoes. Spray the cooker with cooking spray, and add the hamburger mixture. Cover and cook undisturbed for 3 hours. Serve over the toasted buns

Serves two to four

SPICY BEEF AND BEANS

This "south of the border" inspired recipe will have you shouting ole! Serve as a substitute for the regular tacos mixture, or wrap in corn tortillas, and garnish with sour cream, chopped onion and tomatoes. A cold beer is a wonderful accompaniment! Salud!

1 lb. sirloin steak, cut into ½" cubes
¼ cup flour
1 small onion, chopped fine (save some for garnish)
1 small green bell pepper, chopped fine
1 tbsp chopped garlic
1 can (7.5oz) Redpack crushed tomatoes in thick puree
1 can (7.5oz) chili beans (do not drain)
2 tbsp Worcestershire sauce
2 tbsp. Tabasco sauce
Salt and freshly ground black pepper to taste
Sour cream for garnish
2 Roma tomatoes, chopped, for garnish
Some additional chopped onion for garnish

Spray the cooker with cooking spray. Dredge the beef in the flour (use a plastic bag). Place the tomatoes in the cooker. Add the beef and all the other ingredients. Mix well. Cover the cooker and let cook undisturbed for 3 hours. Test the beef with your thermometer – it should be 145 degrees or higher for medium rare. Serve as described above.

Serves two to four

SWISS STEW

This take off on Swiss Steak has about the same end result except that the meat is cubed. It is best served over noodles and with crusty country bread.

1 lb beef round steak, cut into ¾" pieces
½ cup all purpose flour
1 can (15.5 oz) Redpack crushed tomatoes in heavy puree
1 medium onion, sliced, approx. ½ cup
1 stalk celery, sliced into ½" pieces
1 medium carrot, sliced thin, approx. ½ cup
1 tbsp Worcestershire sauce
Salt and pepper to taste
Chopped parsley for garnish

If you want to brown the beef before putting it into the cooker then do so, but it is not necessary. Dredge the beef in the flour, coating it well. Spray the cooker with cooking spray. Add the beef and the prepared vegetables with the tomato puree. Stir well. Cover and cook undisturbed for 3 hours or longer if you want. The beef will be well done and the vegetables will be tender-crisp.

Serves two to four

WYLER'S HEARTY BEEF STEW

This is probably one of the easiest recipes to make in the entire book. You cannot really over-cook this recipe. So if you have something to do like goin' fishin' or antiquin,' then go - come back in four or five hours and you will have a luscious and hearty stew to serve. Best served over noodles or rice, but if you don't have a stove to cook those on thick slices of country bread will do just as well.

1 lb. good beef (sirloin or any good cut), cut into ½" to ¾" pieces
1 pkg. (5.58 oz) Wyler's Soup Starter Hearty Beef Stew Mix
1 can (10.5 oz) beef broth
1 cup water
1 bay leaf
1 tbsp Worcestershire sauce
Salt and freshly ground black pepper to taste

Spray the cooker with cooking spray. Cut the beef as described above and remove all the gristle and fat. Pour the contents of the Wyler's package into the cooker. Add the beef broth and the water and stir well. Add the beef and stir. (Note: If you are unsure about adding uncooked beef to the mixture, then saute it before hand.) The contents will be about 1" below the top of the cooker liner. Do not over fill, as the stew vegetables will expand during the cooking. Cover and cook the stew undisturbed for 4 hours. The stew will thicken during the last hour of cooking. The stew should be just at the top of the liner when done. Serve as described above.

Serves two to four

PORK AND HAM

Caribbean Pork Casserole
Creamy Pork Casserole
Endive with Ham and Cream Sauce
Ham, Black Beans and Rice
Ham Havana
Ham Jambalaya
Ham Loaf
Ham and Macaroni Bake
Ham, Peppers and Rice Casserole
Ham and Potato Casserole
Ham Ragout Caribbean Style
Ham Rolls
Ham Tetrazzini
Islands Style Pork Loin
Pork Barbecue and Potato Casserole
Pork and Black Bean Chili
Pork with Black Beans Cuban Style
Pork Cassoulet
Pork Chops and Scalloped Potatoes
Pork Loin with Prunes and Apples
Pork Loin and Red Cabbage
Pork with Pineapple
Pork and Sweet Potato Casserole
Pork Tenderloin Oriental
Pork in Tomato Sauce with Oregano
Red Bean Stew with Pork
Scalloped Potatoes and Ham Casserole
Sweet and Sour Pork

CARIBBEAN PORK CASSEROLE

The people of the Caribbean love pork and fruit and often mix the two in their favorite dishes. This hearty casserole should be served with white rice and a tossed green salad with sliced avocado and mango.

1 lb boneless pork for stew, cut into ½" to ¾" pieces
1 can (14.5 oz) kidney beans, drained
1 can (7.5 oz) Redpack crushed tomatoes in thick puree
1 green bell pepper, diced, approx. ½ cup
4 scallions, cut into ½" pieces
1 can (7 oz) pineapple chunks, drained and chopped roughly
1 tsp brown sugar
1 tbsp soy sauce
1 tbsp Worcestershire sauce
1 tsp ground allspice
Salt and freshly ground black pepper to taste
Grated coconut for garnish (optional)

Spray the cooker with cooking spray. Mix all the ingredients except the pineapple in a bowl. Pour the mixture into the cooker. Cover and cook undisturbed for 3 hours. Check the pork for doneness with a quick read thermometer. It should be 145 degrees or more for well done. Do not overcook the pork, or it will become tough and stringy. Serve the casserole directly from the cooker and sprinkle some of the pineapple chunks and grated coconut on each serving.

Serves two to four

CREAMY PORK CASSEROLE

Some would consider this an odd combination but the pork cut into bite size pieces and served with the potatoes is a hearty dish. Serve with a fresh green salad beforehand, and good crusty bread and a fresh green vegetable as an accompaniment.

1 lb. boneless pork loin, cut into ¾" pieces
2 cups potatoes, roughly diced
1 medium onion, diced, approx ½ cup
1 cup frozen peas, thawed
2 tbsp garlic, chopped fine
1 can (10.5 oz) condensed cream of celery soup
½ cup water
Salt and pepper to taste

Spray the cooker with cooking spray. In a medium bowl mix all the ingredients and toss well. Pour the mixture into the cooker. Cover and cook undisturbed for 3 hours. Check the pork with an instant read thermometer. It should be 145 degrees or more, but still slightly pink for maximum flavor and texture.

Serves two to four

ENDIVE WITH HAM AND CREAM SAUCE

This is a light and elegant luncheon dish that is also easy to prepare. Serve with a fresh green salad and slices of French baguette. A cold dry white wine is a suitable beverage for a special occasion.

4 endive – select nice fat ones free of brown leaves
4 slices country ham, or smoked ham, sliced 1/8" thick
1 can (10.5 oz) condensed cream of mushroom soup
½ cup dry white wine (or water as desired)
Salt and freshly ground black pepper to taste
Grated Parmesan cheese for garnish

Cut and trim the endive so they will stand upright in the cooker, about 3½" long. Wrap a piece of the ham around each endive and secure with a toothpick. Spray the cooker liner with cooking spray and stand the endive upright in the cooker. Dilute the soup with the white wine and pour it over the endive. Cover and cook undisturbed for 3 hours. Check the endive for doneness with a fork – they should pierce easily. Remove the toothpicks and serve each endive on a plate with the sauce over and garnish with the grated Parmesan cheese.

Serves two to four

HAM, BLACK BEANS AND RICE

This is a simple and easy recipe to make and it is also healthy and inexpensive. The combination of rice and beans is a staple of a large part of the world. Rice provides the starch and the beans provide the protein. The addition of ham and diced onion makes it into a one dish meal.

1 pkg. "Vigo Brand" black beans and rice
2 tbsp oleo
3¼ cups hot tap water
1 lb. cooked Virginia or smoked ham, cut into bite size pieces
1 medium onion, cut into small dice
Salt and freshly ground black pepper to taste

Spray the cooker with cooking spray. Start the cooker and let it heat up for 15 minutes. Add the package of black beans and rice. Add the oleo and 3¼ cups hot tap water. Stir. Cover and cook undisturbed for 2 hours. Uncover and add the ham and chopped onion. Stir well. Cover and cook for 1 hour more, or until the rice is fully cooked and tender.

Serves two to four

HAM HAVANA

This dish will evoke sunny days and starlit nights in the tropics. Since all of the ingredients are pre-cooked (except the green pepper) it does not require long cooking in the slow cooker. Serve with rice and a green salad.

1 lb. fully cooked ham sliced ¼" thick, cut into ¾" pieces
1 can (8oz) pineapple chunks, drained
1 medium green bell pepper, cut into 3" batons
1 can (15.5 oz) Bruce's Cut Yams in heavy syrup (or equal)
½ cup dark raisins
½ tsp ground cloves
2 tbsp cornstarch
Salt and freshly ground black pepper to taste

Spray the cooker with cooking spray. Drain the yams, and reserve the juice. Cut the yams into approx. ½" pieces. Drain the pineapple juice and combine with the yam juice. Combine the ham, yams, green pepper, pineapple and raisins. Mix well and pour into the cooker. Mix the combined juice with the cornstarch and the ground cloves, and pour over the mixture. Cover the cooker, and let cook undisturbed for 3 hours. The juice will thicken as it cooks.

Serves two to four

HAM JAMBALAYA

This is a wonderful way to use up some leftover ham by creating another totally different dish. You probably have all the ingredients in your pantry. Serve with a green salad and good country bread.

2 cups cooked ham, cut into bite size pieces
1½ cups instant enriched long grain rice
1½ cups hot tap water
1 medium onion, chopped fine, approx. ½ cup
1 medium green bell pepper, chopped fine, approx. ½ cup
1 can (7.5 oz) chopped tomatoes, in thick puree
2 tbsp garlic chopped
1 tsp dried thyme
1 tsp Tabasco sauce
Salt and pepper to taste

Spray the cooker with cooking spray. Add the rice and the hot tap water along with the onion, garlic and pepper. Cover and cook undisturbed for 2 hours. Stir and add the tomatoes and the cooked ham, thyme and Tabasco sauce. Cover and cook for 1 more hour. Check for seasoning and add salt and pepper as necessary.

Serves two to four

HAM LOAF

Buy good quality cooked ham from your deli and grind it yourself or use a food processor. This loaf is good either warm or cold. Serve with Dijon mustard and small pickles. With a green salad, it makes a wonderful luncheon dish. Chilled and sliced thin this makes a good pate as an appetizer. Super as a delicate sandwich also.

1 lb. cooked Virginia ham, ground or chopped very fine
1 cup bread crumbs, freshly made if possible
1 large egg, slightly beaten
¼ cup milk
1 small onion, chopped fine, approx. ½ cup
1 celery stalk, chopped fine, approx/ ½ cup
1 tbsp chopped garlic
1 tbsp Worcestershire sauce
1 tbsp dry English mustard
Salt and pepper to taste

In a medium size bowl combine all the ingredients. If using a stand mixer use the paddle attachment. Spray the cooker with cooking spray and place the mixture into the liner. Pack it down well. Cover and cook undisturbed for 3 hours. To un-mold the loaf, use a thin knife and go all around the outside of the loaf to loosen it. Invert over a serving plate. Slice and serve.

Serves two to four

HAM AND MACARONI BAKE

If you want comfort food, then this is it! Ham with macaroni has always been a favorite combination. Rolls and a salad would make a fine dinner, and kids will love it!

1 lb fully cooked ham, cut into bite size pieces
1 cup elbow macaroni (uncooked measure)
1 can (10.5 oz) condensed cream of mushroom soup
½ cup water
¼ cup pimento, cut into small dice
1 cup frozen peas, thawed
Salt and pepper to taste

Cook the macaroni according to package directions until just soft. Do not cook fully, as it will cook again in the slow cooker. Dilute the soup with the ½ cup water. In a medium bowl mix the ham, peas, mushroom soup and the pimento. Taste for seasonings and add salt and pepper as necessary. Spray the inside of the cooker with cooking spray and add the mixture. Cover and cook undisturbed for 2 hours. Add the cooked macaroni and cook for 1 hour more. Stir well. Adjust seasonings and serve directly from the cooker.

Serves two to four

HAM, PEPPERS AND RICE CASSEROLE

This is an easy casserole to make and inexpensive too! The only thing missing is a green vegetable or a salad on the side.

2 cups cooked ham, cut into bite size pieces
1 cup instant enriched long grain premium rice
1 cup hot tap water
1 medium green bell pepper, diced*
1 medium red bell pepper, diced*
1 tsp dried thyme
Salt and pepper to taste

Spray the cooker with cooking spray. Put the rice into the cooker and add the hot water. Cover and cook for 2 hours or until the rice is fluffy and tender. Add the other ingredients and stir well. Cover and cook for 1 hour more. The peppers will still be tender crisp.

Serves two to four

*You can change the vegetables in this recipe; for instance substitute canned peas (drained) for the peppers.

HAM AND POTATOES CASSEROLE

This is a quick and easy dish and a great way to use leftovers. Serve it over toast points or on corn bread. A good luncheon dish, but hearty enough for dinner also.

1 lb. cooked ham, cut into bite size pieces
1 can (15.5 oz) cooked potatoes, cut into small dice
1 can (10.5 oz) condensed mushroom soup
¼ cup water
Small onion, diced, approx. ½ cup
Pimento, diced, approx. ¼ cup
Stalk celery, diced, approx. ½ cup
Salt and pepper to taste

In a medium bowl dilute the soup with the water. Add all the other ingredients. Mix well. Spray the cooker with cooking spray. Pour the soup mixture into the cooker. Cover and cook undisturbed for 3 hours or until the casserole is warm enough to serve.

Serves two to four

HAM RAGOUT CARIBBEAN STYLE

Ham and fruit have a natural affinity for each other. The peoples of the Caribbean exploit those qualities and frequently combine ham or pork with various fruits. Serve this ragout with a fresh tropical fruit salad on the side.

1 lb fully cooked ham slice, cut into ¾" pieces
1 cup instant long grain premium rice
1 cup hot tap water
1 tsp oleo or butter
1 can (8 oz) pineapple chunks, drained
1 medium orange peeled, sectioned, and cut into ½" pieces
1 medium green bell pepper diced, approx. ½ cup
3-4 scallions, cut into ½" pieces
¼ cup dark seedless raisins
Salt and freshly ground black pepper to taste

Spray the cooker with cooking spray. Start the cooker and melt the oleo on the bottom. Stir in the rice and add the hot tap water. Cover and cook undisturbed for 2 hours. Fluff the rice with a fork and add all the other ingredients. Stir well. Cover and cook for 1 more hour. The bell pepper will still be crunchy, and the rice should be tender and fluffy

Serves two to four

HAM ROLLS

Since all the ingredients in this recipe are pre-cooked, you can place them in the cooker for a shorter period of time. Buy the best quality cooked ham from your deli, and have it sliced about 1/8" thick. Trim it to about 3" x 6" so it can stand upright in the cooker.

8 slices cooked ham, trimmed as noted above.
8 slices provolone cheese, trimmed to the same size as the ham
1 can (7.5 oz) Bruce's (or equal) yams, in thick syrup
1 can (6 oz) pineapple bits – do not drain
¼ cup chopped walnuts
Dijon mustard
Salt and pepper to taste

Spray the cooker with cooking spray. Place the canned yams on the bottom of the cooker. Sprinkle the chopped walnuts and pineapple bits over. Place the eight ham pieces on a piece of waxed paper. Cover generously with the Dijon mustard. Place the provolone cheese on top. Salt and pepper well, and roll them up as tight as you can. Use a toothpick to secure the rolls. They should just fit into the cooker on top of the yams. Cover and cook undisturbed for 2 to 3 hours or to serving temperature. Be sure to serve some of the yams, pineapple and walnuts on each plate with the ham rolls.

Serves two to four

HAM TETRAZZINI

Like the Chicken Tetrazzini in the poultry section of this book this is an easy dish to prepare. The only preliminary preparation is the cooking of the elbow macaroni so that they are ready for the cooker. Have some freshly shredded Parmesan cheese ready for the topping.

2 cups fully cooked ham, cut into bite size pieces
2 cups cooked elbow macaroni (cooked measure)
1 can (10.5 oz) condensed cream of mushroom soup
½ lb fresh mushrooms, sliced
½ cup frozen peas, thawed
1 tbsp dry English mustard
1 tbsp Worcestershire sauce
Salt and pepper to taste
Freshly grated Parmesan cheese for garnish.

In a medium bowl mix all the ingredients together (except the macaroni cooked al dente), and toss well. Spray the cooker with cooking spray and pour the mixture into the cooker. Cover and cook undisturbed for 2 hours. Add the macaroni and stir well. Cover and cook 1 hour more.

Serves two to four

ISLANDS STYLE PORK LOIN

Pork Loin with fruits and vegetables could be from Hawaii, or any of the Caribbean Islands. Take you choice. The combination is a marriage made in heaven! There is going to be a further culture clash however, as Oriental seasonings are used in this recipe, so now we are on the far Pacific Rim! Whatever, the slow cooking in the cooker produces a succulent and juicy pork loin. Serve this with white rice and Oriental condiments like Japanese Wasabi, Chinese mustard, Indian shredded coconut, yes, and even peanuts!

1 small boneless pork loin – about 1½ lbs.
1 can (7.5 oz) pineapple chunks (reserve the juice)
1 green bell pepper, cut into thin batons about 3" long
1 cup soy sauce
½ cup of the reserved pineapple juice
2 tbsp sesame oil
2 tbsp Chinese stir fry sauce
1 tbsp garlic, minced fine
½ cup sweet and sour duck sauce
Salt and pepper to taste

Spray the cooker with cooking spray. Put a layer of the pineapple on the bottom of the cooker, and lay the pork loin in a spiral on top of it. In a non-reactive bowl, combine all the other ingredients and mix well. Pour the marinade over the pork and into the pineapple. Pour the green pepper on top of the pork, with the remaining pineapple. Cover and cook undisturbed for 2 hours. Check the pork with your quick read thermometer – it should read 145-150 degrees. Do not overcook – the pork should still be a slightly pink color. Slice the pork into ½" slices, and serve over rice with the pineapple and pepper slices on top.

Serves four to six

PORK BARBECUE AND POTATO CASSEROLE

Hardly seems possible that one could barbecue in the slow cooker, but the taste will be there. Marinate the pork in the barbecue sauce for as long as you can, overnight in the refrigerator if possible. Serve with the potatoes and traditional cole slaw.

1 lb. boneless pork cut into bite size pieces
2 cups baking potatoes, peeled and cut into small dice
½ cup barbecue sauce (your choice of flavor)
½ cup water
1 small onion, diced fine, approx. ½ cup
1 tbsp brown sugar
1 tbsp wine vinegar
Salt and pepper as necessary

Combine the water, barbecue sauce, brown sugar and vinegar in a non-reactive bowl and marinate the pork pieces in the mixture as long as you can. Spray the cooker with cooking spray, and pile the potatoes on the bottom. Place the sliced onion on top, and then put the marinated pork on top of the onions. Leave as much of the barbecue sauce on the pork as you can, or even better pour the remainder over the pork. Cover the cooker and cook undisturbed for 3 hours. Test the pork with a quick read thermometer – it should read 145-150 degrees or more.

Serves two to four

PORK AND BLACK BEAN CHILI

This chili is a favorite in Latin American countries and in many parts of the Caribbean. It is a one-dish meal so serve it with rice and a salad of avocado and thin sliced red onion.

1 lb boneless pork for stew, cut into ¾" pieces
1 can (7.5 oz) black beans, drained
1 medium onion, diced, approx. ½ cup
1 green bell pepper, diced, approx. ½ cup
1 can (7.5 oz) diced tomatoes in heavy puree
2 tbsp garlic, chopped
3 tbsp chili powder (or more if you want)
1 tbsp Tabasco sauce
1 tsp red pepper flakes (optional)
Salt and freshly ground black pepper to taste
Sour cream for garnish

Spray the cooker with cooking spray. Mix all the ingredients in the cooker. Cover and cook undisturbed for 3 hours. Check the pork for doneness with a quick read thermometer. It should read about 150 degrees for well done. Serve the chili in bowls over the rice with a dollop of sour cream on top.

Serves two to four

PORK WITH BLACK BEANS CUBAN STYLE

This delicious dish is easy to prepare and is a good way to use left over pork. Serve with a tropical fruit salad such as mangos and avocado. Crispy fried plantains would be a delicious added extra.

1 pkg (8 oz) "VIGO" seasoned black beans and rice
3½ cups hot tap water or beef broth
2 cups cooked pork, cut into ½" to ¾" cubes
1 tsp mixed Italian seasonings
1 tsp minced garlic
½ tsp ground cumin
Salt and pepper to taste

Spray the cooker with cooking spray. Add the hot tap water (or beef broth) and the bean and rice mixture. Stir well. Cover and cook undisturbed for 2 hours. Add the cooked pork and the seasonings. Cook for 1 hour more. Fluff the rice and pork mixture and serve.

Note: If you do not have left over pork, this dish is equally delicious using cooked sausage such as kielbasa or any other spicy sausage. Prepare the recipe in the same manner as above.

Serves two to four

PORK CASSOULET

This easy to make cassoulet is based on the heart warming French dish, without all the fuss. Serve with a crusty French baguette and lots of butter. Start this Provence style dinner with a tossed green salad with fresh tomatoes and a lusty mustard-based vinaigrette. Don't forget some Dijon style mustard for added taste.

1 cup fully cooked ham, cut into bite size pieces
½ lb fully cooked pork sausage, sliced thin (about ¾ cup)
1 can (15 oz) navy beans (do not drain)
1 small onion, sliced
2 Roma tomatoes, roughly chopped, approx. ½ cup
2 cloves garlic, chopped fine
2 bay leaves
1 tsp herbs de Provence
Salt and pepper to taste

In a medium bowl combine all the ingredients. Do not drain the beans. Spray the cooker liner with cooking spray and place the ingredients in the cooker. Cover and cook for 3 hours or longer, or until warm enough for serving. Serve in warmed soup bowls.

Serves two to four

PORK CHOPS AND SCALLOPED POTATOES

This dish is an adaptation of an old family favorite, and the slow cooker is the absolutely best way to make it. When cooked in the oven, the pork chops tend to dry out, but in the slow cooker they remain moist and tender. Use a mandolin, if you have one, to slice the potatoes as thin as possible. Do not be afraid to use plenty of pepper, salt and garlic powder, the potatoes can take it.

1 or 2 baking potatoes, approx. 2 cups, sliced
4 pork chops, boneless about ½" thick (about 1¼ lbs)
1 can (7.5 ox) onion soup (do not dilute)
Salt, Pepper and Garlic powder
½ cup shredded Swiss cheese
½ tsp. rosemary leaves

Spray the cooker with cooking spray. Slice the potatoes and begin layering them into the cooker. Add onion soup and salt, pepper, garlic powder, and Swiss cheese as you build the layers of potatoes. The potatoes should be about 1" thick. End with Swiss cheese on top. Place the pork chops on top of the potatoes and salt and pepper them well. Sprinkle the rosemary over the chops. Cover and cook the chops undisturbed for 3 hours. Check for doneness by using an instant read thermometer. The chops should read 145-150 degrees. Test the potatoes with a fork – they should be tender but not mushy. If necessary, cover and cook for another ½ hour or so.

Serves two to four

PORK LOIN WITH PRUNES AND APPLES

Pork has a special affinity with prunes and apples. They have both been traditional in pork recipes for years. With the addition of raisins the combination reaches new heights. Serve this dish with small roasted potatoes and a green vegetable. A salad of sliced tomatoes and red onion, with good country bread, would make a fine dinner.

1 lb boneless pork tenderloin
½ cup flour for dredging
2 tbsp ground cumin
1 cup dry red wine
1 can (10.5 oz) chicken broth
1 small onion, chopped fine, approx. ½ cup
12 pitted prunes, cut in half or quartered. approx. ½ cup
1 medium cooking apple, cored and cut into medium dice
½ cup seedless raisins
1 tbsp rosemary leaves
Salt and pepper to taste

Spray the cooker with cooking spray. Dredge the pork loin in a mixture of the flour and cumin. Take half the prunes and lay them on the bottom of the cooker. Lay the pork on top of the prunes in a spiral. Sprinkle the remaining prunes, the apple, the onion and raisins on top. Cover and cook undisturbed for 3 hours. Check the pork with your instant read thermometer – it should be 145-150 degrees for medium rare. Do not overcook. Slice the pork into ½" slices and serve with the prunes, apple and raisins on top.

Serves two to four

PORK LOIN AND RED CABBAGE

Red cabbage and pork have a natural affinity. In this recipe the addition of apples makes a luscious "sweet and sour" combination. Buy a small boneless pork loin and separate the two loins, reserving one for another time.

1 small boneless pork loin, approx. 1 lb.
1 small red cabbage, shredded fine, approx. 3 to 4 cups
1 cup beef broth
¼ cup red wine vinegar
1 tsp. caraway seeds
5 pepper corns
1 small Granny Smith apple, chopped fine, approx ½ cup
Salt, pepper, rosemary leaves and garlic powder to taste.

Slice the cabbage into quarters. Remove the center core, and shred the cabbage finely. There should be approx. three to four cups tightly packed. Spray the cooker with cooking spray. Pack the cabbage into the cooker. It may seem like a lot, but it will cook down. Arrange the pork loin over the cabbage in a spiral. Quarter and core the apple, then chop into small dice. Combine the beef broth, vinegar, caraway seeds and pepper corns. Pour over the pork and into the cabbage. Coat the pork loin with salt, pepper, rosemary and garlic powder. Place the diced apple on top. Cover and cook undisturbed for 3 hours. Check for doneness with an instant read thermometer. The pork should read 140 to 150 degrees. Remove the pork to a serving platter and slice into ½" pieces. Serve with the cabbage and apples.

Serves two to four

PORK WITH PINEAPPLE

Pork and sweet fruits have a natural affinity. In this recipe the pork is first marinated with the fruit and then cooked on top of it. Serve with rice and steamed snow peas. Cut the pork into 1" slices.

1½ lb pork tenderloin (if large use one portion)
1 can (10.5 oz) crushed pineapple
2 tbsp red wine vinegar
2 tbsp chopped garlic
½ cup soy sauce
1 tsp red pepper flakes
2 tbsp brown sugar

Spray the cooker with cooking spray. In a non-reactive bowl prepare the marinade using all the ingredients above. Mix well. Marinate the pork for 1 hour or more turning frequently. Pour the marinade into the cooker and coil the pork on top of it. Cover and cook for 2 hours. Check the pork with a quick read thermometer – it should read 145 degrees or more. If not done cover and cook for 1 hour more. Serve the pork over rice with the pineapple marinade on top.

Serves two to four

PORK AND SWEET POTATO CASSEROLE

Pork and sweet potatoes have a natural affinity as does the addition of apples and raisins. This may have to cook more than the three hours noted in the recipe but the wait will be well worth it.

1 lb approx. boneless pork loin, cut into 1" pieces.
2 cups sweet potatoes peeled, cut into ½" pieces
1 cooking apple, diced fine, approx. ½ cup
¼ cup seedless dark raisins
½ cup apple cider
1 tsp butter or oleo
2 tbsp brown sugar
Salt and pepper to taste

Spray the cooker with cooking spray. Put the butter on the bottom of the cooker. Pile the cubed sweet potatoes over. Sprinkle the brown sugar over the potatoes, and pour the cider over them. Sprinkle the apple pieces and the raisins over. Pile the pieces of pork on top, and generously salt and pepper them. Cover the cooker and cook undisturbed for 3 hours. Check the pork with a quick read thermometer – it should read 145 degrees or more. Stir the casserole well before serving.

Serves two to four

Note: You may use canned sweet potatoes if you wish.

PORK TENDERLOIN ORIENTAL

Pork cooks quicker in the slow cooker than most people think. Actually vegetables take longer in many cases. In this recipe the pork loin is put on top of the oriental vegetables, and coated with any of the Chinese marinades which are readily available in any supermarket. Serve with white rice of course.

1 small pork tenderloin (half a package approx 1 to 1¼ lb)
1 green pepper, sliced into ¼" x 3" batons
1 red pepper, sliced as above
1 celery stalk, sliced diagonally
5 scallions, chopped diagonally
1 can (5 oz) sliced water chestnuts, drained
1 can (5 oz) sliced bamboo shoots, drained
1 can (5 oz) pineapple chunks (do not drain)
1/3 cup Chinese marinade (Mee Tu garlic flavored is good)
3 tbsp water or rice vinegar

Prepare the vegetables as directed above. Spray cooker with cooking spray and place the vegetables, pineapple, water chestnuts, and bamboo shoots in a pile on the bottom in no particular order. Place the pork loin on top in a spiral, and pour the marinade mixed with the rice vinegar over all, and down into the vegetables. Cover and cook undisturbed for 3 hours. Check the pork with a quick read thermometer – it should be 145 degrees or higher. Remove the pork from the cooker and slice into 1" pieces. Serve with the rice and the oriental vegetables on top.

Serves two to four

Note: You may use frozen oriental vegetables if you wish. Buy a 16 oz package and bring to room temperature before proceeding with the recipe.

PORK IN TOMATO SAUCE WITH OREGANO

This dish commonly called "a pizzaiola" is found in many Italian cookbooks. This could be served over pasta or rice, and as a main course with a green salad and good bread.

1 lb to 1½ lb boneless pork loin, cut into 1" bite size pieces
1 can (15.5 oz) Redpack crushed tomatoes in thick puree
1 medium onion, diced fine, approx. ½ cup
1 medium green bell pepper, chopped fine, approx. ½ cup
½ lb fresh sliced mushrooms, approx. 1 cup
2 tbsp oregano
Salt and pepper to taste

Pour the tomato sauce into the cooker. Add the onion, green bell pepper and oregano. Cover and cook undisturbed for 1 hour. Add the pork and stir well. Cover and cook for 2 more hours. Test the pork for doneness with an instant read thermometer. It should be 140-150 degrees or more and still slightly pink in the middle. Do not over cook as it will become tough and dry.

Serves two to four

RED BEAN STEW WITH PORK

This is a common type of dish in the Caribbean. There it would be cooked for hours, but we have simplified it by using canned beans and left-over cooked pork. Serve this savory dish with rice, and a salad of tropical fruits.

1 can (15.5 oz) red kidney beans (do not drain)
1½ cups cooked pork, cut into bite size pieces
1 can (7.5 oz) diced tomatoes in heavy puree
1 small green bell pepper, coarsely chopped, approx. ½ cup
1 medium onion, coarsely chopped, approx. ½ cup
1 celery stalk, sliced in ¼" slices
2 tbsp garlic, chopped
2 tbsp paprika
1 tsp Tabasco sauce
Salt and pepper to taste

Spray the cooker with cooking spray. Combine all the ingredients in the cooker and stir well. Cover and cook undisturbed for 3 hours. Test for seasonings and add salt and pepper as necessary.

Serves two to four

SCALLOPED POTATOES AND HAM CASSEROLE

This potato dish has an added kick with the smoked ham and onions in the layers. Use plenty of pepper and garlic as the potatoes can take it. Be careful with the salt if the ham is already quite salty.

2 cups fully cooked smoked ham cut into bite size pieces
2 cups potatoes, sliced thin
1 cup onion, sliced thin
1 can (10.5 oz) beef broth
3 tbsp garlic, chopped
Salt and pepper as needed

Spray the cooker with cooking spray. Start layering the potatoes putting some garlic and onion in between until it is about 1" high. Add a good layer of ham. Repeat until all the ingredients have been used up. Pour the beef broth over until it covers the potatoes. If there is not enough broth add water. Cover and cook undisturbed for 3 hours. Test to see if the potatoes are done. They should be tender but not mushy. Serve directly from the cooker.

Serves two to four

SWEET AND SOUR PORK

Always a favorite, this version is not quite like you'd get in your favorite Chinese restaurant but it comes close. And you don't have to stand over a wok to do it! Serve with white rice of course.

1 lb boneless pork loin, cut into ½" to ¾" cubes
1 can (10.5 oz) chicken broth
½ cup all purpose flour
1 green bell pepper, sliced into 3" batons
1 can (8 oz) pineapple chunks, drained
1 medium onion, sliced, approx. ½ cup
¼ cup brown sugar
¼ cup cider vinegar
1 can (6 oz) sliced water chestnuts, drained
2 tbsp cornstarch, or Pillsbury Shake and Blend Flour
2 tbsp cold water

Spray the cooker with cooking spray. In a plastic bag coat the pork pieces with the flour. Set aside. In the cooker mix the chicken broth, pepper, onion and pineapple and water chestnuts. In a separate cup mix the vinegar and brown sugar and add to the mixture. Add the coated pork and mix well. Cover and cook for 3 hours. Mix the cornstarch or flour with the cold water and add to the cooker and cook for 1 hour more until the sauce thickens and the pork is done.

Serves two to four

LAMB

Lamb and Bean Casserole
Lamb Couscous
Lamb Curry
Lamb Fricassee
Lamb Stew
Lamb Stew with Dill and Paprika
Lamb Stew with Lemon and Oregano
Lamb Stew Mediterranean Style
Moroccan Lamb Stew
Savory Lamb Stew
Simple Irish Stew
Sweet and Sour Lamb

VEAL

Creamy Veal Stew
Veal Birds
Veal Curry
Veal Ragout
Veal in Red Wine with Mushrooms
Veal Stew
Veal Stew with Mustard Cream Sauce
Veal Stew with Tomatoes and Olives

LAMB AND BEAN CASSEROLE

Lamb and beans have a natural affinity for each other. Since this is a one-dish meal you should serve it with a fresh green tossed salad and good crusty bread to sop up the juices.

1 lb lamb for stewing, all gristle removed and cut into ¾" pieces
½ cup all purpose flour
1 can (7.5 oz) white kidney beans (or cannellini), drained
1 can (7.5 oz) stewed tomatoes in thick puree
1 medium onion, diced, approx ½ cup
1 tbsp garlic, chopped
1 can (10.5 oz) beef broth
1 celery stalk, diced, approx ¼ cup
1 tsp thyme
2 bay leaves
Salt and pepper to taste

Spray the cooker with cooking spray. Dredge the lamb pieces in the flour to coat well. In a medium bowl mix all the ingredients. Pour into the cooker and stir well. Cover and cook undisturbed for 3 hours. Test the lamb for doneness with your quick read thermometer; it should read 140-150 degrees for medium rare. Taste for seasonings and add salt and pepper as needed.

Serves two to four

LAMB COUSCOUS

As I have said before do not be afraid to use prepared grains and other mixes to facilitate easy preparation of many of these dishes. In this recipe I have used "Near East" brand couscous (which comes in many flavors) to make the preparation easier. This is a one-dish meal. Serve with a green salad with sliced tomato, cucumber and red onion with a sour cream dressing.

1 lb lamb shoulder or shank, cut into ½" pieces
1 medium onion, diced, approx. ½ cup
1¼ cups beef broth (hot but not boiling)
1 pkg. (5.7 oz) "Near East" couscous mix (any flavor you like)
½ cup carrot, cut into ¼" slices
½ cup seedless dark raisins
1 tsp ground ginger
1 can (7.5 oz) chickpeas, drained
Salt and pepper to taste

Spray the cooker with cooking spray. Add the coucous and the hot beef broth. Cover and cook undisturbed for 1 hour. Add the lamb cubes and all the other ingredients except the chickpeas. Cover and cook undisturbed for 2 hours. Uncover and add the chickpeas. Stir well and check for seasonings. Cover and cook for 1 hour more. Serve directly from the cooker.

Serves two to four

LAMB CURRY

Lamb is the meat of choice in Middle Eastern countries where curried dishes are a mainstay. Serve this dish over rice or couscous, with pita bread, and condiments like chutney, raisins, cubed mango, shredded coconut, and unsalted peanuts.

1 lb boneless lamb stew meat, cut into ½" to ¾" cubes
1 small onion, chopped fine, approx. ½ cup
¼ cup all purpose flour
2 Roma tomatoes, chopped fine, approx. ½ cup
¾ cup chicken broth
1 Granny Smith apple, chopped into ¼" cubes, approx ¾ cup
¼ cup seedless dark raisins
2 tbsp curry powder (or more to taste)
Salt and freshly ground black pepper to taste
1 tbsp Cornstarch or Pillsbury Shake and Blend Flour
2 tbsp chicken broth or water

Dredge the lamb well in the flour. Mix the chicken broth with the curry powder. Add the raisins and the chopped apple. In a bowl, mix the lamb with the chopped tomatoes, and then with all the other ingredients. Place into the slow cooker. Cover and cook undisturbed for 3 hours. Use a quick read thermometer to test the lamb; it should read 135 to 140 degrees for medium rare. Do not over cook as the lamb will become stringy and tough. If the curry is too thin, make a mix of the broth or water and cornstarch or flour. Add to the curry and cook for ½ hour more to thicken.

Serves two to four

LAMB FRICASSEE

This is a slightly different version of a lamb stew. The addition of the tomato base gives it an entirely different character. Serve it with a fresh lettuce and tomato salad with an assertive vinaigrette, and good country bread to sop up the juices.

1lb boneless shoulder of lamb, trimmed and cut into ½" cubes
1 can (10.5 oz) diced tomatoes in thick puree
3 small new red potatoes, cut into ½" dice, approx 1 cup
1 small onion, chopped, approx. ½ cup
2 small carrots, sliced fine, approx ½ cup
1 bay leaf
2 cloves
Salt and pepper to taste

Pick over the lamb, trim as needed and cut into ½" cubes. In a medium bowl combine the lamb and the canned tomatoes. Add the other ingredients. Pour into the cooker. Cover and cook undisturbed for 3 hours. Check for doneness with your quick read thermometer. The lamb should be 135-140 degrees for medium rare. Do not over-cook as it will get tough and stringy.

Serves two to four

LAMB STEW

This hearty stew is perfect on a cold wintry day. Serve it with white beans in the French style. A loaf of French bread to sop up the juices would be a fine accompaniment.

1 lb lamb stew meat, cut into bite size pieces, approx. ½"pieces
1 medium onion, chopped, approx ½ cup
2 small carrots, cut into ¼" slices, approx. ½ cup
2 small potatoes, cut into ½" cubes, approx. ½ cup
2 medium Roma tomatoes, chopped roughly, approx. ½ cup
1 can (7 oz) beef or chicken gravy
½ cup water
½ tsp ground cumin
½ cup flour
2 tbsp garlic chopped
Salt and pepper, to taste

Spray the cooker with cooking spray. Chop the onion, potato and carrots as directed. Place them on the bottom of the cooker. Prepare the stew meat as directed, and dredge it in the flour. (Use a plastic bag.) Place it on top of the vegetables. Chop the tomato and mix it with the stew meat. Mix the cumin, garlic, salt and pepper into the gravy. Add the ½ cup water, stir well and pour over the meat. Cover and cook undisturbed for 3 hours. Stir the vegetables up into the stew before serving. Use your instant read thermometer to check the lamb – it should read 140-150 degrees for medium. Serve directly from the cooker into warm bowls.

Serves two to four

LAMB STEW WITH DILL AND PAPRIKA

Dill (or dill weed as it is sometimes known) is not used as much in America as it is in some European kitchens especially those of Sweden and Hungary. This dish along with the ubiquitous sour cream brings out the essence of these two national cuisines. Serve with noodles and good dark pumpernickel or rye bread.

1 lb boneless lean lamb, cut into ½" pieces
1 can (10.5 oz) beef gravy
½ cup flour (in a plastic bag)
1 medium onion, sliced, approx. ½ cup
1 can (15.5 oz) whole potatoes, drained and cut into ½" dice
½ lb mushrooms, sliced, approx. ¾ cup
1½ tbsp fresh chopped dill or dried dill weed
2 tbsp Hungarian or sweet paprika
½ cup sour cream (or more if needed)
Salt and pepper to taste

Dredge the lamb in the flour. Spray the liner of the cooker with cooking spray and add all the ingredients except the mushrooms and the sour cream. Cover and cook undisturbed for 3 hours. Add the mushrooms and cook for 1 hour more. Test the lamb with y our quick read thermometer – it should read 135-150 degrees for medium to well done. Add the sour cream and stir well. Serve as described above.

Serves two to fou

\

LAMB STEW WITH LEMON AND OREGANO

This stew is just the thing for a Spring dinner. The lemon gives the meat a new dimension, and the oregano adds a Greek taste to the dish. Serve this stew with small boiled potatoes and spinach as a surprise green vegetable. A salad of sliced tomatoes and red onion would be a suitable accompaniment.

1 lb lamb for stew, preferably shoulder, cut into ½" pieces
½ cup flour for dredging
1 can (10.5 oz) chicken stock
1 cup dry white wine
2 leeks, cleaned and sliced thin into 3" batons (white part only)
½ cup lemon juice
Zest of 1 lemon
2 tbsp oregano
2 bay leaves
1 tbsp minced garlic
Salt and pepper to taste

Spray the cooker with cooking spray. Add the chicken stock, the wine and the lemon juice. Stir well. Dredge the lamb in the flour – use a plastic bag. Add the lamb and the remaining ingredients. Cover and cook undisturbed for 3 hours. Check the lamb with your instant read thermometer – it should read 145-150 degrees for medium rare. Do not overcook. Serve as suggested above.

Serves two to four

LAMB STEW MEDITERRANEAN STYLE

This delicious stew could be from any of the countries bordering the Mediterranean Sea. Serve with new red potatoes or couscous and good rustic country style bread.

1 lb lamb for stew, cut into ½" to ¾" pieces
½ cup all purpose flour, for dredging the lamb
1 can (7.5 oz) diced tomatoes
1 small eggplant, cut into ½" dice, approx. 1½ cups
1 small zucchini, cut into ½" dice, approx. ¾ cup
1 onion, cut into ½" dice, approx. ½ cup
½ cup pitted Calamata olives, sliced in half
1 tbsp chopped garlic
½ tsp ground cumin
Salt and pepper to taste

Spray the cooker with cooking spray. Put the lamb in a plastic bag with the flour and shake well to coat. In a medium bowl combine the vegetables and the diced tomatoes. Add the olives, garlic and spices. Combine with the lamb and pour all into the cooker. Cover and cook undisturbed for 3 hours. Check the lamb for doneness with your instant read thermometer; it should read 135-140 degrees for medium rare. Do not overcook, as the lamb will become stringy and tough. Serve with the potatoes or the couscous.

Serves two to four

MOROCCAN LAMB STEW

Lamb has been the national dish of Morocco since Biblical times. Although not made in a "tagine" this recipe gives a good approximation of the traditional dish. Serve with couscous and pita bread for dipping. A salad of cucumbers with sour cream is a traditional accompaniment.

1 lb stewing lamb, all gristle removed and cut into ½" pieces
½ cup all purpose flour, for dredging the lamb
1 medium onion, diced, approx. ½ cup
2 tbsp garlic, chopped
1 tsp ground ginger
1 tsp ground cinnamon
1 can (7.5 oz) tomatoes in thick puree
¼ cup pitted prunes, cut into small dice
¼ cup dark seedless raisins
¼ cup dried apricots, diced
Salt and pepper to taste

Spray the cooker with cooking spray. Dredge the lamb in the flour coating well. Combine all the other ingredients in the cooker. Add the lamb and mix well. Cover and cook undisturbed for 3 hours. Check the lamb for doneness with your instant read thermometer. It should read 135-140 degrees for medium rare. Serve with the couscous and the pita bread.

Serves two to four

SAVORY LAMB STEW

This is a savory stew as the name implies. Serve it over rice or couscous. Have a loaf of good country bread at hand to sop up the juices.

1 lb stewing lamb, cut into ½" dice
½ cup all purpose flour
1 medium onion, diced, approx ½ cup
2 medium size carrots cut into thin slices, approx. ½ cup
1 stalk celery cut into thin slices, approx ¼ cup
½ lb fresh mushrooms, sliced thin, approx. ½ cup
2 tbsp garlic, minced
½ cup red table wine
1 cup beef broth
½ cup dark seedless raisins
1 tbsp cornstarch, dissolved into ¼ cup water
Salt and pepper to taste

Spray the cooker with cooking spray. Put the lamb into a plastic bag along with the flour and shake to coat well. In a medium bowl mix the vegetables with the red wine, the beef broth, and the raisins. Add the lamb and pour it all into the cooker. Cover and cook undisturbed for 3 hours. Check the lamb with your quick read thermometer – it should read 140-150 for medium rare. Do not overcook. If the stew is too thin, add the cornstarch mixture, and stir until the sauce thickens.

Serves two to four

SIMPLE IRISH STEW

This easy to make stew can cook in the mini cooker as long as you want. It will only get mellower and tastier as it cooks. Serve with soda bread and a green salad on the side.

1lb stewing lamb, cut into ½" pieces
½ cup all purpose flour, for dredging the lamb
1 can (10.5 oz) beef gravy
½ cup water or beef broth
1 medium onion, diced, approx. ½ cup
1 medium carrot, cut into ¼" slices, approx ¼ cup
New potatoes, cut into ½" pieces, approx 1½ cups
Salt and pepper to taste
2 tbsp Worcestershire sauce
1 tbsp dried thyme
2 tbsp tomato paste
Chopped parsley for garnish

Spray the cooker with cooking spray. Toss the lamb with the flour in a plastic bag to coat well. Mix the lamb with the potatoes and onion in the cooker. Add the beef gravy mixed with water and the Worcestershire sauce, tomato paste and thyme. Stir well. Cover and cook undisturbed for 3 hours. Check for doneness with your instant read thermometer. The lamb should be 140-150 degrees for medium rare, although you can cook this as long as you want. Serve in warmed bowls with the chopped parsley on top for garnish and color.

Serves two to four

SWEET AND SOUR LAMB

Although this recipe has tropical and oriental overtones, there is no reason that lamb cannot be treated, in this case, like pork. Lamb of today does not have the gamey flavor once associated with it, and mutton is a thing of the past. I would serve this lamb with rice and an avocado and red onion salad.

1 lb lamb, cut into ¾" cubes
½ cup flour, for dredging
1 can (10.5 oz) chicken broth
½ cup water
½ cup Hoisin sauce
¼ cup white wine vinegar, or rice vinegar
½ cup dark soy sauce
1 can (5 oz) crushed pineapple
1 can (5 oz) pineapple chunks, drained
1 can (5 oz) water chestnuts, drained and sliced
2 tbsp rosemary leaves
Salt and pepper to taste

Spray the cooker with cooking spray. Make a marinade of the chicken broth, water, Hoisin sauce, vinegar and soy sauce. Place the lamb in the marinade and let it stand in the refrigerator for 2 to 3 hours. Remove the lamb from the marinade, and dredge it in the flour. (Use a plastic bag.) Put the crushed pineapple on the bottom of the cooker. Place the lamb on top. Pour the marinade over all and sprinkle the rosemary on top. Cover and cook undisturbed for 3 hours. Check the lamb with your instant read thermometer – it should read 140-150 degrees for medium rare. Serve with the rice and the pineapple chucks on the side.

Serves two to four

CREAMY VEAL STEW

I could not in all good conscience call this dish a Blanquette de Veau, that luscious French dish which requires hours of preparation. However, this is an approximate interpretation. Serve with early spring peas and small boiled potatoes. A crusty French baguette and a good red or white wine would make a great accompaniment.

1 lb stewing veal, cut into ½" pieces
1 can (10.5 oz) condensed cream of mushroom soup
½ cup water
2 carrots, sliced thin, approx. ½ cup (more if you want)
1 cup frozen small onions, thawed
1 celery stalk, chopped fine, approx ¼ cup
1 tsp ground cloves
1 bay leaf
1 tsp thyme
2 tbsp lemon juice
Salt and pepper to taste

Pick over the stew meat. Remove all gristle and cut into ¾" pieces. In a medium bowl dilute the soup with the ½ cup water and add all the remaining ingredients. Spray the cooker with cooking spray. Add the stew mixture. (Note: Normally veal stew meat will give off a lot of scum as it heats up, but in the slow cooker this will not happen. If there is some scum, just remove it quickly with a spoon.) Cover and let cook undisturbed for 3 hours. Check the veal with a quick read thermometer – it should read 145 degrees or higher. Serve as suggested above.

Serves two to four

VEAL BIRDS

This elegant, but easily prepared dish will become a family favorite. Buy the best quality veal you can find, it's expensive but worth it! Serve the Veal Birds with rice and a green vegetable.

1 lb veal, sliced thin and pounded to 1/8" thick, 8 pieces.
8 slices turkey pastrami, sliced thin
8 slices Swiss or Provolone cheese, sliced thin
1 can (10.5oz) mushroom soup (thinned with ½ cup water)
Salt and pepper to taste

Prepare the veal as directed. Trim the veal to 4" x 3" (so it will stand up vertically in the cooker liner when rolled.) Salt and pepper each piece, and place one slice of the turkey pastrami and the cheese on each. Trim to fit the veal slices. Roll each piece tightly and tie with kitchen string or a toothpick. Place the veal birds upright in the slow cooker, and pour the mushroom soup over. Cover and cook undisturbed for 3 hours. Test the veal birds with your quick read thermometer – it should read 140 degrees for rare, or 150-160 for well done. Place two veal birds on each of four plates and pour the sauce over.

Serves two to four

VEAL CURRY

Some people have an aversion to veal. But in all honesty their reasons are unfounded. It is one of the most delicate meats available and in this curry it shines forth. Serve this dish with white rice and a tossed green salad.

1 lb stewing veal, cut into ½" pieces
½ cup all purpose flour, for dredging the veal
1 can (10.5 oz) chicken broth, use only 1 cup, reserve the rest
1 can (10.5 oz) condensed cream of mushroom soup
1 medium onion, diced fine, approx. ½ cup
1 Granny Smith apple, diced into bite size pieces, approx 1 cup
½ cup seedless raisins
2 tbsp Madras curry powder (or more if you want)
1 tbsp cornstarch (optional)
½ tsp dried thyme
1 bay leaf
Salt and pepper to taste

Spray the cooker with cooking spray. In a plastic bag toss the veal with the flour. In a medium bowl mix the chicken broth with the mushroom soup and the curry powder. Stir well and add all the other ingredients except the cornstarch. Add the mixture to the cooker. Cover and cook undisturbed for 2½ hours. If the curry is too thin, mix 2 tbsp of the broth with the cornstarch and add to the cooker stirring to thicken. Cook for 1 hour more

Serves two to four

VEAL RAGOUT

This is a snap to make with just about all the preparation done for you. Serve with rice or herbed new red potatoes and a salad on the side.

1 lb stewing veal, cut into bite size pieces, approx. ½" to ¾"
½ cup all purpose flour, for dredging the veal
1 pkg. (16 oz) frozen mixed vegetables, thawed
½ lb mushrooms, sliced, approx. ¾ cup
2 tbsp garlic, chopped
1 can (10.5 oz) condensed chicken broth
Salt and pepper to taste
1 tbsp cornstarch

Spray the cooker with cooking spray. In a plastic bag mix the veal with the flour and coat well. Mix the veal with the thawed vegetables and mushrooms. Pour into the cooker. Add the chicken broth and chopped garlic and stir. Cover and cook undisturbed for 3 hours. Check the veal for doneness. If still too rare cover and cook for ½ hour more. Remove the stew with a slotted spoon and put into a serving dish. Stir the cornstarch mixture into the sauce and cook until it thickens. Pour the sauce over the ragout and serve.

Serves two to four

VEAL IN RED WINE WITH MUSHROOMS

Veal is a delicate meat and needs to be handled with care. Although you could use white wine in this recipe the body of the red wine gives the dish the necessary character. I would serve this with oven-fried potatoes and fresh green peas. A tossed green salad with a robust vinaigrette and a French baguette would complete a wonderful meal.

1 lb boneless shoulder of veal, cut into ½" to ¾" pieces
½ cup flour for dredging
1 cup red table wine
1 can (10.5 oz) beef broth
4 slices bacon, fried crisp and chopped fine
½ lb fresh mushrooms, quartered, stems on, approx. ¾ cup
1 medium onion, chopped fine, approx. ½ cup
2 tbsp garlic, minced
½ cup carrots, diced fine
2 tbsp dried thyme
½ cup fresh parsley, chopped fine, for garnish
Salt and pepper to taste

Spray the cooker with cooking spray. Dredge the veal in the flour (use a plastic bag), and set aside. Combine all the other ingredients, except the veal and the mushrooms. Pour into the cooker, cover and cook undisturbed for 1 hour. Add the veal and the mushrooms and stir well. Cover and cook for an additional 2 hours. Test the veal with your instant read thermometer – it should read 140-150 for medium rare. Do not overcook. Serve as suggested above.

Serves two to four

VEAL STEW

This heart warming but subtle dish is perfect for a snappy Fall day. Serve with a tossed green salad and good crusty bread.

1 lb stewing veal, cut into ½" cubes
½ cup flour, for dredging the veal
3 small red potatoes, cut into ½" cubes, approx 1 cup
2 carrots, sliced thin. Approx. ½ cup
1 small onion, chopped roughly, approx. ½ cup
2 cloves garlic, chopped fine
2 Roma tomatoes, chopped roughly, approx. ½ cup
1 can (10 oz) beef broth
½ lb fresh mushrooms, quartered, approx ¾ cup
2 bay leaves
3 cloves
Salt and pepper to taste

Dredge the veal in the flour (use a plastic bag). Prepare the vegetables as directed and place them in layers on the bottom of the slow cooker. Add the veal. Mix the beef broth with the garlic and the cloves and pour over all. Cover and cook undisturbed for 3 hours. Check the veal for doneness. It should be pink on the inside and very tender. Stir the vegetables and the veal together before serving. Serve in warmed bowls.

Serves two to four

VEAL STEW WITH MUSTARD CREAM SAUCE

This delicate stew gets its punch from the mustard, which is added near the end of the cooking. Serve this with garlic mashed potatoes, or rice and small garden peas. A fresh green salad and some good country bread are always welcome. A young red wine, like a new Beaujolais, would make a festive addition.

1 lb. stewing veal, cut into ½" to ¾" pieces
½ cup flour, for dredging the veal
½ cup chicken stock
½ cup dry white wine
½ lb fresh mushrooms, cut into quarters, stems on, approx 1 cup
1 tsp dry thyme
1 tsp dried rosemary
3 tbsp Dijon style mustard
¼ cup heavy cream, or half and half (more if you want)
3 tbsp capers, drained
Salt and pepper to taste

Spray the cooker with cooking spray. Dredge the veal in the flour (use a plastic bag). Add the veal, the stock and the wine to the cooker. Cover and cook undisturbed for 2 hours. Add the mushrooms, cover and cook for 1 hour more. Mix the mustard with the cream, and add it to the cooker, stirring it well into the stew. Cover and cook for ¼ hour more. Serve from the cooker onto warm plates, with the potatoes or rice and peas.

Serves two to four

VEAL STEW WITH TOMATOES AND OLIVES

This subtle and easy to make dish is best served with rice or noodles. You don't have to pay much attention to this as it gets going. Serve with green salad with sliced tomatoes and red onions. A dollop of sour cream on top would be a nice added touch.

1 lb stewing veal, picked over and cut into bite size pieces
1 can (7.5 oz) diced tomatoes in thick puree
1 medium onion, diced fine, approx. ½ cup
1 celery stalk, cut into ¼" slices, approx ¼ cup
½ cup pitted Calamata olives, sliced in half
¼ cup dry white wine
1 tbsp garlic, chopped fine
½ cup dried thyme
Salt and freshly ground pepper to taste
Cornstarch, as necessary

Add the tomatoes, onion, celery, olives, garlic, white wine and the spices to the cooker. Mix well. Cover and cook undisturbed for 1 hour. Add the veal and stir well. Cover and cook for 2 hours more. Check the veal for doneness. It should still be medium rare. Test the seasonings and add salt and pepper as necessary. Stir in the cornstarch with some of the broth to thicken the sauce.

Serves two to four

SPECIALTY MEATS

Albert's Gentle Bolognese Sauce
Italian Sausage and Peppers
Italian Sausage in Spicy Tomato Sauce
Kielbasa with Cabbage and Raisins
Kielbasa and Red Cabbage
Kielbasa and Sauerkraut in Beer
Meatball and Sausage Casserole
Sausage and Black Beans
Sausage and Cannellini Casserole
Sausage Chili
Sausage with Couscous and Vegetables
Sausage Gumbo
Sausage Jambalaya
Sausage and Sauerkraut
Sausage and Spanish Rice
Sausage with Tomatoes and Orzo
Venison Stew

SPECIALTY MEATS

I have made this a special section as there are so many good recipes here. Using pre-cooked meats in specialty recipes not only saves time but makes the cooking easier.

Most pre-cooked specialty meats only require refrigeration, and those that are canned can be stored without refrigeration. Most of the other ingredients are boxed or canned so there is no worry about storage there. This is especially important if you are using your mini slow cooker in an RV, trailer, motor home, or on a boat.

Some of these recipes combine fresh or boxed ingredients. They will all cook well together. If you like robust flavors then the use of Kielbasa in many of these recipes will suit you well. You won't get the charred flavor as if cooked on a grill or under a broiler but the spices in the meat will come through.

Of course, all of these recipes require minimum preparation and "pot watching" – so you can go on with your other activities without worrying about the dinner to come.

Some of the recipes use totally prepared foods so you are using the mini slow cooker as a convenient way to bring the food up to serving temperature and melding the flavors. You cannot really overcook any of these recipes so go antiquing or fishing and forget about the delicious dinner which is being prepared for you! Plus, no heat in the kitchen!

ALBERT'S GENTLE BOLOGNESE SAUCE

Although you have to do this in three steps, the results are worth it. The trick is getting the sweet Italian sausage well mixed into the sauce. If you do this in a frying pan it generally seizes up and becomes lumpy. The addition of the cream at the end takes "the red out" and leaves a gentle flavor. Use it on top of y our favorite pasta.

1 can (24 oz) crushed tomatoes in thick puree
¾ lb ground beef – 10% fat, if you can get it
2 sweet Italian sausages – pre-cooked if possible, or cook on high in the micro-wave oven for 4 minutes
1 small onion, diced, approx.1/2 cup
1 carrot, cut into 1" pieces
1 tbsp dried basil
¼ cup half and half (more if you want)
Salt and pepper to taste

Step 1. Spray the cooker with cooking spray. Saute the beef in a pan until it is no longer red. Combine it with the tomato sauce in the cooker.
Step 2. If the sausage is not cooked, then cook it in the micro wave as directed above. Put the sausage, onion and carrot into the bowl of a food processor, and process until fine. Add this to the mixture in the cooker. Stir well to combine.
Step 3. Cover and cook undisturbed for 2½ - 3 hours. Check for seasoning and adjust as necessary. Add the half and half – be careful as the cooker will be full.

Serves four or more on top of pasta

ITALAIAN SAUSAGE AND PEPPERS

This has been an American favorite for years. Buy any good pre-cooked Italian style sausage and only the Italian style cooking peppers – the long pointed kind, which no one seems to know what to do with. Serve with spaghetti and crusty Italian bread.

1 lb. pre-cooked Italian sausage, cut into ½" pieces
2 cups green Italian peppers, cored and cut into chunky pieces about   1" or so
1 can (7.5 oz) spaghetti sauce – your choice
3 tsp chopped garlic
1 tbsp dried basil leaves
Salt and freshly ground pepper to taste
Grated Parmesan cheese for garnish

Pasta of your choice, cooked al dente.

In a small bowl mix all the ingredients. Spray the cooker with cooking spray and pour all the ingredients (except the pasta) into it. Cover and cook undisturbed for 3 hours. Serve the sausage and peppers over your favorite pasta, with lots of the sauce and the grated Parmesan cheese.

Note: You can also serve this over Italian bread for a sausage and pepper hero. Your choice!

Serves two to four

ITALIAN SAUSAGE IN SPICY TOMATO SAUCE

Easy to prepare and a fulfilling dinner, this zesty dish will be a welcome addition to your kitchen favorites. Serve over your favorite pasta with plenty of freshly grated Parmesan or Romano cheese on hand. Start with a simple antipasto of sliced tomatoes, sliced red onion, canned artichoke hearts, and a few slices of pepperoni. Have some slices of hearty Italian bread at hand

1 can (15.5oz) spaghetti sauce or stewed tomatoes in thick puree. (I use Redpack)
1 lb pkg. pre-cooked Italian sausage, cut into ½" pieces
1 green bell pepper, diced, approx ¾ cup
1 small onion, diced. Approx. ½ cup
½ cup pitted Calamata olives, cut in half
1 tbsp chopped garlic
1 tbsp Tabasco sauce
1 tbsp Worcestershire sauce
Salt and pepper to taste
1 tbsp dried basil leaves

Spray the cooker with cooking spray. Pour the tomato sauce into the cooker liner and add all the other ingredients. Mix well. Cover and cook undisturbed for 3 hours. Taste for seasonings and adjust as necessary. Serve in bowls over your favorite pasta with plenty of grated cheese on top.

Serves two to four over pasta or on a hero sandwich

KIELBASA WITH CABBAGE AND RAISINS

This is a hearty German or Polish related dish. Serve with dark rye or pumpernickel bread and a glass of cold beer.

1 lb. pre-cooked Polish Kielbasa, cut into 1" pieces
1 can (10.5 oz) chicken broth
4 cups cabbage, shredded
½ cup dark seedless raisins, (or more if you want)
2 tbsp caraway seeds, (or more if you want)
½ tsp dried thyme
Salt and pepper to taste

Spray the cooker with cooking spray. Toss the shredded cabbage with the caraway seeds and raisins. Pack the cooker with the cabbage and pour the broth over. Arrange the Kielbasa on top (you may have to push it down hard to get it all in). Cover and cook undisturbed for 3 hours. Arrange the Kielbasa on a serving platter and remove the cabbage with a slotted spoon.

Serves two to four

KIELBASA AND RED CABBAGE

An easy to prepare dish that has robust flavor. Serve with a fresh tossed green salad and pumpernickel bread with lots of good creamery butter and a good cold beer.

1 pkg. (16 oz) fully cooked Kielbasa (or sausage of your choice)
1 small red cabbage, cored and sliced thin, about 4 cups
1 cup beef broth
2 tbsp caraway seeds
¼ cup dark seedless raisins (More if you want)
1 Granny Smith apple, cored and diced, approx. ¾ cup
Salt and pepper to taste

Prepare the cabbage. Mix in the caraway seeds, apple and raisins. Pack the cabbage into the bottom of the cooker and pour the beef broth over. Cut the Kielbasa in 1" pieces and place on top of the cabbage. The cabbage will sink down into the cooker as it cooks, so don't worry that there seems to be too much at this point. Cover and cook undisturbed for 3 hours. Serve directly from the cooker.

Serves two to four

KIELBASA AND SAUERKRAUT IN BEER

This is a slightly different recipe for cooking kielbasa and sauerkraut. Buy the sauerkraut in the refrigerated deli section of your supermarket – the canned kind just does not work well. The beer will give the dish a slightly sweeter flavor. Serve with dense dark pumpernickel bread and lots of good butter. Have some good Dijon type mustard available.

1 bag (32 oz) sauerkraut (refrigerated)
1 kielbasa, (16 oz) precooked and cut into ½" slices
1 can (10 oz) beer of your choice (dark or light)
1 tbsp caraway seeds (or more if you like)

Rinse the sauerkraut well. Mix the sauerkraut, kielbasa and caraway seeds in the cooker. Add the beer. The cooker will be full – just push the sauerkraut down with a spoon. Cover and cook undisturbed for 3 hours. Serve directly from the cooker.

Serves two to four

MEATBALL AND SAUSAGE CASSEROLE

This hearty combination will become a family favorite. Serve with new red potatoes and a green vegetable. If you prefer, you can serve this over your favorite pasta, with a good loaf of crusty Italian style bread.

1 pkg (16 oz) frozen pre-cooked meatballs, defrosted (use half)
1 pkg (16 oz) pre-cooked sausage, cut into 1" pieces (use half)
1 can (7.5 oz) crushed tomatoes in thick puree
1 cup red wine
1 medium green pepper, cut into 3" batons, approx. ½ cup
1 cup onion, diced, approx. ½ cup
1 tbsp garlic, chopped
2 tsps dried chopped basil leaves
1 bay leaf
Salt and pepper to taste

Spray the cooker liner with cooking spray. In a medium bowl mix together all the ingredients and pour them into the cooker. Cover and cook undisturbed for 3 hours. Check for seasonings and serve hot directly from the cooker as suggested above.

Serves two to four

SAUSAGE AND BLACK BEANS

This hearty dish is quick and easy to prepare, and since all of the ingredients are pre-cooked you do not need a long cooking time. You can change this dish at will by adding some favorite spices to give it a different flavor. I've added some chili powder for some heat, but you can omit it if you want. This is a good luncheon dish but also hearty enough for a satisfying dinner. Garnish each serving with some sour cream on top.

1 pkg. (16 oz).fully cooked Kielbasa (or sausage of your choice)
1 can (15.5 oz) black beans (do not drain)
1 small onion, chopped, approx ½ cup
1 stalk celery, chopped, approx. ½ cup
1 green pepper, chopped, approx. ½ cup
1 tbsp hot chili powder (or more if you want)
Salt and pepper to taste
Sour cream for garnish

Spray the cooker with cooking spray. Cut the sausage into 1" pieces. Put all the ingredients into the cooker and stir well. Cover and cook undisturbed for 3 hours. Serve directly from the cooker into large bowls.

Serves two to four

SAUSAGE AND CANNELLINI CASSEROLE

You can make this dish with any type of sausage you want, but Polish Kielbasa or any other spicy sausage works best. Use the turkey Kiellbasa to cut down on the fat and the calories. This is truly a one-dish meal, and needs only a fresh green salad and some crusty bread to complete a satisfying dinner or hearty lunch.

1 lb. pre-cooked sausage of your choice, cut into ½" slices
1 medium onion, diced, approx. ½ cup
2 tbsp garlic, minced
1 medium zucchini, cut into ¼" slices, about ¾ cup
1 can (7.5 oz) cannellini beans, drained
1 can (7.5 oz) crushed tomatoes, in thick puree
1 tsp dried oregano
Grated Parmesan cheese, for garnish (optional)
Salt and pepper to taste

Spray the cooker with cooking spray. Add all the ingredients and stir well. Cover and cook undisturbed for 3 hours. Check for seasonings and adjust accordingly. Serve directly from the cooker onto warm plates or bowls.

Serves two to four

SAUSAGE CHILI

This simple and easy dish is a heart warming winter treat. Use Polska Kielbasa or any other pre-cooked sausage of your choice. Serve with a green tossed salad on the side and good French or Italian bread to sop up the juices.

1 pkg. (16 oz) pre-cooked sausage, cut into ½" pieces.
1 can (14.5 oz) red kidney beans (do not drain)
1 medium onion, chopped fine, approx ½ cup
2 tbsp chili powder (more if you want)
1 tsp cumin
2 tbsp garlic, chopped
Salt and pepper to taste
Sour cream (optional)
Chopped onion, as garnish (optional)
Shredded Mexican style cheese, as garnish (optional)

Spray the cooker with cooking spray. Add the kidney beans, sausage, onions and the remaining ingredients. Stir well. Cover and cook for a minimum of 2 hours, or until the chili is hot enough to serve. Serve in warm bowls with a dollop of sour cream on the top along with the onion and cheese, if using.

Serves two to four

SAUSAGE WITH COUSCOUS AND VEGETABLES

Couscous is a wheat based grain which is the staple of many African and Middle Eastern countries. There are endless ways of preparing it from main dish specialties to fruit based desserts. This is simple and easy to prepare and makes a savory and satisfying meal. Serve with pita bread and garnish with sour cream.

1 pkg (5.7 oz) "Near East" brand couscous – original flavor
1 cup chicken or beef stock, heated if possible
1 lb pre-cooked sausage of your choice cut into ½" pieces
1 can (7.5 oz) crushed tomatoes
1 can (7.5 oz) whole kernel corn, drained
1 cup frozen peas, defrosted
½ lb fresh mushrooms, sliced, approx. ½ cup
1 tbsp chopped garlic
Salt and freshly ground black pepper to taste

Spray the cooker liner with cooking spray. Add the couscous and the hot tap water. Cover and cook undisturbed for 2 hours, or until the couscous is puffed and ready. Stir the couscous and add all the other ingredients. Mix well. Cover, and cook for 1 hour more, or as long as you want before serving.

Serves two to four

SAUSAGE GUMBO

Do not serve this spicy mix of sausage and gumbo to the faint of heart. This is a wonderful dish for a cold winter day, but for only those who like it hot! You can, of course, use a less spicy sausage, but if you can get the Aidells Smoked Chorizo you will have a really authentic New Orleans Gumbo. Serve with a green salad preceding and with good French bread. How about a good cold beer?

1 pkg. (7 oz) "Zatarains" New Orleans Style Gumbo Mix
1 pkg. (13 oz) "Aidells" Smoked Chorizo, or sausage of your choice, cut into ¼" slices
3½ cups water (or a mix of canned beef broth and water)
1 green pepper, cut into ¼" x 3" batons, approx. ½ cup
1 red pepper, cut into ¼" x 3" batons, approx. ½ cup
Salt and freshly ground black pepper to taste

Spray the cooker with cooking spray. Add the gumbo mix, peppers and water to the cooker. Add the sausage and stir well. Cover and cook undisturbed for 3 hours. Note: You really cannot overcook this dish, as the sausage is pre-cooked. The longer it cooks in the slow cooker the more the flavors meld together.

Serves two to four

SAUSAGE JAMBALAYA

A "jambalaya" is defined as a dish of Creole origins using onions, peppers and plenty of herbs and spices, generally with rice as a base. This is a spicy dish using Polish Kielbasa as the sausage. However, you may use any fully cooked sausage of your choice. Serve with a fresh tossed green salad and biscuits.

1 pkg. (16 oz) fully cooked Kielbasa (or other sausage)
1 cup instant long grain rice (dry measure)
1 cup hot tap water
½ cup onion, chopped fine
½ cup celery, chopped fine
½ cup green pepper, chopped fine
2 tbsp garlic, chopped fine
1 can (7.5 oz) spicy tomato sauce
1 tbsp Tabasco (or more if you want)
1 tbsp basil
Salt and pepper to taste

Spray the cooker with cooking spray. Pour the rice and the vegetables into the cooker and add the hot tap water. Stir well. Cover and cook undisturbed for 2 hours. Cut the sausage into 1" pieces. Add to the cooker with all the remaining ingredients. Cover and cook undisturbed for 1 hour more.

Serves two to four

SAUSAGE AND SAUERKRAUT

This is one of the easiest recipes to prepare, since all of the ingredients are pre-cooked. However, the slow cooking in the cooker infuses the sauerkraut with a subtle flavor of the sausage and the caraway seeds. Serve with a tossed salad and rustic rye or pumpernickel bread. Garnish with Dijon mustard or horseradish.

1 lb. pkg. pre-cooked Italian sausage or Polish style Kielbasa
2 lb. pkg. sauerkraut (from the dairy case if available)
1 tbsp. caraway seeds (more if you want)
Salt and pepper, to taste

Put the sauerkraut into a colander and rinse well with cold water. Drain, add caraway seeds and toss. Cut kielbasa (or other sausage) into ½ inch pieces. Add to sauerkraut, and place into the slow cooker. Cover and cook undisturbed for 2 hours or as long as you want. You cannot overcook this dish.

Serves two to four

SAUSAGE AND SPANISH RICE

This is a dish which is easy to prepare and will yield a satisfying dinner. Follow the directions for cooking the rice and you will not be disappointed in the results. Serve with a tossed green salad, good crusty bread, and cold beer.

1 cup instant enriched long grain rice (dry measure)
1 cup hot tap water
1 lb Chorizo or other fully cooked sausage of your choice
1 can (7.5 oz) spicy tomato sauce
½ cup diced green pepper
½ cup diced onion
½ cup salsa, medium or hot, your choice
1 tbsp chopped garlic
1 tsp thyme
Salt and pepper to taste

Spray the cooker with cooking spray. Pour the rice into the liner along with the green pepper, onion, thyme and garlic. Pour the hot water over the rice mixture and stir well. Cover and cook undisturbed for 2 hours. Cut the sausage into 1" pieces. Add the tomato sauce, sausage and salsa to the rice. Stir well. Cover and cook for 1 hour more, or longer if you want.

Serves two to four

SAUSAGE WITH TOMATOES AND ORZO

This easy to prepare recipe is delicious and a welcome change from the usual pasta dish. You can use any kind of sausage you want, but a pre-cooked Italian sausage would be the best. Serve this one-dish meal with a tossed green salad and good Italian bread.

1 lb. pre-cooked Italian type sausage, or sausage of your choice
1 can (14.5 oz) crushed tomatoes in thick puree
½ cup orzo (dry measure)
1 onion, chopped fine, approx. ½ cup
½ lb fresh mushrooms, sliced fine, approx. ½ cup
1 small can (8 oz) small peas, drained
1 tsp crushed red pepper flakes
Salt and pepper to taste
Grated Parmesan cheese, for garnish

Spray the cooker with cooking spray. Cut the sausage into ½" pieces. Add all the ingredients (except the peas) to the cooker and stir well. Cover and cook undisturbed for 2 hours. Add the peas and cook for 1 h our more. Test the orzo – it should be done but still al dente. Serve directly from the cooker into warm bowls with the grated Parmesan cheese sprinkled on top.

Serves two to four

Note: If you want to eliminate the orzo add 1 can (7.5 oz) Pinto Beans or Great Northern Beans instead, drained of course.

VENISON STEW

Now forget your Bambi complex! All venison available in the market is farm raised and has been fed with the finest feed that money can buy. Venison is no longer the "gamey" meat of yesteryear. So unless you have a hunter in the family you can serve this at any time of the year. Serve this with long grain and wild rice, and a puree of cooked rutabaga. In France, venison is always served with pureed Chestnuts – a real treat!

1 lb farm raised venison, shoulder or shank cut into ½" pieces
½ cup all purpose flour
1 medium onion diced, approx. ¾ cup
2 medium carrots diced, approx ¾ cup
1 can (10.5 oz) beef broth
1 can (10.5 oz) sliced potatoes, drained
2 tbsp Worcestershire sauce
1 tbsp cornstarch
1 tbsp cold water
Salt and pepper to taste

Spray the cooker with cooking spray. Dredge the venison in the flour. Pour the venison into the cooker. Add the broth and all the vegetables. Mix well. Cover and cook undisturbed for 3 hours.
The venison should be medium rare – if you want it well done, then cover and cook for 1 hour more. Taste for seasonings and add salt and pepper as needed. Remove the venison to a serving platter and keep warm. Make a slurry of the cornstarch and water and add to the sauce stirring all the while until it thickens. Puree with a stick blender (the potatoes will help to make a thicker sauce) and taste again. Pour over the venison or serve on the side with the vegetables you have selected.

Serves two to four

POULTRY

Arroz Con Pollo
Brunswick Stew
Chicken and Black Bean Chili
Chicken Breasts in Spicy Sauce
Chicken Cacciatore
Chicken Curry
Chicken Fricassee
Chicken with Green Olives
Chicken Hash
Chicken "Hong Kong"
Chicken Jambalaya
Chicken Legs with Apricot Glaze
Chicken with Lemon and Caper Sauce
Chicken Livers in Tomato Sauce
Chicken Marengo
Chicken and Mushroom Risotto
Chicken with Onions and Olives
Chicken Piccata
Chicken Pot Pie
Chicken and Saffron Rice
Chicken and Sausage Casserole
Chicken and Sausage Tex-Mex
Chicken "Shanghai"
Chicken and Shrimp
Chicken Stew
Chicken Tetrazzini

continued next page

POULTRY CONTINUED

Chicken Tex-Mex Casserole
Chicken Thighs with Pineapple
Chicken Thighs, Tomatoes and Olives
Chinese Chicken in Orange Sauce
Chinese Chicken and Vegetables
Coq au Vin
Country Captain
Creamed Chicken
Curried Chicken and Rice
Curried Turkey Pot Pie
Hungarian Chicken Paprika
Mexican Chicken Casserole
Mustard Chicken with Mushrooms
Oriental Chicken with Peppers
Provencal Braised Chicken
Rolled Stuffed Chicken Breasts
Sesame Chicken Nuggets
Southern Succotash with Chicken
Spicy Chicken with Anchovies
Turkey Chili
Turkey Loaf
Turkey Noodle Casserole
Turkey Roulades

POULTRY

You cannot cook a whole chicken in the mini slow cooker! But you can cook a wide array of wonderful dishes using chicken parts.

Chicken thighs are made for the mini slow cooker. They fit well, cook to perfection and attain a juiciness not obtainable by other cooking methods.

Chicken breasts are another chicken part which is wonderful in the mini slow cooker. They can be stuffed and rolled or cut into pieces to fit the cooker. They never dry out in the mini slow cooker like they can do with high heat cooking.

Use your instant read thermometer to test to see if the chicken is finished cooking. The recommended temperature is between 165 and 170 degrees, and the juices should run clear. Again, you cannot overcook chicken in the mini slow cooker, so if some other activity takes you away from the cooker longer than the suggested cooking time do not worry about it. Longer cooking will meld the flavors and make the chicken fork tender.

Chicken legs are generally too long to fit into the mini slow cooker. The inside dimension of the cooker is about 3½" high- 4" to the underside of the dome lid. If using chicken legs take a cleaver and chop off the bone end of the leg to fit the cooker.

I bring your attention to my all-time favorite chicken recipe "Chicken Thighs with Tomatoes and Olives" which draws raves every time I make it. You will have your favorites too.

ARROZ CON POLLO

This chicken and rice dish is a favorite in Latin American countries. You can make the rice ahead of time on the stove or start from the very beginning in the slow cooker. If you use cooked chicken as I have in this recipe you will save considerable time. This is a one-dish meal but a side salad of mixed greens with sliced avocado and mango would be a suitable accompaniment.

1½ cups cooked chicken cut into ½" pieces, white or dark meat
1 pkg (5 oz) "Mahatma" saffron yellow rice
1¼ cup hot tap water
1 tsp oleo
1 small onion, diced, approx. ½ cup
1 small green bell pepper, diced, approx. ½ cup
1 red bell pepper, diced, approx. ½ cup
2 Roma tomatoes, diced, approx. ½ cup
½ cup smoked ham, diced
½ cup stuffed green olives, cut in half
¼ cup capers, drained
1 small can (8.5 oz) peas, drained (optional)
¼ cup pimiento, diced (optional)
Salt and pepper to taste
Grated Parmesan cheese, for garnish

Spray the cooker with cooking spray. Add the Mahatma rice and the hot water, along with the oleo, diced peppers and onion. Cover and cook undisturbed for 2 hours. Add the cooked chicken, the peas, capers and pimiento. Stir well. Cover and cook for 1 hour more. Pour the arroz con pollo into a shallow ovenproof gratin dish. Sprinkle with the Parmesan cheese and heat in the oven until the cheese melts.

Serves two to four

BRUNSWICK STEW

A famous version of this Old Southern favorite is served at Chownings Tavern in Colonial Williamsburg. This recipe omits the traditional okra and adds thin slices of zucchini instead. Serve this in a bowl or over rice for a hearty dinner. Don't forget the cornbread for an additional treat.

1 lb. cooked boneless chicken, cut into bite size pieces
1 can (7.5oz) diced tomatoes in thick puree
1 can (7.5 oz) lima beans, drained
1 medium zucchini, sliced thin, approx ¾ cup
1 can (7.5 oz) whole kernel corn, drained
1 tbsp tarragon
2 tbsp barbecue sauce
Salt and pepper to taste

In a medium size bowl mix all the ingredients. Spray the cooker with cooking spray. Add the mixture. The cooker will be full and there may be some spill-over as the stew cooks. Cover and cook undisturbed for 3 hours, or longer if you wish. Adjust the seasonings and serve as suggested above.

Serves two to four

CHICKEN AND BLACK BEAN CHILI

This piquant dish is a winner when beef and other meats are not wanted. Use as much chili powder as you want so you can adjust the amount of "heat" you can stand. Serve with a green salad as a starter, and with rice as an accompaniment, or on a hamburger bun like a "Sloppy Joe."

1 lb. chicken breast, cut into ½" cubes*
1 medium onion, chopped, approx. ½ cup
1 can (7.5oz) black beans, drained
1 can (7.5oz) diced tomatoes in thick puree
1 green bell pepper, diced, approx. ½ cup
1 tbsp chopped garlic
½ cup salsa, hot or medium, your choice
1 tbsp chili powder (or more, to your taste)
1 tsp ground cumin
Salt and pepper to taste

In a medium bowl mix all the ingredients well. Do not taste until the mixture has been cooked as directed. You can adjust the seasonings later. Cover and cook undisturbed for 3 hours. Test the chicken for doneness with a quick read thermometer. The chicken should be 165 degrees or more, and the juices should run clear. Adjust the seasonings and serve.

Serves two to four

* You can use cooked chicken if you wish – just add it during the last hour of cooking.

CHICKEN BREASTS IN SPICY SAUCE

This recipe will take you "South of the Border" with its spicy sauce. Serve this over rice and with warm tortillas and a dish of sour cream to cut the heat. Cold Mexican beer would be a nice accompaniment!

1 lb boneless skinless chicken breast, cut into ½" pieces*
1 can (14.5 oz) spicy tomato sauce
1 small onion, diced fine, approx. ½ cup
1 small green bell pepper, chopped fine, approx. ½ cup
½ cup salsa (medium or hot, it's up to you)
2 tbsp Tabasco sauce
Salt and pepper to taste

Spray the cooker with cooking spray. Add all the ingredients and cover and cook undisturbed for 3 hours. Test the chicken with a quick read thermometer – it should read 165 degrees or higher and the juices should run clear. Taste for seasoning and add salt and pepper if necessary.

Serves two to four

* You can use cooked chicken if you prefer – just add it to the dish during the last hour of cooking.

CHICKEN CACCIATORE

This famous Italian dish is easy to cook and makes a robust meal. Serve with your favorite pasta with lots of freshly grated Parmesan cheese and a loaf of good crusty bread.

4 chicken thighs, skin removed (approx. 1 lb)
1 can (7.5 oz) diced tomatoes in thick puree
1 medium onion, sliced thin, approx. ½ cup
1 tbsp chopped garlic
¼ cup dry white wine
1 tbsp dried basil leaves
Salt and pepper to taste

Spray the cooker with cooking spray. Mix the tomatoes with the remainder of the ingredients except the chicken. Pour 1" of the sauce on the bottom of the cooker. Arrange the chicken thighs on top of the sauce. Depending on their size you may have to push them down hard. Pour the remaining sauce over the thighs. Cover and cook undisturbed for 3 hours. Test the chicken with a quick read thermometer – it should read 165 degrees or more, and the juices should run clear. Serve with your favorite pasta.

Serves two to four

CHICKEN CURRY

The word curry strikes terror in the hearts of many Americans, as they think it is hot, hot, hot! Nothing could be further from the truth. This "curry" recipe with the raisins and apples develops a wonderful sweet-sour taste. Perfect served over white rice, with a green salad on the side.

1 boneless chicken breast approx. 1 lb. cut into bite size pieces
1 can (10.5 oz) condensed cream of mushroom soup
½ cup water or chicken broth
½ lb fresh mushrooms, sliced, approx ½ cup
2 tbsp. curry powder (more if you want)
½ cup seedless raisins (more if you want)
1 Granny Smith apple, cored and chopped, approx ¾ cup
Salt and pepper to taste

Wash and trim the chicken breast and cut into bite size pieces. Mix the mushroom soup with ½ cup water. Add the mushroom soup and the chicken pieces to the slow cooker. Cover and cook undisturbed for 2 hours. Chop the apple into ¼" pieces. Mix the mushrooms, curry powder, raisins and apple. Add to the cooker, stir, cover and cook for 1 hour more. Serve over rice as directed.

Note: You may use cooked left-over chicken for this recipe if you desire. Use 2 cups of chicken cut into bite size pieces. Add the chicken during the last hour of cooking.

Serves two to four

CHICKEN FRICASSEE

Chicken in a creamy sauce has always been an old fashioned comfort food. In this recipe the cream of mushroom soup acts as the base but the other ingredients are traditional. Serve with rice and a fresh green salad with warm country rolls.

1½ cups cooked boneless chicken, cut into bite size pieces
1 can (10.5 oz) condensed cream of chicken soup
¼ cup water
1 small onion, chopped fine, approx. ½ cup
2 celery stalks, chopped fine, approx. ½ cup
2 carrots, sliced thin, approx ½ cup
½ lb fresh mushrooms, sliced thin, approx. ¾ cup
½ cup frozen peas, thawed
1 tbsp lemon juice
1 bay leaf
Salt and pepper to taste

In a medium bowl dilute the chicken soup with the water. Add all the other ingredients. Spray the cooker with cooking spray. Add the mixture. Cover and cook undisturbed for 3 hours or until the fricassee is warm enough to serve.

Serves two to four

CHICKEN WITH GREEN OLIVES

This easy to make dish should be served with white rice or couscous. Use large pitted green olives and cut them in two lengthwise.

4 fresh chicken thighs, skin removed, approx. 1 lb total
1 can (7.5 oz) crushed tomatoes in thick puree
1 medium onion, diced, approx. ½ cup
4 scallions, sliced in 1" pieces
1 medium green bell pepper, diced, approx. ½ cup
½ cup pitted green olives, sliced in half
1 tbsp garlic, chopped
1 tbsp dried thyme
½ cup dry white wine
Salt and pepper to taste

Spray the cooker liner with cooking spray. In a medium bowl mix all the ingredients except the chicken. Pour 1" of the mixture into the liner and arrange the chicken thighs on top. Pour in the rest of the mixture. Cover and cook undisturbed for 3 hours. The chicken should have a temperature of 165-170 degrees and the juices should run clear. Serve over rice or couscous and with lots of the sauce.

Serves two to four

CHICKEN HASH

This is a wonderful way to use up leftovers. Since everything is already cooked you can use the cooker just to bring it to temperature. If you want the hash served in the traditional way you will have to fry it until a brown crust forms on the bottom. Cover each serving with a poached or fried egg on top. Serve with cornbread or Southern biscuits – and ketchup if you must!

2 cups cooked chicken, diced
2 cups cooked potatoes, diced
1 small green pepper, diced, approx. ½ cup
1 small onion, diced, approx. ½ cup
2 tbsp garlic, diced
1 tbsp parsley, chopped
Salt and pepper to taste

Spray the cooker with cooking spray. In a medium bowl combine all the other ingredients and place into the cooker. Cover and cook undisturbed for 3 hours or until the hash is at serving temperature. Remove the hash to a 10" frying pan and cook over medium heat until a crust forms on the bottom. Flip the hash over and fry on the other side. Cut the hash cake into four wedges. Serve each wedge with a poached or fried egg on top. If you are not frying the hash, just serve it directly from the cooker onto plates and serve the eggs on top or on the side.

Serves two to four

CHICKEN "HONG KONG"

Hong Kong is one of the most exciting cities in the world, with a cuisine that encompasses probably every known style of cooking. It is impossible to make an authentic "stir-fry" in the slow cooker, but this recipe will give you an approximate rendition. Serve over white rice with unsalted peanuts, chopped coriander, and additional soy or sesame oil as garnish.

1 lb. chicken breast or tenders, cut into bite size pieces
½ cup snow peas, trimmed
1 medium carrot, sliced thin or in batons
1 can (7oz.) bamboo shoots, drained
1 can (7oz.) sliced water chestnuts, drained
1 can (7oz.) pineapple chunks, drained
1 small green pepper, sliced into small strips
3 scallions, trimmed and chopped into 1" pieces on the bias
½ lb fresh mushrooms, sliced
I pkg. "Sun-Bird" or equal, stir-fry mix

Prepare stir-fry mix according to package directions, set aside. Spray the cooker with cooking spray. Prepare the vegetables, and trim the chicken as necessary. Layer the chicken, vegetables and all other ingredients into the cooker. Pour the stir-fry mix over. Cover the cooker and cook undisturbed for 3 hours. Check to see if the chicken is done by using your quick read thermometer. The temperature should be 165-170 degrees and the juices should run clear. If the sauce is too thin, thicken with a mixture of ¼ cup water and 1 tsp. cornstarch. Cook for an additional ½ hour to thicken. Toss well before serving.

Serves two to four

CHICKEN JAMBALAYA

If you have any qualms about cooking rice in the slow cooker lay them aside. If you use instant long grain premium rice you will get excellent results. Since all the meats are pre-cooked only the vegetables have to be cooked along with the rice. Serve with corn bread and iced tea!

1 lb cooked boneless chicken, cut into bite size pieces
½ lb cooked ham, cut into bite size pieces
1 cup instant long grain rice (dry measure)
1 cup hot tap water
½ cup onion, chopped
½ cup celery, chopped
½ cup green pepper, chopped
2 tbsp garlic, chopped
1 can (7.5 oz) tomato sauce, or spaghetti sauce of your choice
1 tsp thyme
Salt and pepper to taste

Spray the cooker with cooking spray. Pour the rice into the cooker. Add the vegetables and garlic. Add the hot water and stir well. Cover and cook undisturbed for 2 hours. Fluff the rice and add the ham, chicken and the tomato sauce. Cover and cook for 1 hour more or until serving temperature.

Serves two to four

CHICKEN LEGS WITH APRICOT GLAZE

This easy to prepare dish is a different take on some recipes using similar ingredients. Since this has some Oriental overtones, this is best served with white rice or with one of the long grain and wild rice combinations readily available. A green vegetable is a nice addition, as would be a fresh tossed green salad.

6 chicken legs (4 if they are extra large)
1 (7.5oz) can apricot halves in heavy syrup
1 small green pepper cut into small dice, approx. ½ cup
3 scallions cut into ½" pieces, white portion only
1 (7oz) can sliced water chestnuts, drained
2 tbsp white wine vinegar
3 tbsp Teryaki sauce
Salt and pepper to taste

With a large cleaver, cut off the bone end of the chicken legs to make them short enough to fit vertically into the cooker approximately 3" to 3¼" long. Arrange them around the outside of the cooker, one up, one down and so on all around. Chop the apricots and the water chestnuts into ½" dice, and add the green pepper and the scallions. Fill the center of the liner with the apricot mixture. Mix the apricot syrup with the Teryaki sauce, and the vinegar and pour over the legs. Cover, and cook undisturbed for 3 hours. Test the legs with an instant read thermometer. It should read 165-170 degrees or more. Serve with the rice, and pour the sauce over the legs.

Serves two to four

CHICKEN WITH LEMON AND CAPER SAUCE

This is a simple yet elegant dish. Serve the chicken with rice and a fresh green vegetable. A note about the chicken thighs; they come in many sizes. If the ones you buy are large then you can expect to get only four into the cooker. If they are small you will get as many as six into the cooker. So judge accordingly.

4 chicken thighs (about 1 lb), skin peeled off
½ cup all purpose flour
1 can (10.5 oz) chicken broth
½ cup dry white wine
¼ cup lemon juice
¼ cup capers, drained
2 tbsp cornstarch
¼ cup water
Chopped parsley for garnish
Salt and freshly ground black pepper to taste

Spray the cooker with cooking spray. Dredge the chicken thighs in the flour and coat them well. Arrange the thighs in the cooker and pour the broth and wine over them. Add the capers and the lemon juice. Cover and cook undisturbed for 3 hours. Test the chicken with a quick read thermometer – it should read 165 degrees or more and the chicken juices should run clear. Arrange the chicken on a serving platter. Mix the water and the cornstarch and add to the sauce stirring all the while to thicken it Pour over the chicken and sprinkle with the chopped parsley.

Serves two to four

CHICKEN LIVERS IN TOMATO SAUCE

Some say chicken livers are an acquired taste but they have many uses in fine cooking. The only problem is that most cooks over-do them and they become tough and stringy. Ideally they should be pink on the inside and just cooked through. Serve with rice and a simple green salad.

1 lb fresh chicken livers
1 can (14.5 oz) whole tomatoes in thick puree
1 medium onion, chopped fine, approx. ½ cup
1 small green bell pepper, chopped fine, approx. ½ cup
1 stalk celery, chopped fine, approx. ¼ cup
1 tbsp dried basil leaves
Salt and freshly ground black pepper to taste

Pick over the chicken livers and remove any of the membranes. Cut them in half if they are very large. Add the tomatoes to the cooker and break them up with a wooden spoon. Add the vegetables and the spices. Mix well. Cover and cook undisturbed for 2 hours. Add the chicken livers, cover and cook 1 hour more. Test one chicken liver to see if it is done sufficiently. Cover and cook 1 hour more if not done to your taste. Adjust the seasonings and serve as suggested.

Serves two to four

CHICKEN MARENGO

This dish supposedly prepared by a harried chef to Napoleon was a pick up recipe – in other words he used what could be found in the farms around the battlefield - hence the name Marengo. There are many versions, but this is pretty close to the original and it is delicious nonetheless. For Napoleon the chef put the poor chicken's last egg, fried and served on top of the dish! Serve the chicken with noodles or simple boiled potatoes.

4 chicken thighs, skinned, about 1 lb.
1 can (7.5 oz) diced tomatoes
1 medium green pepper, chopped, approx. ½ cup
1 medium onion, chopped, approx. ½ cup
½ lb fresh mushrooms, sliced
½ cup cooked ham, diced (optional)
3 tbsp garlic, chopped fine
Salt and pepper to taste
Parsley for garnish, chopped fine

Spray the inside of the cooker with cooking spray. In a medium bowl combine all the ingredients and stir well. Add the mixture to the slow cooker. Arrange the chicken thighs in the mixture. Cover and cook undisturbed for 3 hours. Test the chicken with a quick read thermometer. It should read 165 degrees or more and the juices should run clear.

Serves two to four

CHICKEN AND MUSHROOM RISOTTO

The mini slow cooker is an ideal way to make a rice dish very much like the famous Italian risotto and without all the stirring and attendance at the pot. Rice cooked in the slow cooker has a more glutinous quality than the "instant" method so it can be enriched with cream at the end of the cooking. The other ingredients can be added at that time, and you will get a very good approximation of the original Italian "risotto."

1½ cups instant enriched long grain premium rice
1½ cups hot chicken broth
2 tsp butter or oleo
1½ cups cooked chicken, cut into bite size pieces
I small can (8 oz) tiny new peas, drained
½ lb fresh mushrooms, sliced
2 tbsp garlic, chopped
1 cup light cream
½ cup grated Parmesan cheese
1 tsp dried basil leaves
Salt and pepper to taste
Chopped parsley for garnish

Spray the cooker with cooking spray. Melt the butter on the bottom of the cooker. Add the rice, hot broth and basil and stir well. Cover and cook undisturbed for 2 hours. Fluff the rice with a fork, and add the chicken and the mushrooms and cook for 1 hour more. With the cooker still plugged in, add the peas and stir in the cream. Gradually add the Parmesan cheese. Stir until the cream is absorbed and the rice is smooth. Garnish with the chopped parsley on top.

Serves two to four

CHICKEN WITH ONIONS AND OLIVES

This delicious casserole is good enough for company! Use the flavorful Calamata olives for extra punch. Serve with rice or mashed potatoes and a green salad.

4 chicken thighs, approx 1 lb, skin removed
1 can (10.5 oz) condensed cream of chicken soup
½ cup water
1 pkg. (16 oz) frozen small onions, thawed
½ cup pitted Calamata olives, sliced in half
1 tsp dried thyme
½ tsp ground paprika
Salt and pepper to taste

Spray the cooker with cooking spray. Dilute the soup with the water. Mix in the onions, olives and the spices. Pour into the cooker and arrange the chicken thighs so that they are covered with the mixture. Cover and cook undisturbed for 3 hours. Check the chicken with an instant read thermometer – it should be 165 –170 degrees or more and the juices should run clear.

Serves two to four

CHICKEN PICCATA

This is a rich and flavorful dish, with the lemon an assertive taste. The addition of the vegetables makes a fine sauce. Serve over linguini or your favorite pasta. A cold dry white wine as used in the recipe would be an elegant and festive beverage.

1 boneless chicken breast approx. 1 lb, cut into ½" pieces
2 Roma tomatoes, sliced fine
1 small onion, sliced fine, approx. ½ cup
1 small zucchini, sliced fine, approx. ½ cup
1 tsp butter or oleo
1 tbsp capers, drained
¼ cup lemon juice
2 cloves garlic, chopped fine
Salt and pepper to taste
½ cup dry white wine (or chicken broth if you prefer)
I lemon, sliced
Pasta of your choice prepared to package directions.

Spray the cooker with cooking spray. Place the vegetables on the bottom over the butter (or oleo). Mix the wine with the lemon juice and pour over the vegetables. Place the chicken on top and spread the capers over. Cover and cook undisturbed for 3 hours. Test the chicken with a quick read thermometer – it should read 165 degrees or more and the juices should run clear. Serve the chicken over the pasta. Mash the vegetables with a fork or stick blender to serve as a sauce. Garnish with lemon slices.

Serves two to four

CHICKEN POT PIE

This chicken pot pie is made without the crust on top, but is served with a baked crust of pastry. The filling itself is a good way to use up any left over chicken. Serve with a fresh green salad and country biscuits.

2 cups cooked chicken cut into bite size pieces
1 can (10.5 oz) condensed cream of chicken soup
½ cup water
1 pkg. (16 oz) frozen mixed vegetables, thawed and drained
Salt and pepper to taste

1 pkg. refrigerated pie crust cut into four 6" circles

Spray the cooker with cooking spray. Dilute the soup with the water and combine with the remaining ingredients in the cooker. Cover and cook undisturbed for 2 hours. While the filling is cooking, bake the 4 crusts according to package directions. Spoon the chicken filling onto each of four plates and place a circle of the crust on top.

Serves two to four

CHICKEN AND SAFFRON RICE

As with some of the other recipes in this book I have used a named product which has given me good results in designing these recipes. Do not be afraid of using these products as they are designed to save time and give the best flavor for the money. This chicken recipe comes as close to the Spanish "arroz con pollo" as you can get with simple ingredients.

1 lb. chicken breast or tenders cut into bite size pieces
1 pkg (5 oz) "Mahatma" Saffron Long Grain Rice
1 small green bell pepper, diced, approx. ½ cup
1 small onion, diced, approx. ½ cup
1 tsp chopped garlic
1 cup chicken broth, heated to near boiling
1 tbsp butter or oleo
½ cup canned peas, drained
¼ cup pimento, diced fine
¼ cup pimento stuffed olives, chopped
Salt and pepper to taste

Pre-heat the cooker for 10 minutes. Add the butter and the rice and stir. Add the heated chicken broth and stir. Cover and cook undisturbed for 2 hours. Stir the rice and add all the other ingredients. Cover and cook undisturbed for 2 hours more. Put the chicken into a flat serving dish, mix well and sprinkle with chopped parsley or cilantro.

Serves two to four

CHICKEN AND SAUSAGE CASSEROLE

This is a hearty dish combining many ethnic sources. I would serve this with noodles or rice and a green salad.

4 chicken thighs, skin removed, approx 1 lb.
½ lb Kielbasa (or sausage of your choice) cut into ¼" slices)
1 small onion, diced, approx. ½ cup
½ cup fresh mushrooms, sliced
1 small green pepper, diced, approx. ½ cup
2 tbsp chopped garlic
1 can (7.5 oz) diced tomatoes in thick puree
1 tsp oregano
Salt and pepper to taste

Spray the cooker with cooking spray. In a medium bowl combine the chicken and all the other ingredients. Pour into the cooker and add enough water to cover the ingredients. Stir well. Cover and cook undisturbed for 3 hours. Check the chicken with a quick read thermometer – it should read 165-170 degrees or more and the juices should run clear. Serve as suggested above.

Serves two to four

CHICKEN AND SAUSAGE TEX-MEX

This spicy casserole will bring cheers from the lucky people who will share it. Serve it with rice and a green salad with sliced avocado. Cold beer would be an appropriate accompaniment!

4 chicken thighs, skinned (approx. 1 lb)
½ lb pre-cooked Andouille type sausage, cut into ½" slices
1 can (7.5 oz) spicy Mexican style chunky tomato sauce
1 can (7.5 oz) chili beans, drained
1 medium onion, chopped, approx. ½ cup
1 green pepper, diced, approx. ½ cup
3 tbsp chopped garlic
1 tbsp chili powder
½ tsp dried basil leaves
½ tsp dried thyme
1 tsp ground cumin
Ground cayenne pepper to taste
Salt and freshly ground black pepper to taste

Spray the cooker with cooking spray. In a medium bowl mix the tomato sauce with the chili beans. Add the remaining ingredients except the chicken and the sausage. Mix well. Arrange the chicken and sausage in the cooker and pour the tomato mixture over. Cover and cook undisturbed for 3 hours. Test the chicken with a quick read thermometer – it should read 165-170 degrees or more and the juices should run clear. If not done, cover and cook ½ hour more.

Serves two to four

Note: After placing the chicken thighs into the cooker, and then pouring the sauce over them, you may have some sauce left over. In any event, the cooker will be full.

CHICKEN "SHANGHAI"

This is about as close as you can get to stir-fry in the slow cooker! The chicken is juicy and has absorbed the flavors of the Hoisin and Soy Sauce. No quick wok-cooked dish this but flavorful all the same. Serve with rice of course.

4 chicken thighs, skin removed (approx 1 lb)
2 tbsp minced garlic
1 carrot, sliced thin or cut into thin julienne, approx. ¼ cup
1 small green bell pepper, cut into thin julienne, approx. ½ cup
1 can (8 oz) pineapple chunks, drained
1 can (10.5 oz) chicken broth
1 can (5 oz) sliced water chestnuts, drained
1 can (5 oz) sliced bamboo shoots, drained
2 tsp soy sauce
2 tsp Hoisin sauce
2 tsp cornstarch mixed with 2 tsp chicken broth
Salt and freshly ground pepper to taste

Coat the cooker liner with cooking spray, and put the prepared vegetables on the bottom. Arrange the pineapple chunks on top of the vegetables. Arrange the chicken thighs on top. Mix 1 cup of the chicken broth with the Hoisin and soy sauces and pour over the chicken. Cover and cook undisturbed for 3 hours. Using an instant read thermometer, check the chicken for doneness. It should read 165 degrees or more and the juices should run clear. Remove the chicken and the vegetables, and add the cornstarch. Cover and let the sauce cook for ½ hour to thicken.

Serves two to four

CHICKEN AND SHRIMP

Some would say this is an unlikely combination but not so. Originally said to have originated in the Basque region of Spain, it is more likely a dish from the Cajun country of Louisiana. Add as many spices as you like. Serve with rice or grits.

4 chicken thighs approx. 1 lb.
½ lb small shrimp, peeled and deveined
1 can (7.5 oz) stewed tomatoes in heavy puree
½ lb smoked (or boiled) ham, cut into small dice
1 small onion, diced, approx. ½ cup
1 tbsp chopped garlic
1 tsp paprika
½ cup dry white wine
Salt and pepper to taste

Spray the cooker with cooking spray. Combine all the ingredients in the cooker except the shrimp and mix well. Cover and cook undisturbed for 3 hours. Add the shrimp and cook for 1 hour more. Test the chicken with a quick read thermometer – it should read 165-170 degrees or more and the juices should run clear.

Serves two to four

CHICKEN STEW

If you have some left over chicken this is a good way to use it up. Serve this with a tossed salad and rustic bread to sop up the juices.

1 cup cooked chicken, cut into 1" pieces
1 can (7.5 oz) diced tomatoes in thick puree
1 pkg. (16 oz) frozen mixed vegetables, thawed*
1 small onion, diced, approx. ½ cup
½ lb fresh mushrooms, sliced, approx. ½ cup
1 tbsp garlic, chopped fine
1 tsp dried basil leaves
Salt and pepper to taste

Spray the cooker with cooking spray. In a medium bowl mix all the ingredients. Pour the mixture into the cooker. Cover and let cook undisturbed for 3 hours. Serve with rice or noodles.

Serves two to four

*Note: Instead of the frozen vegetables you can use 1 can (15 oz) "Veg-All" mixed vegetables, drained. Add them to the stew 1 hour before the end of cooking. Not as good as the frozen but a time saver and they are acceptable.

CHICKEN TETRAZZINI

Adapted from a dish named for the famed Italian soprano Luisa Tetrazzini (1874-1940) this dish has many variations. It is a wonderful way to use leftovers. This dish is usually made with spaghetti or linguini, but because of the shape of the cooker it is best to use elbow macaroni. The effect and taste is the same. If you do not have leftover elbow macaroni then you will have to make some before proceeding with this recipe. Serve with a fresh tossed green salad and Italian bread.

1½ cups cooked chicken, in bite size pieces
1 can (10.5 oz) condensed cream of chicken soup
2 cups of elbow macaroni (cooked measure)
½ cup water
½ lb fresh mushrooms, sliced, approx. ¾ cup
½ cup frozen peas, thawed
¼ cup pimento, chopped
Pinch of freshly ground nutmeg
Salt and pepper to taste
Grated Parmesan cheese for garnish

In a medium bowl dilute the mushroom soup with the water. Add the remaining ingredients, except the pasta. Spray the cooker with cooking spray and add the mixture. Cover and cook undisturbed for 2 hours. Add the cooked pasta and stir well. Cover and cook for 1 more hour. Serve with the grated Parmesan cheese on top.

Serves two to four

CHICKEN TEX-MEX CASSEROLE

This lusty dish will satisfy the most avid Tex-Mex afficionados. Serve with tortillas, sour cream, chopped onion and chopped tomato for a true Southwest flavor. Serve with warm tortillas or crisp tortilla chips.

1½ cups cooked boneless chicken, cut into bite size pieces
1 can (7.5 oz) diced tomatoes in thick puree
1 medium onion, diced, approx. ½ cup
1 green pepper, diced, approx. ½ cup
1 can (7.5 oz) whole kernel corn, drained
½ cup salsa (hot or mild -your choice)
2 tbsp chopped seedless green chilis (canned are fine)
1 tsp ground cumin
Salt and freshly ground black pepper to taste
Grated cheese for garnish

In a non-reactive bowl combine all the ingredients. Spray the cooker with cooking spray and add the mixture. Cover and cook undisturbed for 3 hours. Spoon directly from the cooker or place into an oval gratin dish and sprinkle grated cheese on top. Place under a broiler for a few minutes or until the cheese melts and browns.

Serves two to four

CHICKEN THIGHS WITH PINEAPPLE

This dish with oriental overtones is easy to prepare and makes a savory dish to serve with white rice and a green salad.

4 chicken thighs depending on size about 1 lb, skin removed
½ cup all purpose flour
1 can (10.5 oz) chicken broth
1 can (8.5 oz) crushed pineapple
1 tbsp Dijon style French mustard
2 tbsp soy sauce
1 tbsp sesame oil
½ cup chili sauce
2 tbsp brown sugar
¼ cup scallions cut into 1" pieces on the bias for garnish
Salt and freshly ground black pepper to taste

Make the sauce by combining the chicken broth, pineapple, mustard, sugar and chili sauce in a small bowl. Dredge the thighs in the flour. Spray the cooker with cooking spray. Pour a small amount of the sauce on the bottom of the cooker. Arrange the chicken thighs on the sauce and pour the remainder over. Cover and cook undisturbed for 3 hours. Check chicken for doneness with a quick read thermometer. The temperature should be 165 degrees or more and the juices should run clear. Serve the chicken over white rice with the sauce, and with the scallions sprinkled on top.

Serves two to four

CHICKEN THIGHS, TOMATOES AND OLIVES

This lusty dish is perfect for a "Provence" inspired dinner. The combination of tomatoes and olives is memorable. Make sure you get the real Calamata olives – regular black olives just will not give the dish the lusty flavor it needs. Serve with rice or boiled potatoes with a green salad on the side. A French baguette is the perfect accompaniment to sop up the juices.

4 chicken thighs, skin removed, approx.1b
1 can (14.5 oz) diced tomatoes in heavy puree
1 medium onion diced fine, approx. ½ cup
2 tsp garlic, chopped
1 tsp oregano
1 tsp dried thyme
½ cup pitted Calamata olives sliced in half
Salt and pepper to taste

Spray the cooker with cooking spray. In a medium bowl mix the tomatoes and all the spices including the olives. Pour ½ cup into the cooker. Start layering the thighs pouring the tomato sauce over them as you go. Cover and cook undisturbed for 3 hours. The cooker will be full and there may be some overflow as the thighs cook. (Mop up around the lid with paper towels.) Test the thighs with an instant read thermometer – it should read 165 degrees and the juices should run clear. If the chicken is not done, recover and cook for an additional ½ hour.

Serves two to four

CHINESE CHICKEN IN ORANGE SAUCE

This is a slightly different take on the usual Chinese chicken dish. Serve over white rice or crisp noodles.

2 cups cooked chicken breast, cut into ¼" x 3" batons
1 pkg (16 oz) frozen "Chinese" style vegetables, thawed
½ cup orange juice
2 tbsp cornstarch
2 tbsp soy sauce
½ tsp red pepper flakes

Spray the cooker with cooking spray. Add the vegetables to the cooker. Cover and cook undisturbed for 1 hour. Add the cooked chicken and the orange sauce and mix well. Cover and cook for 1 hour more. For the orange sauce: in a small saucepan mix the orange juice, cornstarch, soy sauce and pepper flakes. Over low heat, stir the sauce until it thickens.

Serves two to four

CHINESE CHICKEN AND VEGETABLES

Left over chicken can be used in many ways and this is just one of them. Serve over white rice with sliced cucumbers in white wine vinegar and olive oil as a side dish.

2 cups cooked chicken, sliced in ¼" x 3" batons
1 pkg. (15 oz) "Oriental" style frozen vegetables, thawed
½ cup cold water
2 tbsp cornstarch
2 tbsp soy sauce
1 tsp sesame oil

Spray the cooker with cooking spray. Put the thawed vegetables and the chicken into the cooker. Cover and cook undisturbed for 1 hour. In a small saucepan mix the water, cornstarch, soy and sesame oil. Stir while the sauce cooks and thickens. If the sauce is too thick add a little more water or soy. Pour over the vegetables and chicken and stir well. Taste and cook for ½ hour more or as necessary. Toss well before serving.

Serves two to four

COQ AU VIN

Because of the shape and size of the mini slow cooker it is nearly impossible to make a "traditional" French Coq au Vin. Nonetheless, this recipe makes a reasonably accurate version. Serve with small boiled potatoes, French bread and a fresh green salad.

4 chicken thighs approx. 1 lb.. skin removed
½ boneless chicken breast cut into approx.2" batons
1 cup frozen pearl onions, thawed (approx 12 onions)
3 slices bacon, fried crisp and chopped into small pieces
2 tbsp garlic, chopped
1 pkg. fresh mushrooms (8 oz), cut into quarters
1 can (10.5 oz) chicken broth
½ cup red wine
Chopped parsley
2 tbsp cornstarch
2 tbsp cold water
Salt and pepper to taste

Mix the broth and the red wine in a small bowl. Add the bacon and the garlic. Arrange the chicken in the cooker mixing the thighs and breasts. Pour the wine and broth mixture over the chicken. Arrange the mushrooms and the onions among the chicken. Cover and cook undisturbed for 3 hours. Check the chicken with a quick read thermometer. It should read 165 degrees or more and the juices should run clear. Remove the chicken and the onions and mushrooms to a serving platter and keep warm. Mix the cornstarch and water and add to the cooker stirring all the while until the sauce thickens. Pour over the chicken to serve.

Serves two to four

COUNTRY CAPTAIN

This dish is famous in the area around Charleston, South Carolina, where in early days it was named for the clipper captains who brought exotic spices and other goods from far away countries. The original featured bacon fat (of course) but we have omitted it here. Serve with white rice and home made cornbread.

1 lb skinless boneless chicken breasts cut into ½" pieces
1 can (7.5oz) diced tomatoes in heavy syrup
1 medium onion, diced, approx. ½ cup
1 green pepper, diced, approx. ½ cup
2 tbsp chopped garlic
2 tbsp curry powder
1 tsp dried thyme
½ cup seedless dark raisins (more if you want)
Salt and pepper to taste
Sliced almonds for garnish

Spray the cooker with cooking spray. Add all the ingredients to the cooker and mix well. Cover and cook undisturbed for 3 hours. Test the chicken for doneness with a quick read thermometer – it should read 165-170 degrees or more and the juices should run clear. Taste the dish for spices and add salt and pepper as necessary. Garnish with the sliced almonds and serve hot.

Serves two to four

CREAMED CHICKEN

This version of the "ladies luncheon" favorite is more robust than the original recipes, generally served in puff pastry shells. I suggest you serve this over rice, and with a fresh green salad. Freshly baked corn bread would be a nice side dish.

1 lb. boneless chicken breast, cut into bite size pieces.
1 can (10.5 oz) condensed cream of mushroom soup
½ cup water
½ lb fresh mushrooms, sliced thin, approx. ½ cup
½ cup frozen peas, defrosted to room temperature
1 small carrot, sliced thin, approx. ½ cup
¼ cup pimento, chopped fine
Salt and pepper to taste

In a medium size bowl, dilute the mushroom soup. Add all the other ingredients, and mix well. Spray the cooker with cooking spray. Add the soup mixture. Cover and cook undisturbed for 3 hours. Test the chicken with a quick read thermometer – it should be 165 degrees or over and the juices should run clear. Adjust seasonings as necessary. Serve as noted above.

Note: If you use leftover cooked chicken add it at the beginning and cook undisturbed for 2 hours total.

Serves two to four

CURRIED CHICKEN AND RICE

In this recipe the rice is cooked along with the other ingredients. An array of condiments is essential to Indian cooking so use your imagination and serve grated coconut, unsalted peanuts, sliced scallions and raisins in small bowls on the side and let diners help themselves.

1 lb chicken breast or tenders, cut into ½" pieces
1 cup instant enriched long grain rice
1 can (10.5 oz) chicken broth, heated if possible
3 scallions, cut into ½" pieces on the diagonal
2 tbsp Madras curry powder
1 tsp cayenne pepper
1 small green bell pepper, seeded and sliced into batons
1 medium Granny Smith apple, cored and chopped fine
½ cup dark seedless raisins (more if you want)
Salt and freshly ground pepper to taste

Spray the cooker with cooking spray. Put the cup of rice into the cooker. Add 1 cup of the chicken broth heated but not boiling. Cover and cook the rice undisturbed for 1 hour. In a medium size bowl mix the scallions, green pepper, cayenne pepper, curry powder and the remainder of the chicken broth. Add the chicken pieces and the chopped apple. Fluff the rice, and add the chicken mixture and stir. Cover and cook undisturbed for 2 hours. Check the chicken with a quick read thermometer – it should read 165 degrees or more and the juices should run clear.

Serves two to four

CURRIED TURKEY POT PIE

A little different from the Chicken Pot Pie, but many of the ingredients are interchangeable. Cooked without a pastry top, the pie is served either over or under a separately baked pastry top. Serve with a fresh green salad and good crusty bread.

2 cups cooked turkey (white or dark meat), cut into bite size pieces
1 can (10.5 oz) condensed cream of chicken soup
½ cup water
1 can (8 oz) mushrooms stems and pieces, drained
1 can (15.5 oz) mixed vegetables, drained*
¼ cup dark seedless raisins soaked in brandy
1 small cooking apple, cored and cut into small dice
2 tbsp curry powder (more if you want)
Salt and pepper to taste

½ pkg. refrigerated pie pastry cut into four 6" rounds

In a medium size bowl dilute the soup with the water. Add the turkey, mushrooms, vegetables, raisins, and apple. Mix well and add the curry powder. Spray the cooker with cooking spray and add the mixture. Cover and cook undisturbed for 2 hours. In the meantime bake the pastry rounds in the oven to package directions. Serve the curry on top of the rounds, or serve it on a plate with a pastry round placed on top.

Serves two to four

*You can use frozen mixed vegetables if you choose – let them come to room temperature before using them. They will take longer to cook than the canned ones, but I must confess they have better flavor.

HUNGARIAN CHICKEN PAPRIKA

Just about every Hungarian dish has paprika – the national spice of that country! This is no exception. Because of the shape of the cooker, not all pieces of the chicken will fit. Thighs are easiest, but if you want to use legs you will have to chop the bone end off to make them less than 3" long to fit into the cooker. You could also use boneless breast, cutting the breasts into 2" or 3" pieces. Anyway you decide to do it this recipe will become a favorite. Serve over noodles.

1 lb or so chicken parts, as noted above
1 medium onion, chopped, approx. ½ cup
1 green pepper, chopped, approx. ½ cup
1 cup chicken broth, or enough to cover the chicken
2 tbsp Hungarian sweet paprika (or more if you like)
1 cup sour cream
2 tbsp cornstarch
Salt and pepper to taste

Spray the cooker with cooking spray. In a small bowl mix the onion, pepper, paprika and the chicken broth. Arrange the chicken pieces in the cooker, and pour the sauce over. Cover and cook undisturbed for 3 hours. Test the chicken with a quick read thermometer. It should read 165-170 degrees or higher and the juices should run clear. Remove the chicken from the cooker, and keep warm. Take 2 tbsp of the broth from the liner and mix with the cornstarch. Add to the broth and stir until it thickens. Add the sour cream to the broth, and pour over the chicken to serve.

Serves two to four

MEXICAN CHICKEN CASSEROLE

This zesty dish should be served with a bowl of salsa and tortilla chips on the side. Flour or corn tortillas can also be used as a base for the casserole.

4 chicken thighs skinned, approx. 1b
1 can (7.5 oz) crushed tomatoes in heavy puree
1 medium onion, diced, approx. ½ cup
1 small zucchini, sliced thin, approx. ½ cup
½ cup canned whole corn kernels, drained
1 green bell pepper, diced, approx. ½ cup
2 tbsp garlic, chopped
1 tsp chili powder
½ cup salsa (your choice)
½ tsp dried oregano
Salt and pepper to taste
Grated Monterey Jack cheese as garnish

Spray the cooker with cooking spray. Mix all the ingredients in a medium size bowl. Pour about 1" mixture into the cooker and then arrange the chicken thighs on top. Pour in the remainder of the mixture to cover the thighs. Cover and cook undisturbed for 3 hours. Test the chicken with your quick read thermometer The temperature should be 165-170 degrees and the juices should run clear. Pour the chicken into a shallow broiler proof serving dish. Sprinkle with grated Monterey Jack cheese and place under the broiler until the cheese melts.

Serves two to four

MUSTARD CHICKEN WITH MUSHROOMS

This piquant dish is wonderful served with white or long grain wild rice and fresh steamed broccoli. Pour the sauce over the chicken and over the vegetable.

1 half boneless skinless chicken breast (approx 1 lb) cut into strips approx. ½" x 3"
1 can (10.5 oz) condensed cream of chicken soup
½ cup water
1 medium green bell pepper, cut into ¼" x 3" batons
1 medium onion, diced, approx. ½ cup
½ lb fresh sliced mushrooms, approx. ¾ cup
¼ cup Dijon mustard
Salt and pepper to taste
Chopped parsley for garnish

Spray the cooker with cooking spray. Dilute the mushroom soup with the water. Add the chicken and the peppers and onion. Cover and cook undisturbed for 3 hours. Add the mushrooms and cook for 1 hour more. Test the chicken with a quick read thermometer. It should read 165-170 degrees and the juices should run clear. Remove the chicken to a serving platter and keep warm. Add the mustard to the sauce and mix well. Serve over the chicken.

Serves two four

ORIENTAL CHICKEN WITH PEPPERS

This is a wonderful way to use leftover chicken. Make the sauce first and add the chicken and vegetables. Serve with rice, of course.

1½ cups cooked chicken, cut into bite size pieces
1 medium green bell pepper, cut into batons (3" x ¼")
1 medium red bell pepper, cut into batons (3" x ¼")
4 scallions, cut into ¼" pieces on the bias, white parts only
1 tbsp garlic, chopped
¼ cup soy sauce
¼ cup ketchup
¼ cup water
1 tsp cornstarch
1 can (5 oz) bamboo shoots, drained
1 can (5 oz) sliced water chestnuts, drained
½ lb fresh mushrooms, sliced

Spray the cooker with cooking spray. Add the peppers, scallions and fresh mushrooms. Cover and cook undisturbed for 1 hour. Make the sauce with all the other ingredients. Add the chicken and the sauce and stir well. Cover and cook undisturbed for 2 hours more. Toss well and serve over rice.

Serves two to four

PROVENCAL BRAISED CHICKEN

Generally made with whole chickens cut up, the size of the mini slow cooker cannot accommodate such size birds. The alternative is to use thighs or breasts cut into chunky pieces. In this recipe I have used both. Serve with herbed potatoes, a green vegetable and crusty country bread.

4 chicken thighs, approx 1 lb total, skin removed
½ chicken breast, cut into 1" pieces, approx 1 lb total
1 small red pepper, diced, approx.1/2 cup
1 small green pepper, diced, approx. ½ cup
1 small onion, diced, approx. ½ cup
1 can (7.5 oz) crushed tomatoes
½ tsp herbs de Provence
2 tsp garlic chopped
Salt and freshly ground pepper to taste
Chopped parsley for garnish

Spray the cooker with cooking spray. Mix the tomatoes with the vegetables and pour into the cooker. Arrange the chicken in the tomato mixture. Be sure that the chicken is all covered. Cover and cook undisturbed for 3 hours. Test the chicken for doneness with a quick read thermometer. It should read 165-170 degrees or more and the juices should run clear. Serve as suggested above.

Serves two to four

ROLLED STUFFED CHICKEN BREASTS

This elegant and easy recipe will become a regular in your cuisine repertory. Serve with a flavored white or wild rice, and a green vegetable such as peas or snap beans, with warm dinner rolls and plenty of good butter!

4 slices chicken breast, approx 1 lb. pounded flat, and trimmed
4 slices Provolone or Swiss cheese
4 slices turkey pastrami (or the real thing if you prefer)
2 medium Roma tomatoes, sliced thin, approx. ½ cup
1 small onion, sliced thin, approx. ½ cup
1 small zucchini, sliced thin. approx. ½ cup
1 tsp dry basil leaves
1 cup chicken br
2 garlic cloves, chopped fine
1 tsp butter (or oleo)
Salt and pepper to taste

Trim the chicken breasts and pound thin between waxed paper or plastic wrap to about 1/8" thick. Season generously with the salt, pepper and basil leaves, and place a slice of the cheese and pastrami on each one. Roll tightly and secure with a toothpick. Spray the slow cooker liner with cooking spray. Put the butter or oleo on the bottom of the cooker. Arrange the vegetables and garlic in layers. Arrange the rolled chicken breasts in the cooker, and pour the chicken broth over. Cover and cook undisturbed for 3 hours. Serve the breasts as directed. The vegetables on the bottom will have formed a very tasty sauce to be poured over them. Mash the vegetables with a fork or use a stick blender.

Serves two to four

SESAME CHICKEN NUGGETS

This is another way of using left over chicken. The sauce is a piquant mix of sweet and sour tastes. Serve over white rice or crisp Chinese noodles.

1½ cups cooked chicken cut into 1" nuggets
1 pkg (16 oz) frozen "Chinese" vegetables, thawed
1 can (7 oz) crushed pineapple, juice drained and reserved
1 cup chicken broth
3 tbsp cornstarch
2 tbsp soy sauce
2 tbsp sesame oil
2 tbsp ground ginger or coarsely shredded fresh ginger
Juice from the drained pineapple
2 tbsp dry sherry
1 tsp dried Chinese peppercorns

Spray the cooker with cooking spray. Put the thawed vegetables into the cooker with the crushed drained pineapple. Cover and cook undisturbed for 1 hour. In the meantime make the sauce. In a small saucepan mix the chicken broth with the cornstarch and all the other ingredients. Over medium heat stir the sauce until it thickens. Add the chicken nuggets and the sauce to the vegetables and stir well to coat. Cover and cook 1 hour more.

Serves two to four

SOUTHERN SUCCOTASH WITH CHICKEN

This is a wonderful dish in which you can use some left over chicken. Serve over beaten biscuits and with lots of iced tea!

1 can (7.5 oz) whole kernel corn, drained
1 can (7.5 oz) baby lima beans, drained
1 can (7.5 oz) whole potatoes, diced
1 small green bell pepper, diced, approx. ½ cup
1 can (10.5 oz) cream of mushroom soup
1½ cups cooked chicken, cut into bite size pieces
½ cup water
Salt and pepper to taste
1 tsp Cayenne pepper
½ tsp thyme

Spray the cooker with cooking spray. Dilute the mushroom soup with the water. Add all the ingredients to the cooker. Stir well. Cover and cook undisturbed for 3 hours. Taste for seasoning and add salt and pepper as needed. Serve warm over the biscuits.

Serves two four

SPICY CHICKEN WITH ANCHOVIES

Many people hate anchovies and others dote on them. Rinse them well before using them in this recipe and you will have taken a big step forward to alleviating the strong taste some hate. Serve this with noodles or rice, with a green salad on the side.

4 chicken thighs, skin removed, about 1 lb
1 can (7.5 oz) tomatoes in heavy puree
1 medium onion, diced, approx. ½ cup
4-6 anchovy filets, rinsed and chopped fine
2 tbsp garlic, chopped
½ cup red wine
3 tbsp capers, drained
2 tbsp red wine vinegar
Salt and pepper to taste

Mix the tomatoes with the onion, garlic, capers, anchovies, red wine and red wine vinegar. Pour into the cooker. Add the chicken thighs and see that they are submerged in the sauce. Cover and cook undisturbed for 3 hours. Check the chicken with a quick read thermometer. It should read 165-170 degrees and the juices should run clear. Serve the sauce over the chicken.

Serves two to four

TURKEY CHILI

A robust chili without the beef! Yes, and this also a good way to use up some of the left-over Thanksgiving bird. Serve in bowls with chopped onion, sour cream and grated Monterrey Jack cheese on the side.

1½ cups cooked turkey, cut in bite size pieces
1 can (7.5 oz) diced tomatoes in heavy puree
1 medium onion, diced, approx. ½ cup
2 tbsp garlic, chopped
1 medium green pepper, diced, approx. ½ cup
1 can (7.5 oz) red kidney beans, do not drain
2 tbsp ground chili powder
1 tsp ground cumin
1 tbsp dried oregano
Salt and pepper to taste

Spray the cooker with cooking spray. Pour the diced tomatoes into a medium non-reactive bowl. Add the remaining ingredients and mix well. Pour the mixture into the cooker. Cover and cook undisturbed for 3 hours or until the chili is hot enough to serve.

Serves two to four

TURKEY LOAF

This is a meatless "meatloaf" and a refreshing change if you are tired of beef. Ground turkey breast is widely available today, so there should be no trouble in finding it. For down home goodness serve this with mashed potatoes and a fresh green vegetable.

1½ lbs fresh ground turkey breast
1 small onion, diced, approx. ½ cup
1 small green bell pepper, diced, approx ½ cup
1½ cups freshly made bread crumbs
¾ cup tomato puree
2 eggs slightly beaten
1 tbsp Worcestershire sauce
Salt and freshly ground pepper to taste

Spray the cooker with cooking spray. In a medium bowl mix all the ingredients. It is easiest if you use your hands. Place the mixture into the cooker. Cover and cook undisturbed for 3 hours. Test the loaf with a quick read thermometer. It should be 160 degrees or more in the center of the loaf and about 170 degrees near the cooker wall. If you turn the cooker off now the loaf will continue to cook. Use oven mitts to handle the cooker. Ease the loaf out of the cooker with a long handled cooking fork. Let the loaf cool slightly for easier slicing. Put the loaf on its side and slice vertically, or stand it up and slice into wedges.

Serves four or more

TURKEY NOODLE CASSEROLE

This recipe can be made with leftover cooked chicken or turkey, and it is a great way to use up some of the Thanksgiving bird. Serve with some of the leftover dressing and vegetables. Pass the cranberry sauce!

1½ cups cooked turkey, cut into bite size pieces
2 cups elbow macaroni (cooked measure)
½ cup celery, chopped
½ cup onion, chopped
½ cup green bell pepper, chopped
1 can (10.5 oz) celery soup
½ cup water
Salt and pepper to taste
Grated cheese for garnish

Cook the elbow macaroni according to package directions until it is just al dente. Drain well. Spray the cooker with cooking spray. Dilute the soup with the ½ cup water. Add all of the ingredients, (except the macaroni) stirring well. Taste for seasoning. Pour the mixture into the cooker. Cover and cook for 2 hours. Add the cooked macaroni, stir well, and cook for 1 hour more. Pour the mixture into an oval ovenproof casserole, cover with grated cheese, and put under the broiler until the cheese melts and the top crisps.

Serves two to four

TURKEY ROULADES

If your have leftover turkey from the holidays use some of the breast from that bird to make this recipe. If not, you can buy sliced turkey breast all year long from your deli counter. Use good smoked ham or turkey pastrami for the filling. Serve this with white rice or couscous and a green salad.

4 slices cooked turkey breast about 1/8" thick and 3¼" x 6" long
4 slices ham or turkey pastrami, about the same size
1 can (10.5 oz) condensed cream of chicken soup
½ cup water
1 medium green bell pepper, diced, approx. ½ cup
1 medium onion, diced, approx. ½ cup
1 celery stalk, chopped fine, approx. ¼ cup
½ lb mushrooms, sliced
1 tbsp garlic, chopped
1 tsp dry thyme
1 bay leaf
Salt and pepper to taste

Spray the cooker with cooking spray. Lay the turkey breast pieces out on a clean surface. Salt and pepper generously. Lay a piece of the ham or pastrami on each slice. They should be of the same size. Roll them up tightly and secure with a toothpick. They should measure 3¼" wide x 1½" diameter. Dilute the soup with the water and add the vegetables. Arrange the turkey roulades in the cooker and pour the soup mixture over. Cover and cook undisturbed for 3 hours.

Serves two to four

VEGETABLES

Broccoli with Cheese
Brussels Sprouts with Bacon
Butternut Squash Casserole
Corn Pudding
Creamed Onions
Creamed Vegetable Melange
Dixie Corn Pudding
Eggplant, Tomato and Cheese Stew
German Potato Salad
Green Bean Casserole
Herbed New Potatoes
Potato Cheese Cake
Potatoes Savoyard
Ratatouille
Red Cabbage with Apples and Raisins
Sauerkraut with Apples
Spiced Green Beans
Spicy Yams
Spinach Cake
Succotash
Sweet Potato Casserole
Sweet Potatoes with Apples and Raisins
Sweet and Sour Red Cabbage
Tricolor Vegetable Timbale
Vegetable Chili
Vegetable Stew
Winter Vegetable Stew
Zucchini Espagnol
Zucchini in the Style of Provence
Zucchini and Tomato Casserole

VEGETABLES

Vegetables are wonderful cooked in the mini slow cooker. The slow cooking brings out and intensifies the flavors.

You will find some vegetables cook slower than meats, but slightly crunchy vegetables are better than ones which are flabby and with no flavor. You will soon notice that vegetables give off a good amount of water in the mini slow cooker, so do not be surprised if there is more water in the bottom of the cooker than what you might have added.

Which brings me to another advantage of the mini slow cooker. In many cases you do not need to add water or other liquids to cook vegetables thus saving even more of the valued nutrients.

Many of the vegetable recipes use canned or frozen vegetables. Do not let this put you off. If you want to use fresh vegetables then do so. I have used the canned and frozen for convenience only. I have to admit that the frozen ones have more natural flavor than the canned ones, so judge accordingly.

I have included some completely vegetarian dishes for those who do not eat meat, fish or poultry – you can add other things to them for additional variety.

If you are cooking vegetables with meats, fish or poultry you will find the vegetables often take longer to cook than the meats. I like my vegetables "tender crisp" but some of you may find them under-done in the times shown with the recipe. If so, just cover the cooker and cook for another ½ hour or so – and test again.

BROCCOLI WITH CHEESE

Broccoli has a natural affinity for cheese. Use any kind of cheese you like, but a strong cheddar seems to work best. Serve as a vegetable side dish with any number of main course meat dishes.

4 cups broccoli florets, washed and trimmed.
1 pkg shredded cheese (16 oz) your choice
2 tbsp butter or oleo cut into small pieces.
Salt and pepper to taste

Spray the cooker with cooking spray. Layer the broccoli in the cooker, spreading some cheese on each layer with pieces of the butter or oleo. Continue, ending with cheese on top. Cover and cook undisturbed for 2 hours. Check the broccoli for doneness. It should be tender crisp and the cheese should have melted throughout it. Serve directly from the liner, or put it into a shallow gratin dish and run it under the broiler until the cheese bubbles and browns on top.

Serves two to four

BRUSSELS SPROUTS WITH BACON

This is a good recipe for preparing fresh or frozen Brussels Sprouts, and even those who dislike them may come around. Buy the freshest and smallest sprouts you can find. However, if they are large there is no harm in cutting them in half. In fact, more will fit into the cooker if they are cut in half, and they will cook quicker.

4 cups Brussels Sprouts, fresh or frozen, at room temperature
4 slices bacon, fried crisp and chopped fine (save the grease)
1 cup beef or chicken broth
1 cup hot tap water
1 tbsp lemon juice
Salt and pepper to taste

Trim the sprouts, removing yellow leaves and stems. Cut them in half if they are large. Pour the broth and the hot water into the cooker. Cover and cook undisturbed for 1 hour, or until the temperature reaches 170 degrees or higher. Add the sprouts and stir well. Be certain all are covered by the broth. Cover and cook for 1 hour more. Test a sprout with a knife – it should be "tender crisp." If the sprouts are still hard, cover and cook for ½ hour more. Pour the sprouts into a medium bowl, and toss with the chopped bacon, the bacon grease and the lemon juice. Add salt and pepper as necessary. Serve warm.

Serves two to four

BUTTERNUT SQUASH CASSEROLE

This may seem a but fussy to begin with but the results will be worth it. This is a wonderful dish for a cold winter night. Serve with crusty French bread and cold beer.

3 cups Butternut squash, peeled and cut into ½" pieces
1 lb Kielbasa, or other fully cooked sausage, cut into ¼" slices
½ cup beef broth
1 Granny Smith apple, cored and diced, approx. ¾ cup
2 tbsp butter or oleo
1 tsp ground sage
1 tsp ground cloves

Prepare squash as noted above and in a medium bowl combine all the other ingredients. Mix well. Spray the cooker with cooking spray and add all the ingredients. Cover and cook undisturbed for 3 hours. Check to see if the squash is done by using a small knife or fork. The squash should be tender but not mushy. If the squash is still not cooked, cover and cook for ½ hour more.

Serves two four as a side dish

CORN PUDDING

This dish originated in Alsace-Lorraine and is still a favorite with Amish families in this country. You can add other ingredients, but I think the original is still the best.

3 large eggs
¼ cup all purpose flour
1 small onion, chopped fine, approx ½ cup
1 can (15.5 oz) creamed corn (do not drain)
1 can (15.5 oz) whole kernel corn, drained
1 tsp paprika
Salt and pepper to taste

In a large bowl, and using an electric mixer, mix the eggs, flour, onion and paprika until smooth. Add the creamed and kernel corn, and stir well. Spray the inside of the cooker with cooking spray. Add the corn mixture. Cover and cook undisturbed for 2 hours or until the pudding is "soft set." Cover and continue cooking if necessary. Serve directly from the slow cooker.

Serves two to four as a side dish

CREAMED ONIONS

The title is a misnomer, as the onions are cooked in the mushroom soup, but the taste is all there. Long a favorite at holiday gatherings, no one will know the difference unless you tell them. Using the frozen packaged onions eliminates the need for painstaking peeling.

1 pkg (16 oz) Frozen Small Onions (Birdseye are the best)
1 can (10.5 oz) condensed mushroom soup
½ cup water
Salt and pepper to taste

Let the onions defrost until they are at room temperature. Dilute the soup with the ½ cup water, and combine the soup and the onions. Add the salt and pepper, and mix well. Spray the slow cooker with cooking spray. Pour the onion mix into the cooker. Cover and cook undisturbed for 2 hours or until the onions pierce easily with a fork. Continue cooking if necessary.

Serves two to four as a side dish

CREAMED VEGETABLE MELANGE

With the marvels of frozen vegetables this dish can be served at any time of the year and it will still feel like spring. Serve with any main meat dish but roast lamb would be extraordinary.

1 bag (16oz) frozen mixed vegetables, thawed and drained
1 can (10.5 oz) condensed cream of mushroom soup
½ lb fresh sliced mushrooms, approx. ½ cup
½ cup water
Salt and pepper to taste
Chopped parsley for garnish

Dilute the soup with the water, and in a medium bowl combine all the ingredients. Spray the cooker liner with cooking spray and add all the ingredients. Cover and cook undisturbed for 3 hours. The vegetables should be "tender crisp." Do not over cook them, or they will get soft and mushy.

Serves two to four as a side dish

DIXIE CORN PUDDING

A favorite throughout the Southern States, this dish is easily made in the slow cooker. Serve it directly from the cooker with Virginia Country Ham and beaten biscuits. Iced tea is the perfect Southern beverage.

1 can (15.5oz) creamed corn
1 can (15.5oz) whole kernel corn
¼ cup pimento chopped fine
3 large eggs beaten well
Salt and pepper to taste

In a bowl combine the canned corn and pimento. Combine the beaten eggs with the corn mixture. Add salt and pepper to taste. Spray the cooker with cooking spray. Add the corn mixture. Cover and cook undisturbed for 2 hours. If the pudding has not set, cover and cook for 1 more hour. Spoon the pudding directly from the slow cooker.

Serves two to four as a side dish

EGGPLANT, TOMATO AND CHEESE STEW

This savory dish would be especially good served with lamb or any other of the more robust meat dishes in this cookbook. Be sure to get some of the mozzarella in each spoonful. Serve directly from the cooker, or put the stew in a low oven-proof dish and run it under the broiler with more mozzarella on top. Broil until the cheese melts and gets brown on top.

1 medium size eggplant, unpeeled and cut into ½" cubes - about 3 cups total
1 can (14 oz) crushed plum tomatoes in thick puree
¼ cup olive oil
3 tbsp garlic, minced fine
3 tbsp dried basil leaves
½ cup grated pr shaved mozzarella – more if you want
Salt and pepper to taste

Spray the cooker with cooking spray. Toss the eggplant cubes in the olive oil, along with the garlic and the dried basil. Start layering the eggplant into the cooker with some of the tomato sauce and the grated mozzarella on each layer. Cover and cook undisturbed for 2 hours. Check the eggplant – it should be done buy not mushy. Serve as directed above directly from the cooker.

Serves two to four as side dish

GERMAN POTATO SALAD

German Potato Salad is usually served warm or at room temperature but this is good cold also. Serve with a hearty German meat dish like Beef Sauerbraten. The slow cooker takes the pressure off your oven and stove.

4 cups red potatoes, washed but not peeled, cut into ½" dice
1 small onion diced, approx ½ cup
¼ cup water

For the dressing:
½ cup beef broth
½ cup white wine vinegar
4 slices bacon, fried crisp, and chopped roughly
1 tsp dry English mustard
1 dill pickle chopped fine (optional)

Prepare the potatoes and onion as directed. Spray the cooker liner with cooking spray and put the potatoes, onion and water in it. Cover and cook undisturbed for 2 hours. The potatoes should still be firm and not mushy. Prepare the dressing in a small non-reactive bowl and set aside. Empty the potatoes into a serving bowl and pour the dressing over and toss gently. Serve warm.

Serves two to four as a side dish

GREEN BEAN CASSEROLE

In the South green beans are called "snap beans." Whatever you call them this tasty all vegetable casserole will be a welcome addition to your recipe file. Serve as a side dish with simple poached chicken breasts and new red potatoes.

1 lb fresh slender green beans, ends trimmed and cut in half
1 small onion, diced, approx. ½ cup
2 cloves garlic, minced fine
3 Roma tomatoes, diced, approx. ¾ cup
1 can (8 oz) tomato sauce, or spaghetti sauce, your choice
Salt and pepper to taste

In a medium bowl mix all the ingredients and stir well. Spray the cooker with cooking spray and add all the ingredients. Cover and cook undisturbed for 2 hours. Check the beans for doneness. They should be tender crisp. If they are still too raw, cover and cook for ½ hour more.

Serves two to four as a side dish

Note: Southerners love these beans tossed in a little bacon grease.

HERBED NEW POTATOES

These little nuggets can be cooked whole and unpeeled, but I think it is better to halve or quarter them so more will fit into the cooker. They are wonderful served with any meat main dish. Don't be afraid of lots of herbs.

1 lb or more small red potatoes cut into quarters, about four cups
3 tbsp butter or oleo melted
2 tbsp dill weed
2 tbsp basil
Salt and pepper

In a medium bowl mix the potatoes with the melted butter and the herbs. Toss to see that all the potatoes are well coated. Spray the cooker with cooking spray. Pour the potatoes into the liner. Cover and cook undisturbed for 2 hours. Check for doneness with a fork. If the potatoes are still too raw recover and cook for another ½ hour or more. Be sure to pour the liquid on the bottom of the cooker over the potatoes when you serve them.

Serves two to four as a side dish

POTATO CHEESE CAKE

This makes a different and delicious accompaniment to any meat main dish. Cut the cake into wedges, it will be about 2" high x 5" in diameter. Use new waxy potatoes if you can find them. The added cheese and egg will help to keep the cake together.

3 cups potatoes shredded in a food processor or on a hand grater
I cup grated cheese – your choice
1 egg beaten
Salt and pepper (don't be afraid of lots of salt)
1 tsp ground nutmeg (optional)

Wring all the water possible out of the grated potatoes – use a hand towel if necessary. In a medium bowl beat the egg and add the potatoes. Mix well and add the grated cheese. Salt and pepper liberally. Spray the cooker with cooking spray and add the potato mixture. Cover and cook undisturbed for 2 hours. Check for doneness and cook for ½ hour or more if necessary. Release the potato cake by running a thin knife around the edge. Note: If you want to brown the cake put it in a skillet with butter and olive oil and brown on one or both sides.

Serves two to four as a side dishr

POTATOES SAVOYARD

This is just another name for scalloped potatoes, except you use beef or chicken stock instead of milk. I have used scalloped potatoes in many recipes in this book, but this is for the potatoes only. Be sure to spray the cooker with cooking spray, as the cheese will melt during the cooking and it will make a mess of the cooker liner. These potatoes are wonderful with hearty meat dishes like beef or lamb.

3 cups of potatoes (baking or Idaho work best), sliced thin
1 medium onion, sliced thin, approx. ½ cup
1 cup grated cheese (your favorite kind)
1 cup beef broth
3 cloves garlic chopped fine
Salt and pepper – plenty of it!

Spray the cooker with cooking spray. Start layering the potatoes, adding onion, garlic, salt and pepper and cheese as you go. The cooker should be about ¾ full. Pour the broth over the potatoes, and sprinkle with some cheese on top. Cover and let cook undisturbed for 3 hours. The potatoes should be firm but well done and not mushy. Spoon the potatoes directly from the cooker onto serving plates.

Serves two to four as a side dish

RATATOUILLE

This famous dish from Provence, "the vegetable garden" of France, is good either warm or cold. Don't be afraid of using plenty of garlic. Serve as a side dish or on top of lettuce for a refreshing salad course. Accompany it with good French bread and cold dry white wine or Sangria.

1 cup eggplant, unpeeled and cut into bite size pieces
1 cup zucchini, sliced thin or chopped into bite size pieces
1 cup Roma tomatoes, chopped rough
1 cup green bell pepper, chopped rough
½ cup pitted black Nicoise or Calamata olives, cut in half
½ cup onion, chopped
1 can (8oz) spicy tomato sauce or spaghetti sauce
4 tbsp garlic, chopped fine
Herbs de Provence or thyme and basil, about 2 tbsp total
Salt and freshly ground black pepper

Spray the cooker with cooking spray. Place the vegetables as above starting with the eggplant on the bottom, and working in layers, ending with the onion on top. The cooker will be full. Sprinkle the garlic and the herbs over each layer as you build. Add the tomato puree. Cover and let cook undisturbed for 2 hours. Check the vegetables for doneness. They should be tender crisp. Pour the vegetables into a bowl and mix well. Serve directly from the cooker, or let cool and serve as a salad course.

Serves two to four as a side dish, or cold as a salad course

RED CABBAGE WITH APPLES AND RAISINS

This wonderful side dish should be served with any hearty German style meat dish like sauerbraten or venison. Pack the cooker as full as you can at first, as the red cabbage will cook down. You should have about 4 cups of cabbage when it is cooked.

4 cups red cabbage, shredded (use a mandolin if you have one)
1 medium onion, sliced fine, approx. 1.2 cup
1 Granny Smith apple, cored and sliced fine, approx. ¾ cup
½ cup golden raisins
½ cup white wine vinegar
½ cup beef broth or water
2 tbsp caraway seeds (more if you want)
Salt and pepper to taste

Spray the cooker with cooking spray. Fill the cooker with the shredded cabbage packing it down as tight as you can. Pour in the vinegar and the broth or water. Cover and cook undisturbed for 2 hours. Add the onion, raisins, apple, and caraway seeds. Stir well. Cover and cook for 1 hour more. Taste for seasonings and add salt and pepper as necessary.

Serves two to four as a side dish

SAUERKRAUT WITH APPLES

This is a wonderful dish to serve with roast pork loin. New red potatoes and country pumpernickel bread make a fine meal.

1 bag (32 oz) sauerkraut from the deli case
1 Granny Smith apple, cored and sliced into thin batons
1 small onion, diced
2 tbsp caraway seeds (more if you want)
½ cup beef broth
1 tbsp red wine vinegar
½ cup dark seedless raisins (optional)

Wash the sauerkraut in a strainer and transfer to a medium bowl. Mix all the ingredients and stir well. Spray the cooker with cooking spray and add the mixture. Cover and cook undisturbed for 2 hours. Serve directly from the cooker.

Serves two to four as a main or side dish

SPICED GREEN BEANS

This recipe is best made if you have fresh green beans from your garden. However, frozen green beans will do just about as well.

1 pkg. (16 oz) frozen green beans, thawed (two cups total)
2 cups new red potatoes, cut into small dice (do not peel)
2 tsp butter or oleo
½ cup hot tap water
2 tbsp dry English mustard
2 tbsp garlic chopped
1 tsp ground tumeric
1 tbsp sesame oil
1 tsp red pepper flakes
Salt and pepper to taste

Spray the cooker with cooking spray. Add the green beans and the potato with the oleo or butter. Cover and cook undisturbed for 1 hour. Mix the spices with the hot tap water. Add to the cooker and stir into the beans and potatoes. Cover and cook for 1 to 2 hours more. Taste for doneness and adjust seasonings as necessary. The beans should be tender crisp and the potatoes should be firm but done.

Serves two to four as a side dishr

SPICED YAMS

Yams are generally served in this country with a sweet garnish such as brown sugar. In the Caribbean yams are served with all sorts of spices and are an every day staple. These delicious yams would be served with pork, ham or a spicy fish dish.

3 cups yams, peeled and cut into bite size pieces
1 can (10.5oz) chicken broth
½ tsp ground cumin
½ tsp ground cinnamon
½ tsp ground paprika
1 tsp chili powder
Salt to taste
Sour cream for garnish
Chopped cilantro for garnish

Spray the cooker with cooking spray. Add the yams, chicken broth, and all the spices. Stir well. Cover and cook undisturbed for 3 hours. Check to see if the yams are done. They should be firm but still easily pierced with a fork. If they are not finished, cover and cook for ½ hour more. Garnish with the chopped cilantro and serve with the sour cream on the side.

Serves two to four as a side dish

SPINACH CAKE

Don't let the name mislead you but this is an unusual way to serve one of the most maligned of all vegetables. Even Popeye would approve. This is a good green vegetable dish with just about any main meat course, especially lamb.

2 pkgs (10 oz each) frozen chopped spinach, defrosted
2 eggs, well beaten
1 tsp grated nutmeg
1 tsp garlic, chopped fine
½ cup feta cheese, crumbled
Salt and pepper to taste

In a colander or strainer drain the spinach as well as you can by pushing the water out with a spoon. In a small bowl combine the spinach with the beaten eggs, the feta cheese and the spices. Salt and pepper generously. Spray the cooker with cooking spray and add the spinach mixture. Cover and cook undisturbed for 3 hours or until the cake is set. Carefully run a thin knife around the outside of the cake to release it. Invert the liner over a serving dish and the cake should release. Cut into wedges and serve. You can also just spoon the spinach from the cooker – not as fancy a presentation but delicious nonetheless.

Serves two to four as a side dish

SUCCOTASH

This combination of corn and lima beans is one of the oldest dishes in America. Perfect as an accompaniment to broiled chicken or grilled steak, it is cold weather favorite. I've added a few new ingredients but the effect is the same as the old traditional.

1 can (15.5oz) whole kernel corn, drained
1 can (15.5oz) lima beans, drained
1 can (7.5 oz) creamed corn
¼ cup pimento, chopped
½ cup heavy cream or half and half (more if you want)
Salt and pepper to taste

Spray the cooker with cooking spray. Add all the ingredients, except the cream. Cover and cook for 2 hrs. Uncover and add the cream. Stir. Taste and add salt and pepper as necessary. Cover and cook for 1 hour more. Adjust the seasonings and spoon directly from the mini slow cooker.

Serves two to four or more as a side dish

SWEET POTATO CASSEROLE

A favorite at holiday time the sweet potato is the quintessential American vegetable. Used year long in the American South it is a staple there. Use the slow cooker to relieve pressure on your stove or oven – these can cook as long as you like and don't require any attention.

4 cups sweet potatoes, peeled and sliced into ¼" slices
2 tbsp butter or oleo
½ cup chopped walnuts
½ cup brown sugar
½ cup orange juice
Orange zest about 2 tbsp.
Salt and freshly ground black pepper to taste

Spray the cooker with cooking spray. Start layering the potatoes adding some walnuts, brown sugar and orange juice as you go along. Cover and let cook undisturbed for 3 hours. Sprinkle the orange zest on top of the potatoes. The potatoes should be firm, but done. Serve directly from the cooker.

Serves two to four as a side dish or vegetable accompaniment

SWEET POTATOES WITH APPLES AND RAISINS

Sweet potatoes, apples and raisins have a natural affinity. If you are in the middle of preparing your Holiday feast, this easy to prepare casserole leaves one of your burners free on the stove. Serve this with ham or a pork roast.

3 cups peeled sweet potatoes, cut into ½" dice
1 cup peeled Granny Smith apple, cut into small dice
2 tbsp cinnamon
½ cup dark seedless raisins
1 cup apple cider
½ cup dark brown sugar
½ cup chopped walnuts, for garnish
Salt and freshly ground black pepper to taste

Spray the cooker with cooking spray. Toss the apple slices with the brown sugar and cinnamon. Pour the sweet potatoes and apples into the cooker with the apple cider. Cover and cook undisturbed for 2 hour. Add the raisins and mix well. Cover and cook for 1 hour more. Check for doneness with a fork. The potatoes should be firm but not mushy. Spoon the sweet potatoes into a flat serving dish, and garnish with the chopped walnuts and pats of butter. Serve warm.

Serves two to four as a vegetable accompaniment

SWEET AND SOUR RED CABBAGE

This dish of German origin is wonderful served with pork. You will have to push the cabbage hard down into the cooker as it will shrink as it cooks. Do not be afraid if it appears to be too much at first.

1 small head of red cabbage shredded, about 5 cups pushed down
¼ cup red wine vinegar
2 tbsp caraway seeds (more if you want)
2 tbsp dark brown sugar
Pinch nutmeg
Salt and freshly ground black pepper to taste

In a medium bowl toss the cabbage with all the other ingredients making sure the cabbage is well coated with the vinegar and the brown sugar. Spray the cooker with cooking spray and add the cabbage. Push down hard to get it all in. Cover and cook undisturbed for 2 or more hours. The cabbage will have shrunk to about half of its uncooked state but there will still be enough for four good servings.

Serves two to four as a side dish or accompaniment

TRICOLOR VEGETABLE TIMBALE

The initial preparations for this spectacular vegetable dish may seem a little fussy but the results are worth it and no one will believe that you made it in the mini slow cooker. Serve the timbale with another French entree worthy of accompanying it. Garnish with homemade mayonnaise.

1 pkg (12oz) fresh or frozen carrots cut into 1" pieces, defrosted
1 pkg (12oz) frozen chopped spinach, defrosted
1 pkg (12oz) fresh or frozen cauliflower florets, defrosted
3 eggs, each beaten separately
Nutmeg
¼ tsp thyme
Salt and pepper

In a saucepan bring some water to a boil and cook the carrots for 8-10 minutes, or until they are tender. Drain well and set aside. In the same pan cook the cauliflower florets until tender, 10-12 minutes. Drain and set aside. In the same pan cook the frozen spinach for 5-8 minutes. Drain the spinach very well – use a towel to wring out the water if you have to. Set aside. Add each vegetable separately into the bowl of a food processor. Add an egg to each vegetable and process well. Add nutmeg to the spinach, thyme to the carrots, and salt and pepper to the cauliflower. Spray the cooker with cooking spray, and layer the processed vegetables starting at the bottom with the carrots, the cauliflower in the middle, and the spinach on top. Cover and cook undisturbed for 2 hours or more or until the vegetables are set. Run a thin knife around the edge of the timbale to release it. Invert the cooker over a serving plate and shake the timbale loose. Repair any leftover vegetable with a knife, and cut the timbale into wedges to serve it. The timbale will have three separate layers and will measure approximately 5" in diameter and will be about 3"-4" high.

Serves two to four as a side dish

VEGETABLE CHILI

Since there is no meat in this chili you can serve it to your vegetarian friends. Tex-Mex cornbread and a salad of lettuce and sliced avocado will make a fine meal.

1 can (7.5 oz) diced or stewed tomatoes in thick puree
1 can (14.5 0z) red kidney beans, drained
1 can (14.5 oz) black beans, drained
1 green bell pepper, diced, approx. ½ cup
1 medium onion, diced, approx. ½ cup
2 tbsp chili powder (or more, to your taste)
1 tsp Tabasco sauce
Salt and pepper to taste

Spray the cooker with cooking spray. In a medium bowl mix all the Ingredients. Pour the mix into the cooker. Cover and cook undisturbed for 2 hours. The vegetables will still be crunchy. Check the seasonings and add salt and pepper and more chili powder if desired. Continue cooking as desired. Serve directly from the cooker or pour into a serving bowl.

Note: You can use packaged chili mix if desired. Choose from mild, medium or hot! It's your choice.

Serves two to four as a main or side dish

VEGETABLE STEW

This easy to prepare stew is a meal in itself. Since all the ingredients are pre-cooked, all you are using the cooker for is to heat everything up and have the flavors meld together. Serve in bowls with warm biscuits and a green salad on the side.

1 can (10.5 oz) condensed cream of mushroom soup
½ cup water
1 can (15.5 oz) mixed vegetables, well drained (I use Veg-All)
1 can (7.5 oz) sliced potatoes, drained and roughly chopped
1 tbsp dry parsley flakes
1 tbsp chopped garlic
1 tsp dry basil leaves
Salt and pepper to taste

Spray the cooker with cooking spray. In a medium bowl dilute the soup with the water and stir well. Mix in all the other ingredients including the spices and pour the mix into the cooker. Cover and cook undisturbed for 2 hours or until the stew is hot enough to serve.

Serves two to four as a main or side dish

Note: If you prefer a tomato base for this stew, use one can (7.5oz) diced tomatoes, instead of the mushroom soup.

WINTER VEGETABLE STEW

In the old days you could have only made this winter stew with vegetables from the root cellar. Now we have fresh (or frozen) vegetables all year long. Serve this with a crusty country loaf with lots of butter.

1 can (7.5 oz) Great Northern beans, drained
1 can (7.5 oz) crushed tomatoes in thick puree
1 medium onion, diced, approx. ½ cup
1 pkg. (16 oz) frozen mixed vegetables, thawed*
1 can (7.5oz) potatoes, drained and chopped roughly
2 tbsp dried basil leaves
Salt and pepper to taste
Grated Parmesan cheese as garnish

Spray the cooker with cooking spray. Add all the ingredients and stir well. Cover and cook undisturbed for 3 hours. Check for doneness. The vegetables should be firm and not mushy. Serve in bowls with grated Parmesan cheese on top.

Serves two to four or more as a side or main dish

*Instead of the frozen mixed vegetables you can use one can (15.5oz) Veg-All mixed vegetables, well drained.

ZUCCHINI ESPAGNOL

This recipe was given to me by a friend who has lived in Spain and says he prepares zucchini this way when his garden is so full he is giving them away. I have sautéed zucchini in a similar fashion, but the slow cooker does a fine job too. There seems to be a lot of spices in this recipe, but the zucchini can take it. Do not overcook the zucchini – they should be "tender crisp" when served.

1½ lb approx. fresh zucchini (approx. 3 cups) cut into ½" slices
1 medium onion, diced, approx. ½ cup
4 slices bacon, fried crisp and chopped
1 can (7.5 oz) crushed plum tomatoes in t hick puree
1 tbsp minced garlic (more if you want)
1 tbsp dried thyme
1 tsp oregano
1 tsp dried basil
Salt and pepper to taste

Wash the zucchini and cut it into slices as directed. Spray the cooker with cooking spray. Add all the ingredients to the cooker, and stir well. Cover and cook undisturbed for 2 hours. Check the zucchini for doneness – if they are still too hard, cover and cook for an additional ½ hour. Do not overcook or the zucchini will get mushy. Adjust the seasonings to your taste.

Serves two to four as a side dish

ZUCCHINI IN THE STYLE OF PROVENCE

In Provence where the sun is hot and the vegetables grow like weeds there is an abundance of fresh vegetables and tomatoes. This wonderful vegetarian dish makes that part of France real in our minds. Serve with slices of a real French Baguette and a fresh salad of tomatoes and red onion with a Balsamic dressing.

3 cups fresh zucchini, sliced thin
1 can (7.5 oz) crushed tomatoes
1 medium red onion, thinly sliced, approx ¾ cup
2 tbsp garlic, chopped fine
½ cup pitted Calamata olives, halved
2 tbsp capers, drained
2 tsp herbs de Provence
¼ cup freshly made bread crumbs (store bought if necessary)
Freshly grated Parmesan cheese
Salt and pepper to taste

Spray the cooker with cooking spray. Add all the ingredients and mix well. Cover and cook for 3 hours. The zucchini should be tender crisp. Pour the zucchini into an oval gratin dish. Sprinkle the bread crumbs and the grated Parmesan cheese on top. Put under the broiler until the cheese melts and the bread crumbs brown. Serve hot or cold.

Serves two to four as a side dish

ZUCCHINI AND TOMATO CASSEROLE

When your garden is full of zucchini and tomatoes then that is the time to make this tasty dish. It's good cold or hot and makes a tasty luncheon entrée with sliced cold meats or chicken.

2 cups of zucchini, cut into bite size pieces
2 cups tomatoes, cut into bite size pieces (with the juices etc.)
1 medium onion, sliced thin, approx. 1.2 cup
1 medium green bell pepper, diced, approx. ½ cup
2 tbsp garlic, chopped
1 tbsp dried basil leaves
Grated Parmesan cheese for garnish
Salt and pepper to taste

Pour all of the vegetables into the cooker. Stir well. Cover and cook undisturbed for 3 hours. Taste for seasonings and add salt and pepper as necessary. Transfer to an oval gratin dish. Add grated Parmesan cheese on top and put under a broiler until the cheese melts and browns.

Serves two to four as a side dish

GRAINS, PASTA, RICE AND BEANS

Beans Cowboy Style
Black Bean Stew
Brazilian Black Beans
Caribbean Rice and Beans
Chicken and Wild Rice Casserole
Confetti Rice
Couscous with Raisins and Red Peppers
Curried Rice
Dogs and Beans
Grits
Hamburger and Noodle Casserole
Hoppin' John
Linguini Puttanesca
Long Grain and Wild Rice
Macaroni and Beef Casserole
Macaroni and Chicken Bake
Manicotti with Puttanesca Sauce
Manicotti in Tomato Sauce
Noodle and Shrimp Casserole
Penne with Mushrooms and Sausage
Penne in Spicy Tomato Sauce
Penne with Tomato and Shrimp
Persian Rice
Red Beans with Virginia Ham
Red Kidney Beans with Bacon
Red Kidney Beans Dominican Style
Rice with Tomatoes and Black Olives
Risi e Bisi
Tabbouleh
Three Bean Stew
Tortellini with Bacon and Peas
White Beans Tuscan Style

GRAINS, PASTA, RICE AND BEANS

Pasta, rice and beans cook surprisingly well in the mini slow cooker. I would not advise adding a bunch of spaghetti into cold water in the cooker – you will probably end up with a pasta cake!

However, using pasta cooked al dente on the stove will yield good results. Putting pasta into a sauce which is hot in the cooker will also be alright. I have cooked Manicotti many times in hot tomato sauce or even broth and they cook fine in about an hour.

The shape and size of the mini slow cooker also determine what types of pasta are suitable. Long strands of spaghetti would have to be cut into lengths which will fit into the cooker. Better to use elbow macaroni or other small shaped pastas which require no other preparation. Small Penne, Bow Ties and Radiatore are also good shapes.

Beans are also good in the mini slow cooker. They can be combined with so many other ingredients to yield an endless array of nutritious dishes. Beans combined with rice, and pre-cooked sausages will yield many full-flavored dishes – use your imagination.

The rice brands I have recommended will give you good results. If you want to try others follow the same general directions. You will find white rice is more glutinous (like Chinese rice) when cooked in the slow cooker. I think you will like it better than the usual method of putting it into boiling water and covering the pot for five minutes. You can cook other things along with the rice and then add other ingredients (like shrimp) at the half cooked stage.

BEANS COWBOY STYLE

There are so many variations of this style of recipe that it is difficult to know where to start. Known in Mexico as Frijoles Rancheros it is a staple of that country. For what it's worth I offer this version. You won't be disappointed. Serve with chunks of sausage or even a well grilled steak!

1 can (7.5oz) black beans (do not drain)
1 can (7.5oz) pinto beans or red beans (drained)
1 can (8 oz) tomato sauce, or spaghetti sauce
1 medium onion, diced fine, approx. ½ cup
1 small green bell pepper, diced, approx. ½ cup
2 tbsp chopped garlic
½ cup salsa (medium or hot - your choice)
Salt and freshly ground black pepper to taste

In a medium bowl combine all the ingredients. Mix well and add to the cooker. Cover and cook undisturbed for 3 hours or until the flavors meld and the beans are at serving temperature.

Serves two to four as a side dish or accompaniment

BLACK BEAN STEW

This is a hearty dish and a perfect way to use some left over ham. Serve it with rice and country bread. Start with a fresh green salad with sliced red onion and sliced Roma tomatoes.

1 can (15.5oz) black beans (or kidney beans if you prefer)
2 cups cooked ham, cut into bite size pieces (more if you want)
1 medium onion, diced, approx. ½ cup
2 Roma tomatoes, diced, approx. ½ cup
1 tsp basil
Sour cream for garish
Salt and pepper to taste

In a medium bowl combine all the ingredients and stir well. Spray the cooker with cooking spray. Add the mixture to the cooker. Cover and cook undisturbed for 3 hours. Adjust the seasonings and serve directly from the cooker. Add a dollop of sour cram on each serving.

Note: Instead of ham you can use any fully cooked sausage of your choice including Polish Kielbasa (or similar) cut into ½" slices.

Serves two to four as a main or side dish

BRAZILIAN BLACK BEANS

This recipe shows what can be done with simple ingredients. Black beans, the staple of Brazilian cooking takes the spotlight. The addition of the sausage makes this a one-dish meal.

1 can (15.5oz) black beans
1 lb pre-cooked sausage of your choice, cut into ½" slices
1 medium onion, diced, approx. ½ cup
1 medium green bell pepper, diced, approx. ½ cup
2 tbsp garlic, chopped
1 tsp ground cumin
1 tsp red pepper flakes
1 tsp Tabasco sauce
Sour cream for garnish
Salt and pepper to taste
Chopped cilantro or parsley for garnish

Spray the cooker with cooking spray. Combine the beans with the sausage, onion, green pepper, garlic and spices. Cover and cook undisturbed for 2 hours. Stir and test for seasonings. Add salt and pepper as necessary. Cover and cook as long as you want or until ready to serve. Put a dollop of sour cream on top of each serving. Sprinkle with chopped cilantro or parsley.

Serves two to four as a main or side dish, with accompaniments

CARIBBEAN RICE AND BEANS

Rice and beans are a staple of Caribbean cooking. Prepared in many ways this is just but one variation. Serve with an avocado and mango salad, and a rustic country bread.

1 can (7.5 oz) red kidney beans, drained
1 can (7.5oz) black beans, drained
3 slices bacon, fried crisp and chopped into pieces
1 can (7.5 oz) crushed tomatoes
1 small onion, diced, approx. ½ cup
1 green bell pepper, diced, approx. ½ cup
1 cup instant enriched long grain premium rice
1 cup hot tap water
2 tbsp garlic chopped
½ tsp ground cumin
½ tsp thyme
1 bay leaf
1 lime, cut into wedges for garnish
Salt and freshly ground black pepper to taste

Spray the cooker with cooking spray. Add the rice and the hot tap water. Cover and cook undisturbed for 2 hours. Fluff the rice, and stir in all the other ingredients. Cover and cook undisturbed for 1 hour more. The vegetables will still be crunchy. Cover and cook for 1 hour more if they are not done to your taste. Serve with lime wedges.

Serves two to four as a main or side dish

CHICKEN AND WILD RICE CASSEROLE

This is a satisfying dish with the nutty flavor of the wild rice. Use the brand I have specified and you will get good results. Although chicken has been indicated here, left over turkey will work just as well. Serve with a fresh green salad and good country bread.

1 pkg (6 oz) "Uncle Bens" long grain and wild rice (any flavor)
2 cups hot tap water
2 cups cooked chicken or turkey, cut into bite size pieces
1 small onion, diced, approx. ½ cup
1 stalk celery, diced, approx ¼ cup
1 can (10.5 oz) condensed cream of chicken soup
½ cup water
1 tsp dry sweet basil
Salt and pepper to taste

Spray the cooker with cooking spray. Pour the rice into the cooker with the hot tap water. Add the diced onion and celery. Cover and cook undisturbed for 2 hours. Fluff the rice and add the diluted soup and the chicken or turkey with the seasonings. Stir to mix well. Cover and cook for 1 hour more. Check for seasonings and adjust as necessary.

Serves two to four as a main or side dish

CONFETTI RICE

This is a colorful dish and one that can be served with just about any main course meat dish.

1 cup instant enriched long grain rice
1 cup hot tap water
1 can (10.5 oz.) whole kernel corn, drained
1 can (10.5 oz) small peas, drained
2 Roma tomatoes, diced (with their juice, approx. ½ cup
3 tbsp pimiento, diced
1 cup chicken broth
2 tbsp garlic, chopped
Salt and pepper to taste
Chopped parsley for garnish

Spray the cooker with cooking spray. Add the rice and the hot tap water and stir well. Cover and cook undisturbed for 2 hours. Add all the other ingredients. Stir well. Cover and cook for 1 more hour.

Serves two to four as a side dish or accompaniment

COUSCOUS WITH RAISINS AND RED PEPPERS

This is a delicious accompaniment to roast lamb and eggplant. Serve with a Middle Eastern style salad of sliced tomatoes, cucumber and red onion with a yogurt dressing. Pita bread makes a wonderful dipping method.

1 pkg. (5.7 oz) "Near East" couscous (any flavor you want)
1 cup hot chicken stock
1 tsp butter or oleo
1 medium red bell pepper, cut into small dice, approx. ½ cup
1 medium onion, cut into small dice, approx. ½ cup
½ cup dark seedless raisins (more if you want)
Salt and freshly ground black pepper to taste

Spray the cooker with cooking spray. Start the cooker and melt the butter. Pour in the couscous and stir well to coat. Pour in the hot chicken stock and stir. Cover and let cook undisturbed for 1 hour. Add the raisins, onion and red pepper to the couscous and stir well. Cover and cook undisturbed for 1 hour more.

Serves two to four as an accompaniment to a meat main dish

Note: If you want this to remain a vegetarian dish, use vegetable stock instead of the chicken stock.

CURRIED RICE

There are many rice products on the market with curry as a prominent flavor, but sometimes you just want to control the flavor yourself. You can add other ingredients to this recipe also. This rice is wonderful served with roast lamb.

2 cups instant enriched long grain premium rice
1 can (10.5 oz) chicken broth
1 medium apple, cored and peeled and diced fine, approx. ½ cup
½ cup golden seedless raisins (more if you want)
1 tbsp garlic, diced fine
2 tbsp curry powder (or more if you prefer)
Salt and freshly ground black pepper to taste
Garnish with sliced almonds

Spray the cooker with cooking spray. Pour the rice, chopped apple, raisins and garlic into the cooker and mix well. Heat the broth on the stove until it is just about to boil. Pour into the cooker and add the curry powder. Stir well. Cover and cook undisturbed for 2 hours. Fluff the rice with a fork before serving.

Serves two to four as a side dish

DOGS AND BEANS

Having a group of kids over for lunch – then they will love this easy to do recipe for hot dogs and beans. A never fail favorite, serve the dogs and beans open faced on the rolls with fresh coleslaw as a side dish.

1 can (7.5oz) baked beans (any brand you like)
1 can (7.5 oz) chili beans
1 lb hot dogs cut into ½" slices (more if you want)
1 tbsp dry English mustard
1 tbsp Worcestershire sauce
Hamburger rolls, toasted, as many as you will need
2 tbsp brown sugar
Salt and pepper to taste

Pour all of the ingredients into the cooker and mix well. Cover and cook undisturbed (you don't have to worry about anything) for 2 hours or more or until the beans come up to serving temperature. You can leave them in the cooker as long as you want.

Serves two to four or more as a party dish

GRITS

Yes, I know what you're thinking. The very name sets Northerners teeth on edge. But grits are a staple in the South and are served for breakfast, for lunch and at dinner. They even become dessert when sugar, fruit and other sweeteners are added. In reality they are finely ground corn, commonly called Hominy. As an accompaniment to many Southern style dishes, they cannot be beat. Made in the slow cooker they are delicious and you can add any number of items to make them your own.

1 pkg. (24 oz) Quaker Old Fashioned Grits (do not use instant)
3 cups hot tap water

Spray the cooker with cooking spray. Add 1 cup of the grits. Pour in the hot tap water and stir well. Cover and cook undisturbed for 1 hour. Stir well. Cover and cook undisturbed for an additional 1 hour. Test the grits, and if you want them finer in texture cover the grits and cook for ½ hour more. The grits will be like a thick porridge. Serve as an accompaniment to ham, yams, collard greens, spiced apples or other Southern specialties. Add butter, honey, raisins, or whatever suits you.

Serves two to four or more as an accompaniment

HAMBURGER AND NOODLE CASSEROLE

Sort of like "Hamburger Helper" but a cut above. You can partially cook the hamburger on the stove just to get the red out! Serve with a green salad and crusty bread or rolls. Kids will love it!

1 lb quality hamburger (10% fat)
1 can (10.5 oz) cheese soup
¼ cup water
2 cups elbow macaroni (dry measure), cooked al dente
1 medium green bell pepper, chopped fine, approx. ½ cup
1 medium onion, chopped fine, approx ½ cup
1 tbsp garlic, chopped fine
1 tbsp Italian seasoning
Grated cheese as a garnish
Salt and pepper to taste

Spray the cooker with cooking spray. Add the cheese soup and dilute with the water. Stir, and add the onion, pepper, garlic and seasonings. Add the partially cooked hamburger. Cover and cook undisturbed for 2 hours. Add the partially cooked macaroni and stir well. Cover and cook undisturbed for 1 more hour. Taste for seasoning and add salt and pepper as necessary. You can put this casserole in a low oven proof serving dish, sprinkle with the grated cheese, and put it under the broiler until the cheese melts.

Serves two to four as main course one dish meal.

HOPPIN' JOHN

There are so many stories surrounding this famous dish in the low country of South Carolina that it is impossible to separate fact from fiction. It is traditionally made for New Years Day Dinner and is supposed to bring good luck in the New Year. Go figure!

2 cups Instant Long Grain Premium rice
2 cups hot tap water
1 can (15.5oz) black beans, drained
½ cup celery, diced
½ cup onion, diced
1 cup smoked, or country ham, cut into bite size pieces
Salt and pepper to taste

Spray the cooker with cooking spray. Pour the rice into the cooker and add the hot tap water. Cover and cook undisturbed for 2 hours. Uncover and fluff the rice with a fork. Add the drained beans, diced onion and the ham. Mix well. Cover and cook for 2 hours more. Serve directly from the cooker or place on a serving plate surrounded with candied yams and slices of smoked ham. (Just like they did at Tara!)

Serves two to four (or more) as a main dish

LINGUINI PUTTANESCA

No need to go into the origins or name of this lusty dish. You will need to make the pasta in a separate pan on the stove and then toss it with the sauce you have made in the cooker. Serve this tasty pasta with a fresh green salad and good Italian bread.

1 lb pasta (I prefer linguini but you can use your favorite)
1 can (14.5 oz) tomato puree, or diced tomatoes in heavy syrup
5 slices bacon, cooked crisp and diced
½ cup pitted Calamata olives, cut in half (more if you want)
6 canned flat anchovies, diced (more if you like anchovies)
2 tbsp capers, drained (more if you like capers)
Grated Parmesan or Romano cheese for garnish
Salt and freshly ground black pepper to taste

Add all the ingredients to the cooker except the pasta. Cover and cook undisturbed for 2 hours. In the meantime prepare the pasta according to the package directions. Pour the sauce from the cooker into a large bowl and toss the pasta with the sauce. Serve in warm bowls and top with the grated cheese.

Serves two to four (or more) as a main dish

LONG GRAIN AND WILD RICE

I have included this recipe only to prove that cooking any rice in the slow cooker will give you superlative results. I have used "Uncle Bens Long Grain and Wild Rice" as a case in point. I have used this product in other recipes as a cooking medium. However, you will find the rice is puffier, more glutinous and more flavorful when cooked in the slow cooker. Use it as a side dish or as an accompaniment for many dishes or main courses.

1 pkg (6 oz) "Uncle Bens Long Grain and Wild Rice" (original flavor)
2 cups water
Butter or oleo (optional)
Salt and pepper to taste

Spray the cooker with cooking spray. Add the water and the rice and stir well. Cover and cook undisturbed for 1 hour. Add the flavor pack and stir well. Cover and cook for 1 hour more. Fluff with a fork and serve with any main course.

Note: Instead of water, use chicken or vegetables stock for additional flavor. You may add other ingredients to the rice including raisins, nuts, chopped fruit or whatever suits the main dish you are serving.

Serves two to four or more as an accompaniment

MACARONI AND BEEF CASSEROLE

This is a very tasty dish and a good way to use up some left over beef. Serve with a fresh green salad and thick slices of crusty bread.

2 cups elbow macaroni cooked "al dente" and well drained
1 can (7.5oz) tomatoes in thick puree
1½ cups cooked beef cut into bite size pieces
1 medium green bell pepper, chopped fine, approx. ½ cup
2 tbsp cornstarch
2 tbsp water
1 tsp oregano
2 bay leaves
Salt and pepper to taste

In a medium bowl combine the tomatoes with the cooked beef, spices and pepper. Spray the cooker with cooking spray. Add the mixed ingredients and stir well. Cover and cook undisturbed for 2 hours. Add the cooked macaroni and stir well into the mixture. Combine the cornstarch with the water to make a slurry. Add it to the casserole and stir well. Cover and cook for 1 hour more. Taste for seasonings and adjust as necessary. Serve directly from the cooker onto warm plates.

Serves two to four as a main dish

MACARONI AND CHICKEN BAKE

This one pot dish is the perfect way to use up leftover chicken. Serve it with a fresh tossed salad and crusty French bread.

2 cups elbow macaroni (dry measure) cooked "al dente"
1½ cups cooked chicken, cut into bite size pieces
1 can (10.5 oz) condensed cream of chicken soup
½ cup water
1 can (8 oz) mushrooms stems and pieces, drained
2 tbsp pimiento, chopped
1 small can (8oz) baby peas, drained
1 tsp thyme
Salt and pepper to taste

In a large sauce pan cook the macaroni in water until it is "al dente." Drain well. Spray the cooker with cooking spray. Dilute the soup with the water. Add the soup, and all the other ingredients (except the macaroni) to the cooker. Mix well. Cover and cook undisturbed for 2 hours. Add the cooked macaroni, and stir well. Cover and cook for 1 hour more. Taste for seasonings and adjust as necessary.

Serves two to four as a main dish

MANICOTTI WITH PUTTANESCA SAUCE

This is a robust dish best served with hearty Italian bread and a green salad on the side. Buy the mini size manicotti – they cook faster and they look like more on the plate! Serve with lots of freshly grated Parmesan cheese.

1 can (15.5oz) whole or diced tomatoes in thick puree
2 cups frozen mini manicotti, thawed, or about 32 pieces
2 tbsp garlic, chopped
1 tsp red pepper flakes
6 anchovy fillets, drained and cut into small dice
5 slices bacon, cooked crisp and chopped fine
½ cup pitted Calamata olives, cut in half
2 tbsp capers, drained (or more if you like)
2 tbsp dried basil leaves
Salt and pepper to taste
Grated Parmesan cheese for garnish

Pour the tomato sauce into the cooker and break up the tomatoes with a wooden spoon. Add all the other ingredients except the manicotti. Cover and cook undisturbed for 2 hours. Add the manicotti and cook for 1 more hour. Test for doneness and seasonings. Add salt and pepper as necessary. Serve with the grated Parmesan on top.

Serves two to four as a side or main dish

MANICOTTI IN TOMATO SAUCE

Cooking pasta in the mini slow cooker can be a challenge especially because of its shape. However, manicotti can be done as well as elbow macaroni and other small pasta shapes. This recipe uses prepared manicotti and the results are delicious. Serve with a tossed green salad and plenty of freshly grated Parmesan cheese.

1 can (15.5oz) Hunt's "no sugar added" spaghetti sauce
I pkg (13 oz) Celentano round cheese Manicotti (or equal)
1 can (7 oz) sliced mushrooms, drained
1 tsp dry basil leaves
Fresh grated Parmesan cheese for garnish
Salt and freshly ground black pepper to taste

Pour the tomato sauce into the cooker. Cover and cook undisturbed for 1 hour. In the meantime defrost the manicotti. Add the mushrooms and the basil and stir the sauce well. Add the manicotti and be sure they are all well covered by the sauce. Cover and cook for an additional 1 hour. The manicotti will have puffed and are done. Taste to see that they are no longer gluey or pasty tasting. Cover and cook for ½ hour more if necessary.

Note: The tomato sauce after one hour registered 160 degrees in the middle and 170 degrees at the edge of the cooker. Be sure to stir the sauce to even out the heat. You may use stuffed Ravioli instead of Manicotti in this recipe.

Serves two to four as a side or main dish

NOODLE AND SHRIMP CASSEROLE

Just when you thought there could never be another "noodle" casserole this one comes along. Easy to prepare and delicious in a simple way this makes a satisfying meal. Serve with a tossed green salad and crusty bread.

1 lb. fresh shrimp, shelled and deveined
1 (8 oz) pkg noodles, cooked al dente
1 can (10.5 oz) condensed mushroom soup
½ cup water
1 small onion, chopped fine, approx ½ cup
¼ cup pimiento, chopped fine
1 small green bell pepper, diced, approx. ½ cup
¼ cup pitted black olives, cut in half
Salt and pepper to taste

Cook the noodles to package directions. Drain well. Dilute the soup with the water and combine with the onion, pimiento, pepper and olives. Mix well. Spray the cooker with cooking spray. Add the mixture. Cover and cook undisturbed for 2 hours. Add the shrimp and cooked noodles and cook for 1 hour more. Check the seasonings and add salt and pepper as necessary.

Serves two to four as a main luncheon dish

PENNE WITH MUSHROOMS AND SAUSAGE

This is an easy to prepare dish with robust flavor. Serve it with a fresh green salad and good Italian bread.

1½ cups penne (dry weight)
1 lb pkg. Kielbasa, or other pre-cooked sausage of your choice
1 pkg (8\oz) fresh mushrooms, sliced, approx ½ cup
1 can (15.5oz) spaghetti sauce, or tomato sauce of your choice
1 tbsp garlic, chopped
Italian seasoning of your choice, as needed
Fresh grated Parmesan cheese
Salt and freshly ground black pepper to taste

In a large saucepan cook the penne until "al dente." Slice the sausage into ¼" slices. Spray the cooker with cooking spray. Add the tomato sauce, sausage, garlic and sliced mushrooms. Check for seasonings. Stir well. Cover and cook undisturbed for 2 hours. Add the penne and stir well. Cover and cook for 1 hour more. Serve directly from the cooker into bowls or platters, and garnish generously with the Parmesan cheese.

Serves two to four as a main dish

PENNE IN SPICY TOMATO SAUCE

This dish is not for the faint of heart. Add as much red pepper as you want. It is best to cook the penne according to package directions on the stove. Cook it "al dente" as it will cook again in the tomato sauce. You can add meatballs or your favorite sausage on the side for a full meal. Other than that, a green salad and tasty bread will suffice.

1 can (15.5oz) plum tomatoes in heavy puree
2 cups penne (cooked measure)
2 tbsp garlic, chopped
1 tsp basil leaves
1 tsp oregano
2 tsp red pepper flakes (or more if you like it hot)
1 tsp Tabasco sauce (or more if you like the heat)
Salt and pepper to taste
Grated Parmesan for garnish

Add the tomatoes and all the spices to the cooker. Break up the tomatoes with a wooden spoon, but leave them "chunky." Cover and cook undisturbed for 1 hour. Add the penne and stir well. Cover and cook for 1 more hour. Taste for seasonings and adjust accordingly.

Serves two to four as a main or pasta dish

PENNE WITH TOMATOES AND SHRIMP

With the addition of shrimp this light penne and tomato dish becomes a one-dish meal. You can cook the penne ahead of time until it is just al dente. The shrimp will cook easily in the time allotted in the sauce.

1 can (15.5oz) tomatoes in heavy puree
¾ lb. fresh shrimp, peeled and deveined
2 cups penne, cooked measure, al dente
2 tbsp garlic, chopped
1 tbsp dried basil leaves
1 tsp dried rosemary
Chopped parsley for garnish
Freshly grated Parmesan cheese for garnish
Salt and pepper to taste

Pour the tomatoes into the cooker and break them up with a wooden spoon. Add the spices and stir. Cover and cook for 1 hour. Add the penne and shrimp. Stir well. Cover and cook for 1 more hour. Test for seasonings and adjust as necessary.

Serves two to four as a main or pasta dish

PERSIAN RICE

This is a simple dish to be served with any skewered meats or chicken. Be sure to soak the raisins in water for an hour or two so they plump up. Buy shelled pistachios to save time and effort.

1 pkg. (5 oz) "Mahatma" saffron yellow long grain rice
2 tsp oleo
1 cup hot tap water
1 small onion, diced, approx. ½ cup
½ cup raisins, soaked until plump
½ cup pistachios, shelled and chopped coarsely
½ tsp ground cloves
½ tsp ground cinnamon
½ tsp ground cumin
Chopped parsley or cilantro, for garnish
Salt and freshly ground black pepper to taste

Spray the cooker with cooking spray. Add the saffron rice and the hot tap water. Add the oleo to melt. Mix in the diced onion. Cover and cook undisturbed for 1 hour. Fluff the rice with a fork and stir in the remaining ingredients. Cover and cook for 1 hour more.

Note: You may use chicken or vegetable broth instead of the water for additional flavor.

Serves two to four as an accompaniment

RED BEANS WITH VIRGINIA HAM

This hearty dish would be served throughout the South on Sunday after church. You can add whatever else you wish to this dish as every Southern cook has her (or his) own version. Collards with bacon would be the usual accompaniment. You may opt for a less caloric (and fattening) side dish. Corn bread is still acceptable!

1 can (15.5 oz) red kidney beans, (do not drain)
1 lb slice country or Virginia ham, cut into ½" pieces
1 can (7.5 oz) diced tomatoes in thick puree
1 medium onion, diced fine, approx ½ cup
1 green bell pepper, diced fine, approx. ½ cup
1 celery stalk, diced fine. Approx. ¼ cup
1 tbsp garlic, minced
1 bay leaf
1 tsp dried basil leaves
Pinch of allspice
1 tsp Tabasco sauce
Chopped parsley for garnish
Salt and freshly ground black pepper to taste

Pour all the ingredients into the cooker and mix well. Cover and cook undisturbed for 3 hours or until the dish is hot enough to serve. The vegetables will still be tender-crisp. You can continue to cook this dish for about as long as you want.

Serves two to four as a main course

RED KIDNEY BEANS WITH BACON

This is a good side dish served with any lusty main course such as roast lamb. Fry the bacon until it is very crisp and add the fat to the beans before serving. Not good for the waistline, but good for the taste!

1 can (15.5 oz) red kidney beans (do not drain)
5 slices good bacon, fried crisp and chopped roughly
1 medium onion, diced, approx. ½ cup
2 tbsp garlic, chopped fine
1 tsp thyme
1 bay leaf
Salt and pepper to taste
Minced parsley for garnish

Pour the beans into the cooker with the onion, garlic and the spices. Cover and cook undisturbed for 1 hour. Add the bacon and stir well. Cover and cook for 1 more hour. Add the bacon fat, stir and adjust the seasonings as necessary.

Serves two to four as a side dish

RED KIDNEY BEANS DOMINICAN STYLE

No Dominican cook worth her salt would use canned kidney beans but since we are trying to save time and effort we are using them here. Serve this dish with roast pork and rice.

2 cans (14.5 oz each) red kidney beans, (do not drain)
4 strips of bacon, cooked and diced (more if you want)
1 medium onion, diced, approx, ½ cup
1 green bell pepper, diced, approx. ½ cup
1 tbsp garlic, chopped fine
2 Roma tomatoes, roughly chopped
1 tsp oregano
½ cup hot salsa
1 tsp red pepper flakes
Salt and pepper to taste

Spray the cooker liner with cooking spray. Add the beans and the remainder of the ingredients and mix well. Cover and cook undisturbed for 2 hours. The vegetables will still be tender-crisp, but you can continue to cook this dish for as long as you want. The flavors will only intensify and meld together. Taste for seasonings and add salt and pepper if necessary.

Serves four to six as a side dish

RICE WITH TOMATOES AND BLACK OLIVES

This is a good side dish when you want something a little more assertive in flavor than just plain rice. Serve this with just about any Mediterranean inspired dish.

2 cups instant long grain premium rice, (uncooked measure)
2 cups hot tap water
1 medium onion, diced fine, approx. ½ cup
4 Roma tomatoes, chopped coarsely, approx. ¾ cup
½ cup pitted Calamata olives, cut in half
1 tbsp dried basil leaves
Salt and pepper to taste

Spray the cooker with cooking spray. Add the rice and the hot water. Cover and cook undisturbed for 1 hour. Flake the rice with a fork and add the onion, tomatoes and olives. Cover and cook for 1 hour more, or until the dish is hot enough to serve.

Serves two to four or more as a side dish

RISI E BISI

This is the famous dish of "rice and peas" which is said to have originated in Venice. No tomatoes this time. Just water or stock and the peas!

2 cups instant enriched long grain premium rice
2 cups hot tap water, or chicken stock
1 small onion, diced fine, approx. ½ cup
1 pkg (10 oz) frozen tiny peas, thawed *
½ cup thinly sliced prosciutto, diced into small pieces
Salt and pepper as needed
Chopped parsley for garnish
Grated Parmesan cheese for garnish

Spray the cooker with cooking spray. Add the rice and the hot tap water or stock, along with the diced onion. Stir well. Cover and cook undisturbed for 1 hour. Fluff the rice with a fork and add the prosciutto and the peas. Cover and cook for 1 hour more. Serve garnished with the chopped parsley and the grated Parmesan cheese.

Serves two to four as a side dish or accompaniment

*You can use 1 small can (8oz) peas instead of the frozen. Add them ½ hour before the recipe is finished cooking.

TABBOULEH

This is a wonderful Middle Eastern dish – just plain as is, or with the addition of meat it becomes something more substantial. There are many variations of this dish – some made with bulgar wheat and some made with rice. I have used a rice and wild rice combination as the basis. You can serve it hot, but traditionally it is served at room temperature, with pita breads to sop up the juices,

1 pkg. (6.6 oz) "Uncle Bens" Long Grain and Wild Rice
2 cups hot tap water
3 ripe plum (Roma) tomatoes, diced, approx. ¾ cup
1 small cucumber, peeled and diced, approx ½ cup
Juice of 1 lemon, approx ¼ cup
¼ cup olive oil
Salt and freshly ground pepper to taste

Spray the cooker with cooking spray. Add the rice and the hot tap water. Cover and cook undisturbed for 1 hour. Stir the rice, and cover and cook for 1 hour more. The rice will be fluffy and done. Turn off the cooker, and let the rice come to room temperature, with the cover off. Remove the rice to a medium size bowl, and add the tomatoes, cucumber olive oil and the lemon juice. Toss well to coat the rice. Serve as suggested above.

Serves two to four as a side dish or accompaniment to meat

Note: If you want to add some meat to this dish use "Tyson's" pre-cooked sliced steak, cut into bite size pieces.

THREE BEAN STEW

Here is a lusty vegetarian stew which, with a side salad, will make a whole meal. Serve with hearty Italian bread.

1 can (7.5oz) black beans, drained
1 can (7.5oz) red kidney beans, drained
1 can (7.5oz) garbanzo beans, drained
1 can (7.5oz) diced tomatoes in thick puree
2 tbsp garlic, chopped
Chopped parsley for garnish
Salt and freshly ground black pepper to taste

Pour all of the ingredients into the cooker and mix well. Cover and cook undisturbed for 2 hours or longer if you want. Pour into a serving bowl and garnish with the chopped parsley.

Note: If you want to add meat to this dish, just select 1 lb. of your favorite pre-cooked sausage, cut it into bite size pieces and add it to the beans as they cook.

Serves two to four as a side or main dish

TORTELLINI WITH BACON AND PEAS

Tortellini are frequently served in a cream sauce. However it is best to use a tomato based sauce in the mini slow cooker. The addition of bacon and peas brings a new dimension to the dish.

2 cups frozen tortellini, defrosted, approx. 16-24 pieces
4 slices bacon, fried crisp and broken into small pieces
1 can (15.5oz) whole tomatoes in thick puree
1 small can (8oz) small peas, drained
Grated Parmesan cheese for garnish
Salt and freshly ground black pepper to taste

Spray the cooker with cooking spray. Add the tomatoes and with a wooden spoon break them up as best you can. Add the bacon. Cover and cook undisturbed for 1 hour. Add the tortellini and stir well. Cover and cook for 1 hour more. Add the peas and cook for ¼ hour to heat through.

Serves two to four as a main course, with accompaniments

WHITE BEANS TUSCAN STYLE

This is one of the basic dishes served throughout the hilly Tuscan part of Italy where beans are served at practically every meal. The addition of the sausage makes this a one-dish meal. Serve with a lettuce, tomato and red onion salad with good olive oil. Don't forget that good Italian bread!

1 can (15.5oz) white northern or cannelini beans
1 lb pre-cooked Kielbasa, or Italian sausage of your choice
2 tbsp garlic, chopped
1 tsp dried basil leaves
1 tsp dried oregano
Freshly grated Parmesan cheese for garnish
Salt and freshly ground black pepper to taste

Cut the sausage into ½" pieces. Pour all the ingredients into the cooker and mix well. Cover and cook undisturbed for 2 hours or until the dish is hot enough to serve. Serve in bowls with the grated Parmesan cheese on top.

Serves two to four as a main dish

DESSERTS

Apple Brown Betty
Apple and Raisin Bread Pudding
Applesauce
Apple Spoon Bread Pudding
Banana Bread
Banana Bread Pudding with Chocolate
Bread Pudding
Brownies
Cheesecake
Chocolate Cheesecake
Chocolate Mint Bread Pudding
Cinnamon Apples
Cinnamon Pears
Cornbread
Cranberry Sauce
Date and Nut Cake
Gingerbread
Pear and Apple Chutney
Pears Poached in Red Wine
Pineapple Upside-Down Cake
Poached Peaches
Rice Pudding with Raisins
Simple Cheesecake
Spice Cake
Spiced Pears
Spicy Pumpkin Pudding
Spoon Bread
Strawberry Bread Pudding
Tex-Mex Cornbread
Triple Chocolate Fudge Cake

DESSERTS

Everyone likes something sweet to end the meal. If you are like me and a Type II Diabetic then this is where we have to tread lightly.

The shape and size of the mini slow cooker dictates to some extent what type of desserts can be made in the cooker. At first when I was developing this cookbook I considered not even having a dessert chapter since there are so many good commercial desserts available in the markets. However, sometimes a homemade dessert just fits the bill and you can make one in a couple of hours.

I have used boxed cake mixes in many of these desserts. A half box will yield a cake the diameter (about 5") of the mini slow cooker and about 2½" to 3" high. You can decorate the top with fresh fruit or ice it in the traditional manner. Cut into 4 or 6 wedges that is enough for any sweet tooth! I sometimes slice the cake horizontally and "ice" the inner layer with sugar free jam or jelly – strawberry really works well with chocolate flavors.

Bread puddings are wonderful in the mini slow cooker. They are moist and flavorful and you can use no-sugar fillings, or sugar substitutes for sweetening. Top the bread pudding with sliced fruit to match for s special treat.

Brownies are extra special made in the mini slow cooker. They are moist and do not develop the crackled top when they are made in the oven. Do not over-cook the brownies – you want to retain that slightly "gooey" center. You may need a spoon to eat it, but it is terrific with ice cream! Enjoy!

APPLE BROWN BETTY

For want of a better name we have called this by its old fashioned name. It will not brown in the cooker, but the apples will be delicious anyway. Wonderful served with vanilla ice cream or whipped cream.

4 cups cooking apples, cut into thin slices.
½ cup sugar (or equal sugar substitute)
3 tbsp ground cinnamon
1 tbsp lemon juice
Brown sugar for topping

Shake the apples with the sugar, cinnamon and lemon juice in a plastic bag to coat well. Pour the apples into the cooker. Cover and cook undisturbed for 1 hour. Sprinkle the top with the brown sugar, cover and cook for 1 hour more. The apples should be well done but not mushy.

Note: For a delicious variation add ½ cup golden raisins, and ½ cup chopped walnuts to the apples.

Serves two to four

APPLE AND RAISIN BREAD PUDDING

This is a down home dish redolent of smells from the old time kitchen. Serve this hot or at room temperature directly from the cooker or un-mold as a cake and cut into wedges. Top with whipped cream if you want or serve with vanilla ice cream.

4 cups day old bread, crusts removed and cut into ¾" cubes
3 eggs beaten
1 cup applesauce (plain or cinnamon flavored)
¼ cup raisins soaked in 2 tbsp brandy (more if you want)
2 tbsp ground cinnamon
¼ cup sugar or sugar substitute

Spray the cooker with cooking spray. In a medium size bowl mix the applesauce with the ground cinnamon and sugar. Beat the eggs and combine with the applesauce mix. Put the bread in the bowl and let it soak in the egg and apple mixture. Add the raisins and stir well. Pour the mix into the cooker. Cover and cook undisturbed for 2 hours, or until the pudding has set. Unplug and uncover the cooker and let the pudding cool for 1 hour. Spoon directly from the cooker or un-mold by running a thin knife around the edge of the pudding and invert the cooker over a serving plate. Cut into wedges and serve as suggested above.

Serves two to four

APPLESAUCE

The slow cooker is a natural for making your own applesauce. You can really never overcook it, and the pot needs no attention. Use tart apples like McIntosh or Macouns. Although it's not absolutely necessary the applesauce will be nicer if the apples are peeled.

4 cups cored and peeled apples, coarsely chopped
½ cup water (or sweet apple cider if you can get it)
2 tbsp ground cinnamon
Zest of one lemon

Put the apples into the cooker with the water or cider. Cover and cook undisturbed for 1 hour. Add the cinnamon and the lemon zest. Stir well. Cover and cook for 1 more hour or until the apples are soft. Mash the apples with a potato masher, or if you want it finer use a stick blender or food processor.

Serves four or more as a garnish for pork or grits

APPLE SPOON BREAD PUDDING

This recipe takes the traditional plain spoon bread, and with the addition of apple sauce lifts it to dessert level. This is wonderful served with vanilla ice cream or Cinnamon Apples, another Southern favorite.

1 pkg (8oz) "Washington" brand Spoon Bread Mix.
1 large egg
1 cup applesauce, or cinnamon flavored applesauce
½ cup water

Measure ¾ cup of the spoon bread mix into a medium size bowl. Add the other ingredients. Mix with a hand held electric mixer until the batter is smooth. Spray the cooker liner with cooking spray. Add the batter, cover and cook undisturbed for 2 hours. Test with a wooden skewer. It should come out clean. If the pudding is not done, cover and cook for ½ hour more. Spoon the pudding directly from the cooker onto serving plates.

Serves two to four

BANANA BREAD

As I have stated before the use of packaged mixes, especially for baking, make cooking easier and more productive. This recipe makes a wonderful cake suitable for breakfast or a luncheon snack. You will get a cake about 5" in diameter and 2" high.

1 pkg. (7 oz) "Jiffy" Banana Nut Muffin Mix
1 large egg
1/3 cup milk
1/3 cup dark seedless raisins (more if you want)
1/3 cup chopped walnuts (more if you want)

Spray the cooker liner with cooking spray. Cover and begin heating the cooker. In the meantime prepare the batter according to the package directions. Add the raisins and the chopped walnuts and stir well. Pour the batter into the cooker. Cover and cook undisturbed for 1½ hours. Insert a cake tester to check for doneness. Let the cake cool in the liner with the cover off. Cut around the outside of the cake with a thin knife to release it. Invert the liner over a serving plate to release it and serve. Cut into wedges.

Serves two to six

BANANA BREAD PUDDING WITH CHOCOLATE

For some weird reason bananas and chocolate have a natural affinity. This recipe is a case in point. In taste it resembles the famous Bananas Foster, the classic recipe from Brennan's Restaurant in New Orleans. It is wonderful served with chocolate syrup and vanilla ice cream.

4 cups day old bread, crust removed and cut into ¾" pieces
3 large eggs, beaten well
½ cup banana, mashed (about 1 large banana)
½ cup chocolate chips
1 tsp vanilla extract
¼ cup sugar or sugar substitute
Chocolate syrup for garnish
Vanilla ice cream

Beat the eggs well and add the mashed bananas, the vanilla and the sugar. Stir the bread into the mixture and soak the bread for at least ½ hour or more. Be sure all of the bread is immersed into the mixture. Add the chocolate chips. Spray the cooker with cooking spray, and add the banana mixture. Cover and cook undisturbed for 2 hours, or until the pudding has set. Unplug the cooker and let the pudding cool with the lid off. When cool enough to handle run a thin knife around the outside of the pudding. Invert the liner over a serving plate and shake. The pudding should release. You will have a cake about 5" in diameter and 2½" high. Cut into four or six wedges.

Serves two to six

BREAD PUDDING

This wonderful dessert is a cinch in the slow cooker. Bread puddings can be as varied as your imagination can make them, but this is a basic and the rest I leave up to your imagination. Serve with vanilla ice cream or whipped cream.

4 cups white bread, crusts removed and cut into ¾" pieces
3 large eggs beaten
1 tbsp vanilla
¼ cup sugar (or use the equivalent sugar substitute)
1 tsp ground nutmeg
1 tsp ground cinnamon
½ cup dark seedless raisins (more if you want)
2 cups low-fat milk

In a medium bowl beat the eggs and the milk. Add the vanilla, sugar, raisins and the spices. Add the bread and soak well, pushing the pieces down into the mixture so that all are covered, approximately ½ hour. Spray the cooker liner with cooking spray and add the bread mixture. Cover and cook undisturbed for 2 hours or until the pudding is set. Serve directly from the cooker or un-mold onto a serving platter and cut into wedges.

Serves two to four

BROWNIES

You'd have to be the ultimate scrooge to say you didn't like them. Made from a box mix this idea will work with any brand. Add nuts or whatever. Cut into six wedges and serve plain or with ice cream or powdered sugar on top! Accompany with a glass of cold milk!

1 pkg. Brownie Mix – your favorite brand
½ of everything in the directions on the box to make the mix
Whatever you want to add – nuts mostly!

Pour the mix into a 4 cup measuring cup. Divide in half with a smaller measuring cup and put that half into a medium size bowl. Save the other half for another batch of brownies. Add ½ of the other ingredients; oil, water, etc. If the recipe calls for three eggs, then just add two eggs - it's difficult to cut an egg in half! Spray the cooker with cooking spray. Add the brownie mix. Cover and cook undisturbed for 2 hours. Use a cake tester to check for doneness. Do not worry if the center is a little soft. Unplug the cooker and let the brownie cool in the cooker. It will continue to cook for awhile. Run a thin knife around the edge of the cooker to release the brownie. Invert the cooker over a serving plate to serve the brownie. Cut in any way you wish, but I suggest 6 wedges. You will have a brownie "cake" about 5" in diameter and 1½" to 2" high.

Serves two to six – not I f you really like brownies!

CHEESECAKE

This simple recipe makes a smooth and creamy cheesecake. You can add other tastes to this basic recipe, such as strawberry or chocolate. Although there is no crust you can add a "crust" of chopped nuts or the traditional crushed graham crackers after the cake has been removed from the cooker. You can decorate the top with fresh fruit or with your favorite jam or jelly.

1½ pkgs (12 oz total) Philadelphia or equal cream cheese
2 eggs, lightly whipped
3 pkgs. sugar substitute approx. 1/8 cup
2 tbsp. vanilla extract
1 tbsp. lemon juice
2 tbsp. sour cream

Let the cream cheese come to room temperature. Cut into large chunks to facilitate creaming. Cream the cheese with a hand held electric mixer. Add all the other ingredients and mix until the mixture is smooth and creamy. Spray the cooker with cooking spray. Add the cream cheese mix and smooth out the top. Cover and cook undisturbed for 2 hours. Check for doneness with a wooden skewer. Unplug the cooker and let the cake cool. Run a thin knife around the outside of the cake to facilitate release from the cooker. Invert over a serving plate and decorate as desired. Slice into wedges. Best if served after being refrigerated.

Note: The cake will rise quite high when cooking. It will sink when cooling off to a regular cheesecake consistency. You will have a cake approximately 5" in diameter and 3" high.

Serves two to six

CHOCOLATE CHEESECAKE

This is a rich and luxurious dessert and sure to satisfy any chocoholics demands. Be sure to use a really good cocoa powder. If you use an already sweetened cocoa you should omit the sugar substitute. Even a diabetic can eat this with impunity (and a great deal of pleasure to boot!).

¼ cup ground cocoa powder
1½ pkgs cream cheese (12 oz total)
2 large eggs
8 pks. (1 gram each) "Equal," or other sugar substitute
3 tbsp sour cream

Bring the cream cheese to room temperate to facilitate creaming it. Use an electric hand mixer to cream the cheese. Add the eggs and continue beating until the mixture is fluffy and creamy. Add the sugar substitute, the cocoa powder and the sour cream. Continue to beat until it is well mixed. Spray the cooker with cooking spray and pour the mixture into the cooker. Use a spatula to smooth out the top. Cover and cook undisturbed for 2 hours. The cake will have risen quite high. Test it with a wooden skewer. It should come out clean. Uncover and let the cake cool in the cooker. It will sink and become real cheesecake in texture. .Use a thin bladed knife and loosen the cheesecake. Hold a serving plate tightly over the cooker and invert. The cheesecake should release easily. Refrigerate until ready to serve. Decorate as you wish. Cut into wedges and serve with whipped cream, ice cream, or plain.

Serves two to six

CHOCOLATE MINT BREAD PUDDING

If you're looking for something to knock their socks off for dessert then this is the ticket. Serve with mint chocolate ice cream for a real winner.

4 cups white bread, crusts removed, cut into ½" cubes
3 large eggs, beaten
2 cups low fat milk
1 tsp vanilla
Baking chocolate (12 oz) chopped (bittersweet or semisweet)
¼ cup crème de menthe
¼ cup sugar (or sugar substitute)

Melt the chocolate in a microwave safe container. In a medium size bowl beat the eggs with the milk and add the chocolate and crème de menthe. Add the vanilla and mix well. Add the bread and let soak for about 30 minutes. Spray the cooker liner and add the bread mixture. Cover and cook undisturbed for 2 hours or until the pudding is set. Let cool in the container. Serve directly from the container or un-mold onto a serving plate. Refrigerate until serving.

Serves four to six

CINNAMON APPLES

Cinnamon Apples are a favorite in the American South, where they are served as a side dish with pork or ham, and as a dessert with ice cream. Either way they are delicious.

5 cups Granny Smith apples, peeled, cored and sliced thin
3 tbsp ground cinnamon
2 tbsp ground cloves
¼ cup sugar, or sugar substitute - "Splenda" or "Equal"
¼ cup water

Spray the cooker with cooking spray. In a bowl mix the apples and sugar, spices and water. Toss well. Put the apples into the cooker. Cover and cook undisturbed for 2 hours. Check for doneness – the apples should be well done, but not mushy. Cover and cook for another ½ hour or more, or until the apples are the consistency you want.

Serves two to four or more

CINNAMON PEARS

This recipe is similar to that of Cinnamon Apples, but the pears give a new taste and a subtle difference. Make this recipe when pears are at their finest in late summer. Use Bosc or Anjou pears, selecting those that are firm and unblemished. This can be served as a dessert with vanilla ice cream or as a condiment with pork dishes.

4 cups pears, cored and peeled, and cut into bite size chunks
¼ cup brown sugar
¼ cup water
¼ cup seedless dark raisins, or more if you want
2 tsp ground cinnamon
2 tsp ground nutmeg
1 tsp lemon zest
1 tsp vanilla

In a medium bowl mix the pears and all the other ingredients and toss well. Spray the cooker with vegetable spray. Pour in the pear mixture. Cover and cook undisturbed for 2 hours. Check for doneness – the pears should be firm but not mushy. Cook for an additional ½ hour if needed.

Serves two to four or six

CORNBREAD

I have never understood why some cooks refuse to use packaged mixes when they can be a great time saver and delicious to boot. This recipe for cornbread is so easy to prepare that you could make it every day. Cornbread is a great favorite in the South. It is sometimes served under creamed dishes, and then for dessert with berries and whipped cream. However you use it, this makes a wonderful cake, which can be sliced into wedges any size you wish. By the way, the final cake will be 2½" high and 5" in diameter – enough to serve six easily.

1 pkg (8.5 oz) "Jiffy" corn muffin mix
1 large egg
1/3 cup milk

Pre heat the cooker for 15 minutes, with the lid on. In a medium bowl prepare the mix according to package directions. Spray the cooker liner with cooking spray. Pour the mix into the cooker. Cover and cook undisturbed for 2 hours. Test the cake with a wooden skewer. If it comes out clean the cake is done. Let the cornbread cool in the cooker for ½ hour. Take a thin knife and run it around the outside of the cornbread to loosen it. Turn the cooker upside down over a plate and the cake should release easily. Serve as above.

Serves two to four or six

CRANBERRY SAUCE

You can make this sauce ahead of time to serve with the Holiday bird. Keep it refrigerated until you use it. It just gets better with time.

1 bag cranberries (16 oz), picked over to remove any bad ones
½ cup sugar or equivalent sugar substitute
1 orange, peeled and chopped, with its juice
¼ cup water (or orange juice)

Put all the ingredients into the cooker. Cover and cook undisturbed for 2 hours, or until the cranberries have popped and are soft. Mash the sauce with a potato masher or use a stick blender or food processor for a finer texture.

Serves two to four or more as a garnish or accompaniment

DATE AND NUT CAKE

This rich and delicious cake is more like a pudding. It is so simple, you probably have all the ingredients in your pantry at this time. Serve it with ice cream or vanilla sauce.

1 box (7 oz) "Jiffy" Banana Nut Muffin Mix
1 egg
½ cup milk
½ cup pitted dates, chopped
½ cup walnuts, chopped

Prepare the batter to the instructions on the box. Add the chopped dates and chopped walnuts. Spray the cooker with cooking spray. Add the batter, cover and cook undisturbed for 1½ hours. Check the cake with a wooden skewer – if it comes out clean the cake is done. Unplug the cooker, and with the lid off let the cake cool. Go around the outside of the cake with a thin knife, then invert the cooker and let the cake drop onto a suitable serving plate. Cut into wedges.

Serves four or six

GINGERBREAD

Who among us does not remember the smell of gingerbread baking? These wonderful memories flood about us. Served with vanilla ice cream or whipped cream, this was a treat to remember. You can make this cake easily and in an hour and a half you will have a cake 5" in diameter and nearly 2" high. This cake will easily serve four, and is adequate for six. Sprinkle powdered sugar on top and cut into wedges.

1 pkg. (14 oz) "Dromedary" brand gingerbread mix
½ cup water

Plug in the cooker with the cover on and let it start to heat up as you prepare the mix. Divide the mix in half (approximately 1 1/3 cups each) and put the reserved mix in a re-sealable plastic bag for another cake. In a small bowl vigorously stir the mix and the water according to package directions. Pour the mix into the cooker. Cover and cook undisturbed for 1½ hours. Test the cake with a wooden skewer. It should come out clean. Do not overcook. Unplug the cooker and remove the lid. Let the cake cool in the cooker. Run a thin knife around the edge of the cake to release it. Invert over a serving plate to serve. Cut into wedges.

Serves four to six

PEAR AND APPLE CHUTNEY

This is a wonderful accompaniment to roast pork. It will keep a long time in the refrigerator and only improves with age.

2 red Bartlett pears, firm but ripe
2 Granny Smith apples
1 cup seedless golden raisins
½ cup rice vinegar
1 tbsp chopped ginger
1 tsp ground cinnamon
1 tsp mustard seeds (optional)

Peel, core and chop the apples and the pears. Put all the ingredients into the cooker and mix well. Cover and cook undisturbed for 2 hours or until the fruit is tender but not mushy. Refrigerate in a covered container.

Serves four or more as an accompaniment

PEARS POACHED IN RED WINE

This approximation of a classic French dessert is just as delicious as the real thing. Buy only pears that are firm and unblemished. They are perfect served with ice cream and a little chocolate sauce dripped over them.

3 pears preferably Bosc, firm but ripe
1½ cups red table wine
1½ cups water
2 tbsp ground cinnamon
1 tsp ground ginger
½ cup sugar or equivalent sugar substitute
Chocolate sauce (optional)

Peel the pears, cut them in half and cut out the core. Arrange the pears in the cooker. Mix the water, wine, sugar and cinnamon. Pour over the pears. They should be covered. Add more water to cover them if necessary. Cover and cook undisturbed for 2 hours. Check for doneness' The pears should be cooked but not mushy. Serve them cold with ice cream and some of the wine and the chocolate sauce.

Serves two to four or six

PINEAPPLE UPSIDE-DOWN CAKE

You might not think this would work, but it does. Be sure to put the wax paper or cooking parchment on the bottom of the cooker or it might be difficult to get the cake out of the cooker. Cut into wedges and serve with whipped cream or vanilla ice cream.

1 pkg "Jiffy" apple-cinnamon muffin mix
1 large egg
1/3 cup milk
1 can (6 oz) pineapple chunks, drained
¼ cup brown sugar
¼ tsp ground cinnamon (or cinnamon sugar)

Spray the cooker liner with cooking spray. Prepare the muffin mix according to package directions. Cut a round of wax paper or cooking parchment to fit the bottom of the cooker. Spray the top of the paper with cooking spray or rub with butter before inserting in the cooker. Arrange pineapple chunks on top and sprinkle with the brown sugar. Pour the muffin mix on top and smooth with a knife. Cover and cook undisturbed for 1½ hours. Check the cake with a wooden skewer to see if is done. If not, cook for ½ hour more. To release the cake, run a thin knife around the outside and invert the cooker liner over a serving plate. Rearrange the pineapple pieces if they do not come out of the cooker with the cake. Cut the cake into wedges.

Serves two to four or six

POACHED PEACHES

The mini slow cooker is the perfect way to poach fresh fruit. You do not need to tend the "pot" and things cannot get burned and rarely overdone. This recipe is perfect when peaches are at their very best. (Do not try it with canned peaches.) Serve cold or at room temperature with whipped cream on top or with vanilla ice cream on the side.

4-5 cups fresh peaches, skinned and cut into bite size pieces
1 small cinnamon stick
2 tbsp ground cinnamon
1½ cup red wine (table wine or Beaujoulais, etc.)
½ cup sugar or equivalent sugar substitute

Bring a pot of water to the boil and dip the peaches into it for 8 to 10 seconds to loosen the skin. Peel and pit the peaches and slice or chop roughly. Pour the peaches into the cooker. Add the wine, spices and sugar. Stir well. Cover and cook undisturbed for 1 hour. Check for doneness. The peaches should be cooked but not mushy. If they are still too firm, cover and cook for ½ hour more.

Serves two to four or six

RICE PUDDING WITH RAISINS

The comfort food of your youth! The mini slow cooker makes wonderful rice because of the low temperature cooking. Regular long grain rice will be more glutinous in the slow cooker than with the usual high temperature cooking method.

2 cups instant enriched long grain premium rice
2 cups hot tap water
1 tbsp vanilla extract
½ cup sugar, or equivalent sugar substitute (or more if you want)
½ cup seedless golden raisins
½ cup whipping cream

Spray the cooker with cooking spray. Add the rice. Start the cooker and add the hot tap water mixed with the vanilla extract. Cover and cook undisturbed for 2 hours. Fluff the rice with a fork and add the raisins and the sugar. Cover and cook for ½ hour more. Uncover, and with the lid off, let the rice cool in the cooker. When at room temperature put the rice into a suitable container. Whip the cream until it has stiff peaks. Fold the whipped cream into the rice in batches if necessary. Refrigerate and serve cold.

Serves two to four or six

SIMPLE CHEESECAKE

This is about as simple as it gets. There are many variations on this recipe but you can use your own imagination. Let the cheesecake set until it is at room temperature to coax it out of the cooker. Cut into wedges to serve.

2 pkgs (8 oz each) cream cheese
½ cup sugar or equal sugar substitute
2 eggs beaten
1 tbsp vanilla

Beat the cream cheese with the sugar and the vanilla until it is creamy. Add the eggs and continue beating. Spray the cooker with cooking spray. Cut a piece of wax paper to fit the bottom of the cooker and spray that also. Pour the mix into the cooker. Cover and cook undisturbed for 2 hours or until the cheesecake is set. The cheesecake will have risen quite high, but will fall as it cools. After the cheesecake is cool, run a thin knife around the outside edge of the cheesecake to help getting the cheesecake onto a serving plate. Invert the cooker over the plate and shake until the cake drops onto the plate. You may decorate the cake with fresh fruit or fruit jam or jelly.

Serves two to four or six

SPICE CAKE

Don't be put off by the name, as "spice" does not mean hot. This is just a wonderful cake served with whipped cream, or ice cream.

1 pkg. (7 oz) "Jiffy" Apple Cinnamon Muffin Mix
1 egg
¼ cup milk
½ cup cinnamon flavored applesauce
1 tbsp ground cinnamon
1 tbsp ground cloves
1 tsp ground nutmeg
1 tsp salt
Note: ½ cup dark seedless raisins (optional)

In a medium bowl mix all the ingredients. Do not over blend and don't be put off if there are a few lumps. Spray the cooker with cooking spray. Add the batter, cover and cook undisturbed for 2 hours. Check the cake with a wooden skewer – it may not come out clean as the cake will be quite moist, but still done. Let the cake cool in the cooker, with the top off. Run a thin knife around the outside of the cake and then invert the cooker over a serving plate and shake the cake loose. Serve as suggested above.

Serves two to four or six

\\

SPICED PEARS

These pears are delicious served as a dessert on their own, or as a topping for ice cream. They will keep well in a covered container in the refrigerator. If you serve them alone top them with whipped cream and a sprig of mint.

4 ripe Bartlett pears, cored and peeled and coarsely chopped
2 tbsp ground cinnamon
1 tsp ground ginger
Freshly grated nutmeg
¼ cup brandy or cognac
¼ cup chopped walnuts
¼ cup golden seedless raisins

Pour all the ingredients into the cooker. Mix well. Cover and cook undisturbed for 1½ hours. The pears should be done but not mushy.

Serves four to six

SPICY PUMPKIN PUDDING

This is really like pumpkin pie without the crust! Easy to prepare and a little different for a Fall dish. Wonderful served with ice cream or with whipped cream on top.

1 can (15 oz) pumpkin puree (Libby's is the most famous)
1 can (12 oz) evaporated skim milk
3 eggs, beaten
½ cup sugar or sugar substitute
1 tsp ground cinnamon
1 tsp ground ginger
½ tsp fresh grated nutmeg
½ tsp ground cloves
Pinch of salt

Spray the cooker with cooking spray. Mix all the ingredients and pour into the cooker. Cover and cook undisturbed for 2 hours. Check to see if the pudding has set. It should still be a bit like Jello; firm but wobbly! If still not firm enough, cover and cook for ½ hour more. Spoon directly from the cooker, preferably at room temperature.

Note: For a variation add ½ cup chopped walnuts.

Serves four to six

SPOON BREAD

Spoon Bread is an old Southern tradition and this rich soft pudding mixture was perfect served with fried chicken, ham and other Southern favorites. It is traditionally served with lots of butter, but some cooks add honey for an extra rich treat. It is also absolutely wonderful with Cinnamon Apples.

1 pkg. (8 oz) "Washington Spoon Bread Mix"
1 large egg
1½ cup water

Measure ¾ cup of the spoon bread mix into a medium stainless steel or pottery mixing bowl. Add the egg and water. Mix with an electric hand held mixer until the batter is smooth. Spray the slow cooker liner with cooking spray. Add the mix, cover and cook undisturbed for 2 hours. Test the spoon bread with a wooden skewer. It should come out clean. If not, cover and cook an additional ½ hour. Serve directly from the cooker with a long handled spoon.

Serves two to four to six as an accompaniment

STRAWBERRY BREAD PUDDING

If you follow the general directions here you can make a bread pudding of just about any fruit you may have on hand. However, this strawberry pudding is light and delicious. Serve it with some of the leftover frozen strawberries and whipped cream, or with strawberry ice cream and strawberry syrup.

4 cups bread, crust removed and cut into ½" to ¾" pieces
3 large eggs well beaten
1 pkg. (16 oz) frozen strawberries with syrup, thawed

In a medium bowl beat the eggs with a whisk or electric hand mixer until they are frothy. Puree 1 cup of the thawed strawberries. Reserve the remainder for garnish. Add the pureed strawberries to the eggs. Soak the bread in the mixture for at least ½ hour. Mix well to see that all of the bread has been soaked. Spray the cooker with cooking spray and add the strawberry mixture. Cover and cook undisturbed for 2 hours. Uncover and unplug the cooker and let the pudding cool in the cooker. You can serve directly from the cooker, or you can un-mold the pudding by running a thin knife around the outside edge. Invert the cooker over a serving plate and shake. The pudding should un-mold easily. You will have a cake about 2" high x 5" diameter. Cut into 4 or 6 wedges and serve as described above.

Serves two to four or six

TEX-MEX CORNBREAD

This spiced up version of regular cornbread will become a family favorite, especially when served with chili. You will get a cake approximately 5" in diameter and 2½" high. Cut into four or six wedges to serve.

1 pkg. "Jiffy" Cornbread Mix
1 large egg
1/3 cup milk
1 jar (3 oz) roasted red peppers, drained and chopped
¼ cup thick salsa – hot or medium, your choice
¼ cup scallions, chopped fine
2 pickled jalapeno peppers, chopped fine
1 tbsp hot red pepper flakes (optional)
1 tsp Tabasco sauce

Spray the cooker liner with cooking spray. Prepare the muffin mix according to package directions. Add the other ingredients and mix well. Pour the mix into the cooker. Cover and cook undisturbed for 1½ hours. Check for doneness by inserting a wooden skewer into the middle of the cake. If it comes out clean it is done. If not, cover and cook for ½ hour more. Run a thin knife around the outside edge of the cake to help release it. Invert the liner over a serving plate and shake until the cake releases.

Serves two to four or six

TRIPLE CHOCOLATE FUDGE CAKE

It is possible to make a really satisfying chocoholics dream come true in the mini slow cooker! If you follow the general directions you will get a moist and delicious cake about 5" in diameter and 2¼" high. After the cake is baked you are on your own to decide how you want to serve it. You can ice it in the traditional manner, or cut it into two layers and put either icing or fruit jam in between. The possibilities are endless.

1 pkg (18.4 oz) Betty Crocker "Super Moist" Triple Chocolate Cake Mix
2 eggs
2 tbsp cooking oil
½ cup water

Divide the cake mix into 2 equal halves. The easiest way to do this is to pour all of the mix into a 4 cup measuring cup, then transfer half of the mix into a 2 cup measuring cup. You will then have 2 equal parts of the mix. Put one part into a plastic bag and reserve for another cake. Proceed by mixing the batter as directed on the package using the amounts as listed above. Cut a circle of wax paper or cooking paper approx 4¾" in diameter to fit the bottom of the cooker. Spray the cooker liner with cooking spray including the wax paper. Pour the batter into the cooker. Cover and cook undisturbed for 2 hours. Test the cake with a wooden skewer. It should be fully cooked. Uncover and unplug the cooker and let the cake cool for at least 1 hour in the cooker. Use a thin knife to go around the outside of the cake to release it from the sides of the cooker. Invert the cooker over a serving plate. The cake will easily release. Decorate the cake as you like and cut into wedges to serve.

Serves two to four or six

350 BIG TASTE RECIPES FOR THE 1½ QUART MINI SLOW COOKER

INDEX

A
Anchovies, Spicy Chicken w., 276
APPETIZERS
  BBQ Meatballs, 3
  Blue Cheese and Caviar Frittata, 4
  Buffalo Wings, 5
  Caponata, 6
  Cheddar, Bacon and Horseradish dip, 7
  Cocktail Onions, 8
  Dates Wrapped with Prosciutto, 9
  Eggplant Caviar, 10
  Hot "Krab" Dip, 11
  Hotsy-Totsy Peanuts, 12
  Kicked Up Velveeta Spread, 13
  "Little Smokies" Spicy Tomato Sauce, 14
  Meatballs in Cranberry Sauce, 15
  Meatballs Strogonoff, 16
  Mushrooms a la Grecque, 17
  Spiced Mixed Nuts, 18
  Spicy Carrot Sticks, 19
  Sweet and Sour Meatballs, 20
  Swiss Cheese Fondue, 21
  Welsh Rarebit, 22
Applesauce, 351
Apple Brown Betty, 349
Apple and Raisin Bread Pudding, 350
Apple Spoon Bread Pudding, 352
Apples, Cinnamon, 360
Apricot, Chicken Legs w. Glaze, 243
Arroz con Pollo, 232

B
Banana Bread, 353
BBQ (Barbeque) Meatballs. 3
BEEF
  Barter's Stew, 125
  Beef and Beans Burritos, 126
  Beef Bourguuignonnne, 127
  Beef Braised in Beer, 128
  Beef Cabbage Rolls, 129
  Beef Creole, 130
  Beef Goulash, 131
  Beef and Ham Loaf, 132
  Beef Hash Tex-Mex Style, 133
  Beef "Monday" Pie, 134
  Beef and Noodle Casserole, 135

  Beef Rolls Stuffed w. Spiced Ham, 136
  Beef Strogonoff, 137
  Beer Stew, 138
  Carbonnade of Beef, 139
  Chipped Beef, 140
  Classic Chili, 141
  Corned Beef and Macaroni Casserole, 142
  Franks and Beans Tex-Mex, 143
  Hamburger and Vegetable Casserole, 144
  Meatballs, 145
  Meatloaf, 146
  Mediterranean Meatballs, 147
  Old Fashioned Beef Stew, 148
  Pepper Steak, 149
  Picadillo, 150
  Roast Beef Hash, 151
  Sloppy Joes, 152
  Spicy Beef and Beans, 153
  Swiss Stew, 154
  Wyler's Hearty Beef Stew, 155
Bean, Lamb and, Casserole, 188
Bean Navy, and Tomato Soup, 54
Bean, Pasta and, Soup, 55
Bean, Three, Stew, 344
Bean, U.S. Senate Soup, 63
Bean, Vegetarian and, Soup, 65
Beans Cowboy Style, 315
Beans, Italian Sausage and Soup, 48
Beans, Beef and, Burritos, 126
Beans, Black, Soup, 37
Beans, Dogs and, 323
Beans, Franks and, Tex-Mex, 143
Beans, Green, Spiced, 299
Beans, Red, w. Virginia Ham, 338
Beans, Red Kidney, w. Bacon, 339
Beans, Spicy Beef and, 153
Beef Braised in Beer, 128
Beef, Cabbage and, 39
Beef, Macaroni and, Casserole, 329
Birds, Veal, 201
Bolognese Sauce, Albert's Gentle, 211
Black Beans, Chicken and, Chili, 234
Black Beans, Ham, and Rice, 161
Black Beans, Sausage and, 218
Blue Cheese and Caviar Frittata, 4
Bolognese Sauce, Albert's Gentle, 211

379

350 BIG TASTE RECIPES FOR THE 1½ QUART MINI SLOW COOKER

Borscht, 38
Bourguinonne, Beef, 127
Brazilian Black Beans, 317

Banana Bread, 353
Bread Pudding 355
Bread Pudding w. Apple and Raisins, 350
Bread Pudding, Cheese, 24
Bread Pudding, Chocolate Mint, 359
Bread Pudding, Strawberry, 376
Bread Pudding, Cheese, 24
Broccoli, w. Cheese, 283
Brunswick Stew, 233
Brussels Sprouts w. Bacon, 284
Buffalo Wings, 5
Burritos, Beef and Bean, 126
Butternut Squash Casserole, 285
Butter, Shrimp in Herbed, 104

C
Cabbage and Beef Soup, 39
Cabbage, Corned Beef and, Casserole, 142
Cabbage and Raisins, Kielbasa w., 214
Cabbage, Pork Loin and Red, 178
Cabbage, Red with Apples and Raisins, 297
Cabbage, Sweet and Sour, 305
Cajun Style Shrimp, 72
Cake, Potato Cheese, 294
Cake, Spice, 372
Cake, Triple Chocolate Fudge, 378
Capers, Swordfish w. Olives, 116
Caponata, 6
Cao au Vin, 263
Carbonnade of Beef, 139
Caribbean Pork Casserole, 158
Caribbean Rice and Beans, 318
Carrot, Creamed Soup, 43
Carrots, Spicy Sticks, 19
Casserole, Mexican Chicken, 269
Casserole, Tuna Noodle, 120
Cassoulet, Pork, 175
Caviar, Eggplant, 10
Cheesecake, 357
Chili, Classic, 141
Chili, Vegetable, 307
Chili, Pork and Black Bean, 173
Cheesecake, 357
Cheesecake, Simple, 371

Cheese Bread Pudding, 24
Cheese Sauce, Eggs in, 26
Cheese Soup w. Vegetables, 40
Chicken Breasts, Rolled Stuffed, 273
Chicken Breasts in Spicy Sauce, 235
Chicken Cacciatore, 236
Chicken Curry, 237
Chicken Soup w. Tortellini, 41
Chicken, Easy Soup, 45
Chicken Fricassee, 238
Chicken w. Green Olives, 239
Chicken Hash, 240
Chicken "Hong Kong", 241
Chicken w. Onions and Olives, 248
Chicken Piccata, 249
Chicken "Shanghai", 254
Chicken and Shrimp, 255
Chicken Stew, 256
Chicken Tetrazzini, 257
Chicken Tex-Mex Casserole, 258
Chicken Thighs w. Pineapple, 259
Chicken Thighs, Tomatoes and Olives, 260
Chili, Chicken and Black Beans, 234
Chicken and Wild Rice Casserole, 319
Chili, Classic, 141
Chili, Sausage, 220
Chili, Turkey, 279
Chinese Chicken in Orange Sauce, 261
Chipped Beef, 140
Chocolate Banana Bread Pudding w., 354
Chocolate Cheesecake, 358
Chocolate, Triple Fudge Cake, 378
Chops, Pork w. Scalloped Potatoes, 176
Chowder, Corn, 42
Chowder, Manhattan Clam, 51
Chowder, Corn, 42
Chowder, Manhattan Clam, 51
Cinnamon Apples, 360
Cinnamon Pears, 361
Confetti Rice, 320
Corn Pudding, Dixie, 289
Country Captain, 264
Couscous, Lamb, 189
Couscous w. Raisins and Red Peppers, 321
Couscous w. Sausage and Vegetables, 221
Cream Sauce, Endive and Ham w., 160
Cream Sauce, Scallops in. 95
Creamed Chicken, 265

350 BIG TASTE RECIPES FOR THE 1½ QUART MINI SLOW COOKER

Creamed Onions, 287
Creamed Vegetable Melange, 288
Creamy Pork Casserole, 159
Creole, Beef, 130
Cuban Style, Pork w. Black Beans, 174
Curried Rice, 322
Curried Shrimp, 76
Curry, Chicken, 237
Curry, Lamb, 190
Curry, Veal, 202
Curry, Shrimp, 101
Cod, Easy Stew, 77
Cod w. Tomatoes and Olives, 73
Cornbread, 362
Corn, Creamy Soup, 44
Corn and "Krab" Soup, 49
Court Bouillon, Poached Salmon in, 87
Cranberry Sauce, 363
Cranberry Sauce, Meatballs in, 15
Creamed Tuna, 74
Creamy Veal Stew, 200
Creole, Frittata, 27
Curried Chicken and Rice, 266
Curried Turkey Pot Pie, 267
Curried "Krab" Casserole, 75
Curried Shrimp, 76

D
DESSERTS
  Apple Brown Betty, 349
  Apple and Raisin Bread Pudding, 350
  Applesauce, 351
  Apple Spoon Bread Pudding, 352
  Banana Bread, 353
  Banana Bread Pudding w. Chocolate, 354
  Bread Pudding, 355
  Brownies, 356
  Cheesecake, 357
  Chocolate Cheesecake, 358
  Chocolate Mint Bread Pudding, 359
  Cinnamon Apples, 360
  Cinnamon Pears, 361
  Cornbread, 362
  Cranberry Sauce, 363
  Date and Nut Cake, 364
  Gingerbread, 365
  Pear and Apple Chutney, 366
  Pears Poached in Red Wine, 367

Pineapple Upside Down Cake, 368
  Poached Peaches, 369
  Rice Pudding w. Raisins, 370
  Simple Cheesecake, 371
  Spice Cake 372
  Spiced Pears, 373
  Spicy Pumpkin Pudding, 374
  Spoon Bread, 375
  Strawberry Bread Pudding, 376
  Tex-Mex Cornbread, 377
  Triple Chocolate Fudge Cake, 378
Dip, Cheddar, Bacon and Horseradish, 7
Dip, Hot "Krab", 11
Dixie Corn Pudding, 289
Dogs and Beans, 323

E
Easy Chicken Soup, 45
EGGS
  Eggs in Cheese Sauce, 26
  Eggplant Caviar, 10
  Eggs Florentine w Mushrooms, 25
  Frittata, Creole, 27
  Frittata, Italian, 29
  Huevos Rancheros, 28
  Quiche Lorraine without the Crust. 30
Eggplant, Tomato and Cheese Stew, 290
Endive with Ham and Cream Sauce, 160
Tex-Mex Salsa Frittata, 31

F
FISH AND SHELLFISH
  Bay Scallops Provencal, 70
  Cajun Style Shrimp, 71
  Cod Fillets w. Vegetables, 72
  Cod w. Tomatoes and Olives, 73
  Creamed Tuna, 74
  Curried "Krab" Casserole, 75
  Curried Shrimp, 76
  Easy Cod Stew, 77
  Fish Veracruz Style, 78
  Flounder Provencal, 79
  Flounder Rolls in Light Tomato Sauce, 80
  Flounder Rolls, w. Prosciutto, 81
  "Krab" Gumbo, 82
  "Krab" Stuffed Flounder Fillets, 83
  Linguini w. Shrimp, 84
  Mediterranean Style Scallops, 85

350 BIG TASTE RECIPES FOR THE 1½ QUART MINI SLOW COOKER

Oyster Stew, 86
Poached Salmon Court Bouillon, 87
Provencal Fish Stew, 88
Quick "Krab" Newburg, 89
Rice with Shrimp and Peas, 90
Rice w. Shrimp and Red Pepper, 91
Salmon Loaf, 92
Salmon Pinwheels, 93
Salmon Steaks and Vegetable Medley, 94
Scallops in Cream Sauce, 95
Scallops Marinara, 96
Scallops Mediterranean Style, 97
Shrimp Creole, 100
Shrimp Curry, 101
Shrimp Fra Diovolo, 102
Shrimp Gumbo, 103
Shrimp in Herbed Butter, 104
Shrimp Jambalaya, 105
Shrimp in Light Tomato Sauce, 106
Shrimp Marinara, 107
Shrimp Newburg, 108
Shrimp w. Oriental Vegetables, 109
Shrimp and Saffron Rice Casserole, 110
Shrimp w. Saffron Rice and Tomatoes, 111
Shrimp with Tomatoes and Pasta, 112
Shrimp Wiggle, 113
Sole Duglere, 114
Sole w. Vegetables, 115
Swordfish w. Capers and Olives, 116
Tuna Loaf, 117
Tuna and Macaroni Casserole, 118
Tuna Nicoise, 119
Tuna Noodle Casserole, 120
Tuna Steak, 121
Tuna Surprise, 122
Fondue, Swiss Cheese, 21
Fra, Diavolo, Shrimp, 102
Franks and Beans Tex-Mex, 143
French Onion Soup, 46
Fricassee, Lamb, 191
Frittata Italian, 29
Frittata, Tex-Mex Salsa, 31
Frittata, Western, 32
Frittata, Zucchini, 33

G
German Potato Salad, 291
Gingerbread, 365

Goulash, Beef, 131
GRAINS, PASTA, RICE AND BEANS
  Beans Cowboy Style, 315
  Black Bean Stew, 316
  Brazilian Black Beans, 317
  Caribbean Rice and Beans, 318
  Chicken and Wild Rice Casserole, 319
  Confetti Rice, 320
  Couscous w. Raisins and Red Peppers, 321
  Curried Rice, 322
  Dogs and Beans, 323
  Grits, 324
  Hamburger and Noodle Casserole, 325
  Hoppin' John, 326
  Linguini Puttanesca, 327
  Long Grain and Wild Rice, 328
  Macaroni and Beef Casserole, 329
  Macaroni and Chicken Bake, 330
  Manicotti w. Puttanesca Sauce, 331
  Manicotti in Tomato Sauce, 332
  Noodle and Shrimp Casserole, 333
  Penne w. Mushrooms and Sausage, 334
  Penne in Spicy Tomato Sauce, 335
  Penne w. Tomatoes and Shrimp, 336
  Persian Rice, 337
  Red Beans w. Virginia Ham, 338
  Red Kidney Beans w. Bacon, 339
  Red Kidney Beans Dominican Style, 340
  Rice w. Tomatoes and Black Olives, 341
  Risi e Bisi, 342
  Tabbouleh, 343
  Three Bean Stew, 344
  Tortellinin w. Bacon and Peas, 345
  White Beans Tuscan Style, 346
Green Bean Casserole, 292
Gumbo, Sausage, 222
Gumbo, "Krab," 82
Gumbo, Shrimp, 103

H
HAM AND PORK
  Caribbean Pork Casserole, 158
  Creamy Pork Casserole, 159
  Endive with Ham and Cream Sauce, 160
  Ham, Black Beans and Rice, 161
  Ham Havana, 162
  Ham Jambalaya, 163
  Ham Loaf, 164

350 BIG TASTE RECIPES FOR THE 1½ QUART MINI SLOW COOKER

Ham and Macaroni Bake, 165
Ham, Peppers and Rice Casserole, 166
Ham and Potato Casserole, 167
Ham Ragout Caribbean Style, 168
Ham Rolls, 169
Ham Tetraazzini, 170
Islands Style Pork Loin, 171
Pork Barbecue and Potato Casserole, 172
Pork and Black Bean Chili, 173
Pork w. Black Beans Cuban Style, 174
Pork Cassoulet, 175
Pork Chops and Scalloped Potatoes, 176
Pork Loin w. Prunes and Apples, 177
Pork Loin and Red Cabbage, 178
Pork w. Pineapple, 179
Pork and Sweet Potato Casserole, 180
Pork Tenderloin Oriental, 181
Pork in Tomato Sauce w. Oregano, 182
Red Bean Stew w. Pork, 183
Scalloped Potatoes and Ham Casserole, 184
Sweet and Sour Pork, 185
Ham, Beef and, Loaf, 132
Hamburger and Noodle Casserole, 325
Hamburger and Vegetable Casserole, 144
Hash, Beef, Tex-Mex Style, 133
Hash, Chicken, 240
Hash, Roast Beef, 151
Herbed New Potatoes, 293
Hoppin' John, 326
Hot "Krab" Dip, 11
Huevos Rancheros, 28
Hungarian Chicken Paprika, 268

I
Islands Style Pork Loin, 171
Italian Frittata, 29
Italian Sausage and Peppers, 212
Italian Sausage in Spicy Tomato Sauce, 213

J
Jambalaya, Chicken, 242
Jambalaya, Ham, 163
Jambalaya, Sausage, 223
Jambalaya, Shrimp, 105

K
Kicked Up Velveeta Spread, 13
Kielbasa w. Cabbage and Raisins, 214

Kielbasa and Red Cabbage, 215
Kielbasa and Sauerkraut in Beer, 216
"Krab", Hot Dip, 11
"Krab" and Corn Soup, 49
"Krab", Curried Casserole, 75
"Krab" Gumbo, 82
"Krab" Stuffed Flounder Fillets, 83
"Krab", Quick Newburg, 89

L
LAMB
Lamb and Bean Casserole, 188
Lamb Couscous, 189
Lamb Curry, 190
Lamb Fricassee, 191
Lamb Stew, 192
Lamb Stew w. Dill and Paprika, 193
Lamb Stew w. Lemon and Oregano, 194
Lamb Stew Mediterranean Style, 195
Moroccan Lamb Stew, 196
Savory Lamb Stew, 197
Simple Irish Stew, 198
Sweet and Sour Lamb, 199

Leeks, Potato and, Soup, 57
Lemon and Caper Sauce, Chicken w., 244
Lentil and Sausage Soup, 50
Linguini Puttanesca, 327
Linguini w. Shrimp, 84
"Little Smokies" in Spicy Tomato Sauce, 14
Livers, Chicken in Tomato Sauce, 245
Loaf, Beef and Ham, 132
Loaf, Ham, 164
Loaf, Salmon, 92
Loaf, Tuna, 117
Loaf, Turkey, 278

M
Macaroni and Cheese Casserole, 329
Macaroni, Ham and, Bake, 165
Macaroni, Tuna and, Casserole, 118
Manhattan Clam Chowder, 51
Manicotti w. Puttanesca Sauce, 331
Masnicotti in Tomato Sauce, 332
Marengo, Chicken, 246
Marinara, Shrimp, 107
Mediterranean Style, Scallops, 97
Meatball and Sausage Casserole, 217
Meatballs, 145

350 BIG TASTE RECIPES FOR THE 1½ QUART MINI SLOW COOKER

Meatballs, BBQ, 3
Meatballs in Cranberry Sauce, 15
Meatballs Strogonoff, 16
Meatballs, Sweet and Sour, 20
Meatloaf, 146
Mediterranean Meatballs, 147
Mediterranean Style, Lamb Stew, 195
Mediterranean Style Scallops, 85
Mexican Chicken Casserole, 269
Minestrone Soup, 52
"Monday" Pie, Beef, 134
Mornay, Scallops and Shrimp, 98
Moroccan Lamb Stew, 196
Mushroom Risotto, Chicken and, 247
Mushroom Soup, 53
Mushrooms a la Grecque, 17
Mushrooms, Veal in Red Wine, w. 204
Mustard Chicken w. Mushrooms, 270

N
Newburg, Quick "Krab", 89
Newburg, Shrimp, 108
Nicoise, Tuna, 119
Noodle, Beef and, Casserole, 135
Noodle, Hamburger and, Casserole, 325
Noodle and Shrimp Casserole, 323
Noodle, Tuna, Casserole, 120
Noodle, Turkey Casserole, 279
Nuggets, Sesame Chicken, 274
Nuts, Spiced Mixed, 18

O
Old Fashioned Beef Stew, 148
Olives, Cod w. Tomatoes, 73
Onion, French Soup, 46
Onions, Creamed, 287
Onions and Olives, Chicken w., 248
Orange Sauce, Chinese Chicken in, 261
Oriental Chicken w. Peppers, 271
Oriental, Pork Tenderloin, 181
Oriental Vegetables, Shrimp w.109
Orzo, Sausage w. Tomatoes and., 226
Oyster Stew, 86

P
Paprika, Hungarian Chicken, 268
Pasta and Bean Soup, 55
Pasta, Shrimp and Tomatoes w., 112

Pea Soup, 56
Peaches, Poached 369
Peanuts, Hotsy-Totsy, 12
Pear and Apple Chutney, 366
Pears, Cinnamon, 361
Pear Poached in Red Wine, 367
Pears, Spiced 373
Penne w. Mushrooms and Sausage, 334
Penne in Spicy Tomato Sauce, 325
Penne w. Tomatoes and Shrimp, 336
Pepper Steak, 149
Peppers, Oriental Chicken w., 271
Persian Rice, 337
Picadillo, 150
Piccata, Chicken, 249
Pineapple, Chicken Thighs w., 259
Pineapple, Pork w. 179
Pineapple Upside Down Cake, 368
Pinwheels, Salmon, 93
Pork and Black Bean Chili, 173
Poached Peaches, 369
Pork Barbecue and Potato Casserole, 172
Pork, Caribbean Casserole, 158
Pork, Cream Casserole, 159
Pork Loin, Islands Style, 171
Pork Loin w. Prunes and Apples, 177
Pork w. Black Beans Cuban Style, 174
Pork w. Pineapple, 179
Potato Cheese Cake, 294
Potato, and Ham Casserole, 167
Potato and Leek Soup, 57
Potato, Onion and Bacon Soup, 58
Potato, German, Salad, 291
Potatoes, Herbed New, 293
Potatoes Savoyard, 295
Potatoes, Scalloped and Ham Casserole, 184
Pot Pie, Curried Turkey, 267
POULTRY
  Arroz con Pollo, 232
  Brunswick Stew, 233
  Chicken and Black Bean Chili, 234
  Chicken Breasts in Spicy Sauce, 235
  Chicken Cacciatore, 236
  Chicken Curry, 237
  Chicken Fricassee, 238
  Chicken w. Green Olives, 239
  Chicken Hash, 240
  Chicken "Hong Kong", 241

Chicken Jambalaya, 242
Chicken Legs w. Apricot Glaze, 243
Chicken w. Lemon and Caper Sauce, 244
Chicken Livers in Tomato Sauce, 245
Chicken Marengo, 246
Chicken and Mushroom Risotto, 247
Chicken w. Onions and Olives, 248
Chicken Piccata, 249
Chicken Pot Pie, 250
Chicken and Saffron Rice, 251
Chicken and Sausage Casserole, 252
Chicken and Sausage, Tex-Mex, 253
Chicken "Shanghai", 254
Chicken and Shrimp, 255
Chicken Stew, 256
Chicken Tetrazzini, 257
Chicken Tex-Mex Casserole, 258
Chicken Thighs w. Pineapple, 259
Chicken Thighs, Tomatoes and Olives, 260
Chinese Chicken in Orange Sauce, 261
Chinese Chicken and Vegetables, 262
Coq au Vin, 263
Country Captain, 264
Creamed Chicken, 265
Curried Chicken and Rice, 266
Curried Turkey Pot Pie, 267
Hungarian Chicken Paprika, 268
Mexican Chicken Casserole, 269
Mustard Chicken w. Mushrooms, 270
Oriental Chicken w. Peppers, 271
Provencal Braised Chicken, 272
Rolled Stuffed Chicken Breasts, 273
Sesame Chicken Nuggets, 274
Souther Succotash w. Chicken, 275
Spicy Chicken w. Anchovies, 276
Turkey Chili, 277
Turkey Loaf, 278
Turkey Noodle Casserole, 279
Turkey Roulades, 280
Pot Pie, Chicken, 250
Prosciutto, Flounder Rolls w., 81
Provencal Braised Chicken, 272
Provencal Fish Stew, 88
Provencal, Flounder, 79
Pudding, Banana Bread w. Chocolate, 354
Pudding, Bread 355
Pudding, Corn 286

Pudding, Spicy Pumpkin, 374

Q
Quiche Lorraine without the Crust, 30
Quick "Krab" Newburg, 89

R
Ragout, Ham, Caribbean Style, 168
Ragout, Veal, 203
Rarebit, Welsh, 22
Ratatouille, 296
Red Bean Stew w. Pork 183
Red Beans w. Virginia Ham, 338
Red Cabbage w. Apples and Raisins, 297
Red Cabbage, Kielbasa and, 215
Red Cabbage, Pork Loin w., 178
Red Kidney Beans w. Bacon, 339
Rice, Curried Chicken and, 266
Rice, Ham, Black Beans and, 161
Rice, Long Grain and Wild, 328
Rice, Peppers and Ham Casserole, 166
Rice, Persian, 337
Rice Pudding w. Raisins, 370
Rice, Spanish, Sausage and, 225
Rice, Tomato and, Soup, 59
Rice w. Shrimp and Peas, 90
Rice w. Shrimp and Red Pepper, 91
Rice, w. Tomatoes and Black Olives, 341
Rice, Wild w. Chicken Casserole, 319
Risi e Bisi, 342
Roast Beef Hash, 151
Rolled Stuffed Chicken Breasts, 273
Rolls, Beef, Stuffed w. Spiced Ham, 136
Rolls, Ham, 169
Roulades, Turkey, 280

S
Saffron Rice Casserole, Shrimp and, 110
Saffron Rice, Chicken and, 251
Saffron Rice, Shrimp and Tomatoes w. 111
Salmon Loaf, 92
Salmon Pinwheels, 93
Salmon Steaks and Vegetable Medley, 94
Salmon in Cream Sauce, 95
Sauce, Albert's Gentle Bolognese, 211
Sauerkraut w. Apples, 298
Sauerkraut, Sausage and, 224
Sausage and Black Beans, 218

Sausage and Cannellini Casserole, 219
Sausage, Chicken and, Casserole, 252
Sausage, Chicken and Tex-Mex, 253
Sausage Jambalaya, 223
Sausage, Italian Bean Soup w., 48
Sausage, Lentil and, Soup, 50
Sausage, Meatball and, Casserole, 217
Sausage, Penne w. Mushrooms and., 324
Sausage, Tortellini and, Soup, 61
Savory Lamb Stew, 197
Savoyard, Potatoes, 295
Scalloped Potatoes and Ham Casserole, 184
Scalloped Potatoes, Pork Chops and, 176
Scallops, Bay, Provencal, 70
Scallops in Cream Sauce, 95
Scallops Marinara, 96
Scallops, Mediterranean Style, 97
Scallops and Shrimp Mornay, 98
Seafood Stew, 99
Sesame Chicken Nuggets, 274
Shrimp, Cajun Style, 71
Shrimp, Chicken and, 255
Shrimp Creole, 100
Shrimp Curry, 101
Shrimp, Curried, 76
Shrimp Fra Diavolo,, 102
Shrimp Gumbo, 103
Shrimp in Light Tomato Sauce, 106
Shrimp, Linguini w., 84
Shrimp Marinara, 107
Shrimp Newburg, 108
Shrimp, Noodle and, Casserole, 323
Shrimp and Oriental Vegetables, 109
Shrimp Wiggle, 113
Shrimp, w. Rice and Peas, 90
Shrimp w. Rice and Red Pepper, 91
Simple Cheesecake, 371
Simple Irish Stew, 198
Sloppy Joes, 152

SOUP
  Black Bean Soup, 37
  Borscht, 38
  Cabbage and Beef Soup, 39
  Cheese Soup w. Vegetables, 40
  Chicken Soup w. Tortellini, 41
  Corn Chowder, 42
  Creamed Carrot Soup, 43
  Creamy Corn Soup, 44

Easy Chicken Soup, 45
French Onion Soup, 46
Fresh Tomato Soup, 47
Italian Bean and Sausage Soup, 48
"Krab" and Corn Soup, 49
Lentil and Sausage Soup, 50
Manhattan Clam Chowder, 51
Minestrone Soup, 52
Mushroom Soup, 53
Navy Bean and Tomato Soup, 54
Pasta and Bean Soup, 55
Pea Soup, 56
Potato and Leek Soup, 57
Potato, Onion and Bacon Soup, 58
Tomato and Rice Soup, 59
Tortellini en Brodo, 60
Tortellini and Sausage Soup, 61
Tuscan Bread and Tomato Soup, 62
U.S. Senate Bean Soup, 63
Vegetable Soup, 64
Vegetarian Vegetable Soup, 65
Wonton Soup, 66

SPECIALTY MEATS
  Albert's Gentle Bolognese Sauce, 211
  Italian Sausage and Peppers, 212
  Italian Sausage in Spicy Tomato Sauce, 213
  Kielbasa w. Cabbage and Raisins, 214
  Kielbasa and Red Cabbage, 215
  Kielbasa and Sauerkraut in Beer, 216
  Meatball and Sausage Casserole, 217
  Sausage and Black Beans, 218
  Sausage and Cannellini Casserole, 219
  Sausage Chili, 220
  Sausage w. Couscous and Vegetables, 221
  Sausage Gumbo, 222
  Sausage Jambalaya, 223
  Sausage and Sauerkraut, 224
  Sausage and Spanish Rice, 225
  Sausage w. Tomatoes and Orzo, 226
  Venison Stew, 227

Spice Cake 372
Spiced Green Beans 299
Spiced Mixed Nuts, 18
Spiced Pears, 373
Spinach Cake, 301
Spoon Bread, Apple, 352
Spread, Kicked Up Velveeta, 13
Squash, Butternut Casserole, 285

Steak, Pepper, 149
Steak, Tuna, 121
Stew, Barter.s, 126
Stew, Beer, 138
Stew, Black Bean, 316
Stew, Brunswick 233
Stew, Creamy Veal, 200
Stew, Chicken, 256
Stew, Easy Cod, 77
Stew, Eggplant, Tomato and Cheese, 290
Stew, Lamb w. Dill and Paprika, 193
Stew, Lamb w. Lemon and Oregano, 194
Stew, Lamb, Mediterranean Style, 195
Stew, Morocccan Lamb, 196
Stew, Old Fashioned Beef, 148
Stew, Oyster, 86
Stew, Provencal Fish, 88
Stew. Red Bean w. Pork, 183
Stew, Seafood, 99
Stew, Savory Lamb, 197
Stew, Three Bean, 344
Stew, Veal, 205
Stew, Veal w. Mustard Cream Sauce, 206
Stew, Veal w. Tomatoes and Olives, 207
Stew, Vegetable, 308
Stew, Venison, 227
Stew, Winter Vegetable, 309
Strawberry Bread Pudding 376
Strogonoff, Beef, 137
Succotash, 302
Succotash, Southern w. Chicken, 275
Sweet Potato Casserole, 303
Sweet Potatoes w. Apples and Raisins, 304
Sweet Potato, Pork and, Casserole, 180
Sweet and Sour Lamb, 199
Sweet and Sour Meatballs, 20
Sweet and Sour Pork, 185
Sweet and Sour Red Cabbage, 305
Swiss Cheese Fondue, 21
Swiss Stew, 154
Swordfish w. Capers and Olives, 116

T
Tabbouleh, 343
Tetrazzini, Ham, 170
Tex-Mex, Chicken Casserole, 258
Tex-Mex, Chicken and Sausage, 255
Three Bean Stew, 344

Tomato and Rice Soup, 59
Tomatoes, Saffron Rice and Shrimp w., 111
Tomato, Fresh, Soup, 47
Tomato Sauce, Flounder Rolls in, 80
Tomato Sauce, Pork in w. Oregano, 182
Tomato Sauce, Shrimp in Light, 106
Tomatoes and Olives, Chicken Thighs w., 260
Tomatoes, Cod w. and Olives, 73
Tortellini w. Bacon and Peas, 345
Tortellini and Sausage Soup, 61
Tortellini en Brodo, 60
Tortellini, Chicken Soup w., 41
Tricolor Vegetable Timbale, 306
Triple Chocolate Fudge Cake, 378
Tuna, Creamed, 74
Tuna Loaf, 117
Tuna Nicoise, 119
Tuna Noodle Casserole, 120
Turkey Chili, 279
Turkey Roulades, 280
Tuscan Bread and Tomato Soup, 62

U

V
VEAL
  Creamy Veal Stew, 200
  Veal Birds, 201
  Veal Curry, 202
  Veal Ragout, 203
  Veal in Red Wine with Mushrooms, 204
  Veal Stew, 205
  Veal Stew w. Mustard Cream Sauce, 206
  Veal Stew, w. Tomatoes and Olives, 207
VEGETABLES
  Broccoli w. Cheese, 283
  Brussels Sprouts w. Bacon, 284
  Butternut Squash Casserole, 285
  Corn Pudding, 286
  Creamed Onions, 287
  Creamed Vegetable Melange, 288
  Dixie Corn Pudding, 289
  Eggplant, Tomato and Cheese Stew, 290
  German Potato Salad, 291
  Green Bean Casserole, 292
  Herbed New Potatoes, 293
  Potato Cheese Cake, 294
  Potatoes Savoyard, 295

Ratatouille, 296
Red Cabbage w. Apples and Raisins, 297
Sauerkraut w. Apples, 298
Spiced Green Beans, 299
Spiced Yams, 300
Spinach Cake, 301
Succotash, 302
Sweet Potato Casserole, 303
Sweet Potatoes w. Apples and Raisins, 304
Sweet and Sour Red Cabbage, 305
Tricolor Vegetable Timbale, 306
Vegetable Chili, 307
Vegetable Stew, 308
Winter Vegetable Stew, 309
Zucchini Espagnol, 310
Zucchini in the Style of Provence, 311
Vegetable Medley, Salmon Steaks and, 94
Vegetable Soup, 64
Vegetarian Vegetable Soup 65
Vegetables, Cheese Soup w., 40
Vegetables, Chinese Chicken and. 262
Vegetables, Cod Fillets w. 72
Vegetables, Sausage and Couscous w., 221
Vegetables, Sole, w., 115
Venison Stew, 227
Veracruz Style, Fish, 78

W

Western Frittata, 32
Wiggle, Shrimp, 113
Wyler's Hearty Beef Stew, 155
Wonton Soup, 66

X

Y
Yams, Spiced, 300
See also: Sweet Potato Casserole, 303
See also: Sweet Potatoes w. Apples and
           Raisins, 304

Z
Zucchini Espagnol, 310
Zucchini Fritatta, 33
Zucchini in the Style of Provence,, 311
Zucchini and Tomato Casserole, 312